Order Without Rules

SUNY series in the Philosophy of the Social Sciences
Lenore Langsdorf, editor

ORDER
WITHOUT
RULES

*Critical Theory and the
Logic of Conversation*

David Bogen

STATE UNIVERSITY OF NEW YORK PRESS

Published by
State University of New York Press, Albany

© 1999 State University of New York

Cover photo: Dance Pattern #3, Imperial County, California, © Marilyn Bridges 1983.

For information, address State University of New York Press,
State University Plaza, Albany, NY, 12246.

Production by Cathleen Collins
Marketing by Nancy Farrell

Library of Congress Cataloging in Publication Data

Bogen, David, 1960-
    Order without rules : critical theory and the logic of
conversation / David Bogen.
        p.   cm. — (SUNY series in the philosophy of the social
sciences)
    Includes bibliographical references and index.
    ISBN 0-7914-4055-9. — ISBN 0-7914-4056-7 (pbk.)
    1. Communication—Social aspects.   2. Conversation—Social
aspects.   I. Title.   II. Series.
HM258.B596   1999
302.2—dc21
                                                                98-7242
                                                                CIP

10   9   8   7   6   5   4   3   2   1

Contents

Acknowledgments

The contents of this study were written over a period of several years, during which I received inspiration and support from a number of different quarters within a changing landscape of colleagues, friends, and academic institutions. The foundations for this study were laid during my years at Boston University, where I worked as a graduate student and university fellow in the Department of Sociology. It is impossible to communicate the nature and degree of my debt to Jeff Coulter, Mike Lynch, and George Psathas, who were faculty leaders during that period of unparalleled intellectual vitality and growth in the Department. Their efforts coalesced around a multiyear seminar in "The Philosophy of the Social Sciences," which set the intellectual course for a generation of graduate students, and has been responsible for no less than six book-length studies at the intersection between Wittgenstein, ethnomethodology, and social theory. My intellectual debt and fond memories extend also to the other members of this extraordinary group of colleagues and friends: Dusan Bjelic, Eileen Crist, Fred Hunter, Kathleen Jordan, Ramona Naddaff, Ed Parsons, Gary Reed, Edith Rosenthal, and Jeff Stetson. I also wish to thank Tom McCarthy, who lead the seminar in Habermas's *Theory of Communicative Action* in the Department of Philosophy at Boston University, and provided detailed criticism of several of the Chapters of this book in their early stages. I am also indebted to Charles Smith, editor of *Journal for the Theory of Social Behavior*, whose editorial support and criticism encouraged the development of these arguments.

Drafts of various chapters were presented at professional society meetings and colloquia including: the International Institute of Ethnomethodology; the American Sociological Society Annual Meetings; the Society for Phenomenology and the Human Sciences; and the MIDAS Seminar at the Center for Literary and Cultural Studies at Harvard University. My thanks to Barry Barnes, Doug Maynard, Jim Schmidt, Lucy Suchman, and Stephen Turner who all read portions of the manuscript and contributed valuable criticisms along the way. In addition, special thanks are due to Wes Sharrock, professor of Sociology and organizer of the International Symposium on the Philosophy of the Behavioral Sciences at the University of Manchester, England, where on two occasions I was provided with the opportunity to air some of the more contentious arguments of this book.

The final stages of this project were supported in part through a series of faculty grants and research leaves from Emerson College. I am extremely grateful to the faculty and administration at Emerson for their support of this project and for their unwavering commitment to faculty research and development as the cornerstone of the academic mission of the College.

To Lenore Langsdorf, editor of the Philosophy of the Social Sciences Series at SUNY Press, my thanks for many hours spent working through drafts of this manuscript and for seeing this project through to completion. Finally, to my wife Pam, who, next to me, spent more time with this manuscript than anyone on earth, my thanks for your patience, perseverance, and willingness to remind me time and again of what matters most . . . and why.

Portions of chapter 2 were originally published as "A Reappraisal of Habermas's *Theory of Communicative Action* in light of detailed investigations of social praxis" in *Journal for the Theory of Social Behavior* (1989) 19:47–77; a version of chapter 3 was published as "Linguistic Forms and Social Obligations: A Critique of the Doctrine of Literal Expression in Searle" in *Journal for the Theory of Social Behavior* (1991) 21:31–62; a version of chapter 4 was published as "The Organization of Talk" in *Qualitative Sociology* (1992) 15:273–295; a version of chapter 5 was published as "Order Without rules: Wittgenstein and the communicative ethics controversy" in *Sociological Theory* (1993) 11:55–71.

Transcription Conventions

Many of the transcripts of conversation in this book use a system of typographic notation that was originally developed by Gail Jefferson, and has come to be used widely within the fields of ethnomethodology and conversation analysis. In addition to the lexical elements of conversation, this notational system takes account of a variety of intonational, rhythmic, and sequential aspects of speech. A brief list of these conventions is included below.

Numbers in parentheses: (0.8) Pauses, gaps, silences measured in seconds and tenths of seconds. Measures are approximate.

Period in parentheses: (.) "Micropause" of less than two-tenths of a second.

Letters, words, or phrases in single parentheses: (tch) Sounds, words, or phrases that are indistinct or otherwise difficult for the transcriber to make out from the recording.

Double parentheses: ((throat clear)) Commentary describing non-lexical or nonverbal actions evident on the tape that the transcriber deems relevant to mention.

Degree sign: °let's see° Barely audible sound, whisper, or word.

Colons: you:: A stretched sound within, or at the end of, a word.

Equals signs: =That's correct "Latching" of utterance; utterance follows unusually quickly after the immediately preceding utterance.

Square brackets: Marking points where talk by different speakers overlaps. Left brackets mark the beginnings of overlaps, and right brackets the ends, for example,
Joan: ch Ye[ah]
Linda: [But,]

Italics: I *did*. Voiced stress on word, phrase, or sound. Stress
    sometimes does not correspond to written syllables.
Hyphen stroke: a- a call Word or sound that is cut off.
Arrow in margin: → Indication that a line or utterance is
    significant for the analysis.

Introduction

> If language is to be a means of communication there must
> be agreement not only in definitions but also (queer as this
> may sound) in judgments. This seems to abolish logic, but
> does not do so.—It is one thing to describe methods of
> measurement, and another to obtain and state results of
> measurement. But what we call "measuring" is partly
> determined by a certain constancy in results of
> measurement.
>
> —Wittgenstein, *Philosophical Investigations*

This book is concerned fundamentally with the relationship between logic and social order. The central foil for this discussion is Habermas's "theory of communicative action,"[1] and the specific moral, political, and analytical burdens which that doctrine places on the workings of ordinary social practice. Before entering into that longer and more detailed argument, it will be useful to give a general overview of the argument of this book and of where it sits within the broad panorama of contemporary social theory.

A leading assumption of the "communicative ethics controversy"[2] in contemporary social theory is that the failure to recover *universal* standards for the validity of everyday speech inevitably leads to a kind of logical free-for-all in which there exist *no* legitimate standards for assessing the intelligibility, cogency, and reasonableness of statements, and hence, no methods by which disputes between competing epistemic positions could ever reasonably be resolved. It is this assumption that seems to force a choice between the enlightenment program of a transcendental ethics of communication, on the one hand, and the subscription to a doctrine of generalized collapse, decay, and decline, on the other; between the search for universally valid rules of thought and social order, or the conclusion that there are no formally valid rules of discursive engagement, and hence, no legitimate order(s). These alternatives frame the modernist/postmodernist, enlightenment/anti-enlightenment debates in contemporary social theory.[3] They also provide the dominant motif of Habermas's effort to revive "the unfinished project of modernity."[4]

This study aims to question the terms of the philosophical discussion in which matters of reason, logic, and social order are reduced to a choice between these alternatives. The central thesis of the book can be summarized by the following two proposals: (1) that the search within philosophy and social theory for universal standards of validity, objectivity, precision, and the like, has fallen on bad times, and will likely end in disappointment; and (2) that there are nonetheless relatively stable, conventional methods by which utterances and actions are understood, arguments are assessed, facts are constituted, and disputes are resolved, and that these practical methods for reasoning and acting provide adequate grounds for persons' conduct irrespective of appeals to universal standards of validity or rules of conduct. Throughout this study I shall attempt to make clear how the theoretical fetishization of a vocabulary of rules within the linguistic and social sciences has led to systematic confusion regarding the relationship between logic and social order. At the same time, I hope to demonstrate that the incoherence of "rules" as a privileged theoretical construct does not require that we abandon our ordinary conceptual apparatus for defining activity, explaining behavior, insisting, correcting, citing, and so forth, in which the vocabulary of rules plays an important part.

The "order without rules" thesis is intended to capture the basic elements of what Wittgenstein characterized as "primitive language-games"[5]: that they are instructable; that their mastery consists in learning how moves within a game "point beyond" any specific instance of its play; and finally, that once learned, the basic principles of primitive language-games need no further justification. The "order without rules" thesis thus marks a point of fundamental departure from the terms and implications of the modernist/postmodernist debates: in place of the philosophical dispute over "rational grounding," this argument directs our attention toward standards of practice and methods of judgment that are endogenous to the lived-and-used orders of everyday life.

This thesis, I will argue, is consistent with Wittgenstein's remarks on rules and rule following and with Garfinkel's rejection of "the prevailing proposal that . . . rational properties of practical activities" can be adequately described "using a rule or a standard obtained outside actual settings within which such properties are recognized, used, produced, and talked about by settings' members."[6] The argument of this book draws heavily on lines of inquiry that emerged relatively independently within these two traditions during the 1970s and '80s. It is part of a growing body of work aimed at making explicit the continuities between Wittgensteinian and ethnomethodological approaches to the topics of reason, logic, and social order.[7] What I will term "practice-based inquiries" refers to this hybrid area of work that draws on neo-Wittgensteinian conceptual analysis and ethnomethodological studies of language use and practical action.

Although there are profound differences between Habermas's philosophical program and the theoretical aims of ethnomethodological and Wittgensteinian studies of language and social life, there are also rich grounds for engagement between the two traditions. For instance, Habermas's development of the concept of "communicative action" is explicitly indebted to Wittgenstein's critique of the idea of a transcendental language, and to his later remarks on the internal relation between language use and "form of life."[8] Moreover, Habermas's emphasis on the pragmatics of human agreement is consistent with the ethnomethodological insistence on the contingent and socially managed character of social order and intersubjective understanding, and his search for a linguistically sensitive, interpretive sociology that would explicate the "protosociological" grounds of social inquiry resonates powerfully with ethnomethodology's standing interest in pretheoretical methods of ordering, reasoning about, and accounting for one's daily activities in social terms.[9] Indeed, when compared with the traditions of transcendental philosophy with which he is commonly associated, Habermas's work is distinguished by his willingness to relinquish the strong claims of universal history in favor of a conception of "communicative rationality" that is open in principle to the historical and practical contingencies of rational action.[10]

Apart from Habermas's own reflections on the methodology of the social sciences[11], a serious theoretical engagement between critical theory and practice-based inquiries has so far failed to materialize. This is no doubt due to a generalized indifference on the part of ethnomethodologists and Wittgensteinians toward the sort of constructive theoretical project that Habermas envisions. This (post-)theoretical posture is the hallmark of Wittgenstein's descriptivist assault on the "calculus" model of language, and is present in equal measure in the various "policy statements" by Garfinkel, and Garfinkel and Sacks,[12] which urge ethnomethodologists to treat the explanatory accounts of professional sociologists on par with other species of sociological reasoning. Although these policies have served these traditions well as a form of methodological resistance to reductionist accounts of social behavior, this posture has also led them to disregard any and all attempts at systematic philosophy, even those, such as Habermas's, that are in general accord with a practice-based conception of logic and social order.

The neglect of Habermas's work by ethnomethodologists and Wittgensteinians has been matched, on the side of critical theory, by an absence of discussion of empirical-analytic studies of language use and practical action, and a near total disregard for the fundamental challenge to the project of philosophical ethics posed by Wittgenstein's later work.[13] This situation is all the more curious given Habermas's extensive reliance on Wittgenstein's remarks on rules, grammar, and social practice and his explicit aim of showing how philosophical criteria of "ideal speech" can be derived from empirical-pragmatic structures of communication.

The aim of this book is to establish the basic terms for a critical discourse between the theory of communicative action and the tradition of practice-based inquiries inspired by Wittgenstein and elaborated within the field of ethnomethodology. It will be argued that such a discourse not only is *possible*, but that it is *essential* if critical theory is to move beyond the crisis caused by the decline of the great rationalist social projects of the past two centuries and the rise of postenlightenment and antirationalist movements within the discourse of philosophy and the social sciences. Put simply, while ethnomethodological and Wittgensteinian investigations raise fundamental questions for critical theory, their effect for theoretical projects that allege the collapse of logic, reason, meaning, and order is, in my view, even more devastating. It is the central argument of this book that (when taken in sufficient doses) practice-based inquiries can remedy some of the well-known complaints of critical theory. Like any successful therapy, however, this one comes at a price.

If Habermas's turn toward language and communication affords him leverage on the traditional aporias of critical theory, it also commits him to a line of argument that culminates, *not,* as he would have it, in the logic of the proposition, but rather, in the socio-logic of everyday practice. This shift in the locus of analysis—from linguistic form to practical action—means that the so-called binding force of lifeworld relations is anchored not in *words,* but in the *deeds.* This insight, I will argue, is at the heart of Wittgenstein's conception of "logical-grammar." It is also central to practice-based conceptions of demonstration and proof within ethnomethodology, and has been thematized within this tradition under a variety of rubrics.[14]

The significance of this "turn toward praxis" for the philosophy of language and the science of linguistics is profound. Whereas, from a formal-analytical perspective, the empirical operations of everyday language appear as a confusing array of syntactically and logically incomplete utterances, from a practice-based perspective what is remarkable—indeed, what is *awesome*—is that natural language is sufficient for the conduct of actions and social relations that comprise the unutterably complex fabric of ordinary social life. In short, "what we say" is adequate to "what we do" just because *utterances do not occur abstractly.* Rather, utterances are produced and understood in immediate connection with socially organized courses of practical action. On this perspective, the supposed *logical* defects of ordinary language (incompleteness, inconsistency, indeterminacy, and context-dependence) are to be construed instead as *praxiological* resources: features of the everyday order of speech that demonstrate—in the course of *doing*—the evident binding of the logic of language with incarnate orders of practice.

ORIGINS OF THE ARGUMENT

In the Spring of 1987, Peter Winch was invited to give a lecture to the seminar on "Wittgenstein and Social Science" in the Department of Sociology at Boston University. Although it is often difficult to trace the origin of particular arguments, it is clear that the central idea for this book first came together during that lecture and the round of questions that followed afterward. The paper Winch delivered was an advanced draft of the argument that would later be published as the "Preface to the Second Edition" of his classic study, *The Idea of a Social Science*.[15] The main purpose of the paper was to clarify points of misunderstanding that had emerged in the three decades since the publication of that earlier study and to correct a number of "excesses" and "distortions" in the argument as it originally had been formulated. Central among these was a series of corrections to his earlier position regarding the place of rules and rules descriptions in our understanding of human behavior.

In *The Idea of a Social Science*, Winch had argued that explanations in the natural sciences are logically distinct from explanations in the social sciences insofar as the former are concerned with *causal* explanations of relationships between physical phenomena, whereas the latter are fundamentally concerned with the *reasons* why persons do things; that is, with the motives and intentions lying behind and guiding human action. This distinction between reasons and causes is fundamental to the *Verstehen* tradition in German sociology, and is most closely associated with Max Weber's famous assertion that, "(a)ction is 'social' insofar as its subjective meaning takes account of the behavior of others and is thereby oriented in its course."[16] For Weber, it followed from this definition that in order to understand the meaning of social action we must have recourse to the actors' reasons for acting, and thus, that explanations of social action inevitably involve the interpretation of persons' subjective states. The issue then becomes whether and how we can generalize about actors' subjective states such that we can identify principles of rational interpretation that will ensure the validity of social scientific explanations. It is this desire to identify general principles for understanding and interpreting social action that lies behind his typology of social action into the four action orientations of purposive-rational, value-rational, affective, and traditional action.[17]

By framing the problem of understanding as that of closing the gap between "what (objectively) is observed" and "why (subjectively) it was done," Weber commits the *Verstehen* tradition to a conception of social action as logically incomplete. Since social actions always include some inner, subjective component, it is always necessary to engage in a process of interpretation in order to understand their meanings. What distinguishes social scientific understanding from other forms of interpretation is that the methodological discourse of the social sciences is explicit about the tension between subjective meaning and the demands of rational explanation, and hence, is uniquely aware of the special burden this tension places on explanatory accounts of social action. Since the subjective states of individual actors are not directly available for analysis, social scientific interpretations will always represent approximations of persons' subjective reasons for acting in particular cases. However, since social scientific explanations are designed to abstract from individual cases in order to understand the behavior of larger groups, their validity does not depend on their faithfulness to individual actors' reasons, but rests instead on their correspondence to the more general social and historical motivations that characterize these larger populations. In this way, Weber transforms the *theoretical* problem of understanding meaning into the *methodological* problem of developing rational procedures for interpreting the subjective meaning of actions.

In *The Idea of a Social Science*, Winch argued that Weber's formulation of the *Verstehen* problematic trades on a confusion concerning the conceptual logic of understanding and its relationship to subjective meaning. Following Wittgenstein, Winch argued that the meaning of actions is not dependent on the "inner" mental life of individual actors. Rather, the concepts with which we recognize and understand the actions of others are the same concepts we use to formulate and understand our own behavior. The language for describing, interpreting, and understanding social action is itself a matter of publicly organized, publicly ratified social convention, and, as such, is constitutively related to the social practices and events of which it forms a part. As Winch wrote:

> The impression given is that first there is language (with words having a meaning, statements capable of being true or false) and then, this being given, it comes to enter into human relationships and to be modified by the particular human relationships into which it does so enter. What is missed is that those very categories of meaning, etc., are *logically* dependent for their sense on social interaction between men.[18]

On this argument, actions occur within practical contexts of social interaction, and are inseparable from the endogenous, public conditions of their production, interpretation, and understanding. Moreover, like a language, social actions are conventionally ordered, and are understood with reference to the expectations and texture of moral commitments that shape what Wittgenstein had called "agreement . . . in form of life."[19]

This is a crucial step in Winch's argument, and forms the core of the conception of "rules" that he later disavows in the "Preface." The general structure of his argument in *The Idea of a Social Science* can be summarized as follows:

1. Language (as Wittgenstein has shown) is organized by social convention, and is—in this nontranscendental, normative sense—rule-governed;
2. As in the case of the meaning of our words, the meaning of our actions is internally related to the language and to the system of social conventions that provide for their recognition and understanding in the first instance;
3. It follows from this that, in Winch's words, "all behavior which is meaningful (therefore all specifically human behavior) is *ipso facto* rule governed."[20]

Implicit in this argument are two fundamental criticisms of Weber's position. First, by maintaining the strong distinction between observable social actions and their subjective meanings, Weber fails to acknowledge the depth to which the reasoning and conduct of individuals—and of individuals' "inner" lives—is conventionally organized and understood. At the same time, by attempting to subject explanations of social behavior to the autonomous logic of the social sciences, Weber is forced to overlook the rational structure of social actions that is internal to the practical context(s) within which they are produced, recognized, and understood. By showing that the logic of understanding is derived from within the ordinary language and lifeworld relations of practical actors, Winch aims to replace Weber's picture—in which meaning can be approached only "from the outside," through the autonomous logic of the social sciences— with the more anthropological image of a conventionally ordered world in which many kinds of cultural practices are possible, and among these, those forms of systematic inquiry we call science. In this way, the rational structure of scientific inquiries is made to depend on methods of reasoning and interpretation that provide the practical foundations for organized social life, and not, as in Weber, the other way around. For Winch, the normative order of practical action is both the object and the medium for social scientific inquiries, and it is the ordinary concepts we use which, in the final analysis, provide us with what leverage we have on the problem of understanding meaning.[21]

WINCH'S REFORMULATION OF THE "RULES ARGUMENT"

I recount this argument in some detail not only as backdrop to Winch's correctives in the "Preface to the Second Edition," but also because the position outlined in *The Idea of a Social Science* has been so prominent in the thinking of a generation of scholars regarding the implications of Wittgenstein's later writings for the philosophy of the social sciences. Of particular concern are the consequences of Winch's "rules argument"—and his insistence that "all behavior which is meaningful . . . is *ipso facto* rule-governed"—for the way in which interpreters after Winch have understood Wittgenstein's notion of "language games." This issue is central to Winch's remarks in the "Preface," where he details a series of significant reformulations and adjustments of this argument. The inspiration for the present study stems from the fact that these reformulations and adjustments fail in several ways to take full account of the more profound objections to Winch's argument in *The Idea of a Social Science*. They nevertheless articulate a direction of movement in the arguments that the present study seeks generally to endorse and extend.

Winch begins this section of the "Preface" by reiterating the general strategy of the rules argument he had pursued in *The Idea of a Social Science*. This argument (which is summarized in the section above) is based on a reading of Wittgenstein that foregrounds a rather narrow conception of "rules" and "rule following" as these apply to language, and then assumes that, like language, other types of human activity can be regarded generally as forms of rule following behavior. In the "Preface" Winch characterizes his earlier position as having been "far from sufficiently careful in the way [it] expressed the relevance of the notion of a rule, both to language and to other forms of behavior."[22] What he means by this is clarified in the subsequent paragraph, where he writes:

> In Chapter I, Section 8, where I first discussed the matter seriously, I did not explicitly write that all uses of language are rule-governed. But in Chapter II, Section 2, I was much less circumspect: the claim . . . that being committed to some future action by what I do now is formally similar to being committed to a subsequent use of a word by a definition, is followed by: 'It follows that I can only be committed to something in the future by what I do now if my present act is the *application of a rule*.' But this does *not* follow from anything said in the previous section, nor do I think it true as it stands. Things become worse in Chapter II, Section 3, where I claimed that 'all behavior which is meaningful (therefore all specifically human behavior) is *ipso facto* rule-governed' (p. 52). I did, it is true, attempt to qualify this late in the

Section by distinguishing different kinds of rules, but I do not now think this is enough to put things right.[23]

In this passage Winch confronts two related problems with his earlier formulation of Wittgenstein's remarks on rules and rule following. The first has to do with the difference between our use of rules to *explain* or *describe* how something is done, and the claim that doing some specific thing necessarily involves the application of a particular rule. It is one thing to provide an account of some activity in terms of rules for acting, reasoning, playing, and so forth, and quite another to actually do something by virtue of "following the rules."[24] The second issue concerns the sheer diversity involved in our vocabulary of rules, and its implications for the philosophical project of making general statements about the nature of rules and rule following. As Gordon Baker has remarked, even within the rather restricted domain of games, rules take many forms:

> There are duty-imposing rules, rules conferring powers or rights, rules granting permissions, rules modifying the application of other rules, ideal rules (e.g., "a goalie should always be alert"), so-called "constitutive" rules (e.g., "a goal is scored when the ball is fairly kicked between two posts"), general and particular rules, conditional and unconditional rules, etc.[25]

Although a number of philosophers and linguists working within the Austinian tradition of speech act theory have attempted to typologize the major categories of rules,[26] the breadth and variety of usage is indicative of the problems encountered in trying to formalize this vast vocabulary of rules and their place within different orders of practice.

The implication of Winch's original argument in *The Idea of a Social Science* was that social practices could be analyzed like games, where a game is constituted by a set of socially agreed conventions, and intelligible play consists in applying those rules in any particular case. Rules are understood to operate as criteria for judging the correctness or incorrectness of behavior with respect to some conventional order of play. This picture of social practice not only depends on an exceedingly narrow conception of games and of how rules operate in game contexts, it also seeks to extend gamelike principles of social organization well beyond the limits of their legitimate application.

Such overextensions of the concept of a "game" are something of a commonplace among interpreters of Wittgenstein, and are no doubt due to confusion surrounding the idea of "language-games" and the related notion of "forms of life." In Winch's original argument, Wittgenstein's notion of a language-game is read through a conception of rules in which discrete areas of practice are defined by sets of governing conventions. As Winch notes in the "Preface," this argument gives the impression "of social practices, traditions, institutions etc., as more or less self-contained and each going its own, fairly autonomous, way."[27] And, indeed, this is precisely how a number of commentators have understood this argument. Habermas, for instance, is clearly reading Wittgenstein through the lens of this argument when he writes:

> In opposition to the positivist bias, Wittgenstein certainly first brought to awareness the fact that the application of grammatical rules is not in turn defined by general rules on the symbolic level but rather can only be learned as a connection between language and practice and internalized as part of a form of life. But he remained positivistic enough to think of this training process as the reproduction of a fixed pattern, as though socialized individuals were wholly subsumed under their language and activities. The language game congeals in his hands into an opaque oneness.[28]

If logic is conceived as the philosophical task of identifying universal rules of thought and action that unite the various modes of social behavior, then the "rules argument" that Winch developed in *The Idea of a Social Science* appears to be in opposition to that project. As a counter to this position, Habermas argues that "(in) actuality, language spheres are not monadically sealed but porous, in relation both to what is outside and to what is inside."[29] Here Habermas interposes the principle of translation as a way of mediating between the different "spheres" of language and cultural practice that he attributes to Wittgenstein's conception of language games. This principle of translation, which Habermas identifies with the tradition of philosophical hermeneutics, is then universalized as a background condition of every act of communication:

> As a limiting case in hermeneutics . . . translation reveals a form of reflection that we perform implicitly in every linguistic communication. In naive conversation it is concealed, for in reliably institutionalized language games understanding rests on an unproblematic basis of agreement—it is "not an interpretive process but a life process."[30]

Once language-games (and, by extension, "forms of life") are conceived as internally ordered, autonomous spheres of linguistic and cultural practice, the problem rather naturally arises of how it is we come to know and understand the operations of one kind of language-game from within the assumptions, practices, and rules of conduct of another. It is this conception of language-games, together with a willingness to extend this model to all other areas of social life, that lies at the heart of Winch's famous "incommensurability thesis": that different cultures are based in fundamentally different orders of belief and social convention, and thus, operate with standards (of reason, cogency, order, and the like) that are, strictly speaking, incomparable.[31] Although this argument is directed primarily against attempts within the philosophy of science to develop methods of reason and proof that serve as universally valid standards for assessing knowledge claims, it also implies that the social world is organized into an array of static, self-enclosed, self-validating orders of practice. The effect of this argument is thus to replace one kind of formal picture with another. From here, it is a rather small step to attribute this conception of the general structure of language games to Wittgenstein.

In chapters 1 and 5, I will discuss in much greater detail how this picture of language-games fits within the broader architecture of the theory of communicative action. For now it is important to see how in general Habermas uses Winch in order to read the *Philosophical Investigations* across the grain of Wittgenstein's own remarks. The point of Wittgenstein's discussion of rules and rule following in the early passages of the *Philosophical Investigations* was not to proffer a conception of social life in which ordinary activities are dependent upon static, internally related sets of rules, but rather, as Baker has so aptly put it, "to render transparently ridiculous the idea of a hidden or unconscious *following* of a *rule*."[32] In Habermas's reading, by contrast, Wittgensteinian language games are seen as "monadically sealed," isolated domains of linguistic and cultural practice. They thus stand in need of supplement by a principle of translation that would allow movement between these different spheres of cultural life. Ironically, in this reading Wittgenstein's "theory" is made to generate a universal principle—the principle of translation—which, according to Habermas, is internalized through the process of communication.

In the "Preface," Winch attempts to sharpen his position in *The Idea of a Social Science* by conceding that his argument as it was originally formulated relied on "an overidealization of logic."[33] By this he means that the picture of autonomous spheres of social activity represented an attempt to generalize, if only in the negative, about the relationship between logic and social action, and, as such, failed to take the full measure of the claim that "criteria of logic are not a direct gift of God, but arise out of, and are only intelligible in the context of, ways of living or modes of social life."[34] The idea that logic is dependent upon concrete social practice does not mean that we must reject *all* standards of understanding, argument, and criticism. On the contrary, it requires only that we reject the philosophical project of identifying *universal* standards for adjudicating between competing epistemic claims. As Winch continues:

> The logico-conceptual difficulties which arise when ways of
> thinking which have their roots in different reaches of human life
> are brought to bear on each other cannot be resolved by any
> appeal to a formal system—whether a God-given system of logical
> principles or a system of modes of social life, each with criteria of
> intelligibility peculiar to itself.[35]

Thus, Winch is ready to foreclose on the enlightenment project of identifying
universal standards of reason, understanding, and criticism whether these
are based in transcendental philosophy, or are, as in the case of Habermas,
justified in terms of a "transcendental-pragmatic" argument regarding the
normative foundations of everyday speech.[36] He nonetheless wants to pull
back from the apparently relativistic implications of his argument in *The
Idea of a Social Science,* and to insist that there are standards by which
beliefs are evaluated, arguments assessed, reasons given, and so forth, and
that these rules of conduct have all the cogency and force of what, in the
enlightenment vision, was associated with the notion of "logic." What is
wanted, then, is not a better explanation of the underlying "core" of human
linguistic behavior, but rather, a thoroughgoing renovation of our conception
of logic in order to accommodate the diversity of standards, rules, principles,
and methods of application, that comprise the practical foundations of
ordinary social conduct (where "ordinary" means: "without recourse to a
singular, formal-analytic conception of 'rules.'")

PLAN OF THE BOOK

In chapter 1 I outline the theoretical basis for Habermas's attempt at
grounding critical theory in the normative foundations of everyday speech. I
then discuss the methodological posture he adopts toward the "problem of
understanding meaning in the social science," and I introduce a series of
critical arguments on behalf of a practice-based approach to these issues.
The aim of this preliminary discussion is to define, in the broadest terms
possible, the bearing that ethnomethodological and neo-Wittgensteinian
approaches to logic and social order have on Habermas's project.

In chapter 2 I begin a more directed discussion of Habermas's formal
pragmatic theory of meaning. Trading off of the methodological discussion
begun in chapter 1, I argue that the distinction he makes between "formal"
and "empirical pragmatics" misunderstands the nature of argument, discovery, and demonstration in the empirical-analytic sciences of action.
Although it is sometimes claimed that grammatical relations can be studied
inductively, on the basis of empirical instances of actual speech, I argue that
even where empirical materials figure centrally to analysis, elucidations of

grammar are to be understood as *logical* results, based ultimately in our rational intuitions as speakers of a natural language. This argument has the effect of collapsing the distinction (implied by Habermas's argument) between formal and empirical pragmatics, and of challenging the assertion that "(a)n empirical pragmatics without a formal-pragmatic point of departure would not have the conceptual instruments needed to recognize the rational basis of linguistic communication in the confusing complexity of the scenes observed."[37] On the contrary, one of the most significant methodological and analytical lessons of the past three decades of work in ethnomethodology and conversation analysis is that the classical project of explanatory theory vastly underestimates the scope, depth, and diversity of analytical resources that are *already present in the field of action*. In short, the task of "recognizing the rational basis of linguistic communication in the . . . scenes observed" is not, in the first instance, a theoretical project. Rather, it is a matter of local, practical, and material concern for persons engaged in talk and social interaction.

In chapter 3 I resume the critique of the formal pragmatic theory of meaning, focusing on Searle's theory of speech acts, and its place within Habermas's larger argument concerning the logical foundations of everyday speech. My aim is to challenge the assumption that the logical force of utterances is bound to the assertoric force of the (literal) proposition. I argue that this conception of logic fails to comprehend the nature and significance of ethnomethodology's claim concerning the radical indexicality of expression.[38] For Habermas, indexicality is understood against the backdrop of a linguistic model of literal and explicit semantic reference. Indexical expressions are thus seen essentially as *elisions* of certain features of the full term of reference that then need to be filled in by the context of the utterance. In this way, the analytical separation between utterance and context is preserved: what is said indexically is a context specific version of a literal and explict, context-independent expression. In the writings of ethnomethodologists and conversation analysts, by contrast, the "indexicality of utterances" functions as an analytic gloss on the general circumstance that utterances work to constitute the local environment for their receipt, interpretation, and understanding. When compared with the linguistic model, this conception of indexicality amounts to a dereification of *utterances* and their *contexts of production* and a consequent shift in analytical attention to the logical properties of utterances in situ.

Chapter 4 represents a turning point in the argument of the book. Having made the case for the relevance of practice-based inquiries to Habermas's program, and having explored in some detail how the findings of ethnomethodology and conversation analysis lead Habermas to recast his conception of the logical foundations of speech, I then consider a series of developments internal to the recent history of conversation analysis. Here I argue that there has been a steady movement within that discipline toward a foundationalist conception of the sequential organization of speech. While this shared interest in identifying the normative foundations of everyday speech makes an alignment between critical theory and conversation analysis all the more attractive, I argue that the foundational claims made by conversation analysts on behalf of certain "base structures" of sequential organization lack the sort of demonstrative warrant they presume. The effect of this argument is to once again throw the project of identifying "ultimate grounds" into question.

In chapter 5 and the conclusion I return to the hermeneutic model of communicative rationality proposed by Habermas, and attempt to locate it within a broader conceptual history of the constitution of the Cartesian subject within modern linguistic thought. I then argue that Wittgenstein's remarks on rules and rule following point a way through the apparent tension between individual subjectivity and structural determination that is a legacy of this tradition. As the argument of this book will make clear, Habermas's conception of logic fails to relinquish its ties to Cartesianism. Yet this is precisely what a thoroughly Wittgensteinian approach to questions of meaning and understanding would require him to do. The consequences of practice-based inquiries for Habermas are thus far more radical than he supposes, and at some point it will need to be reckoned whether the cure is worth the cost of treatment: whether it is possible to sustain a critical theory grounded in normative structures of communication and practical action, or whether, as Rorty has suggested, critical theory should give up entirely on the program of seeking independent justification for an ethics of communication.[39]

1

The "Binding Force" of Everyday Speech

> If a distinction works well for practical purposes in
> ordinary life (no mean feat, for even ordinary life is full of
> hard cases), then there is sure to be something in it, it will
> not mark nothing: yet this is likely enough to be not the
> best way of arranging things if our interests are more
> extensive or intellectual than the ordinary. . . . Certainly,
> then, ordinary language is not the last word: in principle it
> can everywhere be supplemented and improved upon and
> superseded. Only remember, it *is* the *first* word.
> —J. L. Austin, "A Plea for Excuses"

The full weight of the theory of communicative action rests on the following claim: That the relationship between the logic of language and moral insight is such that, in submitting to the force of the former, one is inevitably drawn into processes of understanding and mutual obligation that underlie the development of the latter. This claim is based in turn on Habermas's central intuition that our use of everyday language presupposes *in principle* the possibility of obtaining intersubjective agreement concerning the basic moral and epistemological texture of a commonly inhabited world. On this view, everyday speech provides the core (socio-)logical medium in which "different participants overcome their merely subjective views and, owing to the mutuality of rationally motivated conviction, assure themselves of both the unity of the objective world and the intersubjectivity of their lifeworld."[1] Habermas's concept of "communicative rationality" is designed to capture precisely this link between the "binding force" of everyday speech, on the one hand, and processes of rational interpretation and argumentation, on the other.

The aim of this chapter is to establish a more rigorous connection between Habermas's theory of communicative action and the tradition of practice-based inquiries inspired by Wittgenstein and elaborated by the ethnomethodologists. I will begin by examining the motivation behind

15

Habermas's attempt to develop a pragmatic theory of meaning that links the formal conditions for communicative rationality to empirical studies of language and social life. Here I trace Habermas's concern with the pragmatic structure of everyday language to his reconstruction of the rationality problematic in Weber, and in particular, to his critique of Weber's thesis regarding the materialization of positive law in modern society. In contrast to Weber, who argued that positive law is characterized by forms of procedural rationality which, in the modern period, becomes increasingly cut off from the traditional authority of customary practice, Habermas argues that the demand for rationality, which is intrinsic to positive law, forces a reliance on processes of practical-moral argumentation that arise *outside* the domain of legal discourse, within the "substantive rationality" of everyday public life. For this argument to succeed, Habermas needs to demonstrate that this "substantive rationality" is linked both with formal processes of argumentation, on the one hand, and with the actual conduct of speech and social activity, on the other. Hence, the ability to link-up with empirically guided analyses of speech and social activity is a crucial test of Habermas's theory, and indeed, of *any* program that would travel down the road mapped by the theory of communicative action.

Following this preliminary discussion, an attempt will be made to deepen the connection between practice-based inquiries and the theory of communicative action through a consideration of Habermas's reflections on "the problem of understanding meaning in the social sciences." Here I contrast Habermas's conception of "rational interpretation" based on the model of philosophical hermeneutics with an approach, common to ethnomethodological and Wittgensteinian investigations, which treats problems of interpretation, translation, understanding, and agreement as occasioned by, and intelligible with respect to, actual courses of practical action.

CRITICAL THEORY AND THE RATIONALIZATION OF MODERN LEGAL SYSTEMS

In his 1971 essay, "Does Philosophy Still Have a Purpose?," Habermas identifies "three urgent tasks" for critical theory: (1) to provide a critique of "the objectivistic self-understanding of the sciences and any scientistic concept of science and scientific progress"; (2) to establish relations with methodological questions in the social sciences such that "the elaboration of adequate basic concepts for systems of communicative action [is] not hindered but promoted"; and 3) to elucidate "the dimension in which the connection of the logic of research and technological development with the logic of consensus-forming communication becomes clear."[2] According to Habermas, only a philosophical program capable of absorbing the late-twentieth-century critique of "totalizing knowledge," while at the same time preserving the utopian content associated with a rationally grounded interest in emancipation, can gain a practical-democratic foothold in the present age. Such a philosophy, he argues, "no longer conceives itself as philosophy," but rather, "understands itself as critique" and "apprehends itself as the reflective element of social activity."[3]

The theory of communicative action attempts to deliver on the emancipatory promise of critical theory by situating the critique of instrumental reason within a formal theory of meaning and argumentation. According to Habermas, the writings of the Frankfurt School had left critical theory at an impasse: by extending Weber's concept of rationalization to the totality of social and economic relations, critical theory was able to expose processes of fragmentation, distortion, and monadization at the core of modernist conceptions of reason. At the same time, the reflexive application of this critique meant that critical theory was itself incapable of providing rationally grounded (nonarbitrary, nonauthoritarian) standards of truth and political will formation. Elsewhere, Habermas summarizes the consequences of this negative critique for the prospects of systematic philosophy:

> Horkheimer and Adorno radicalize Lukács' critique of reification. They do not consider the rationalization of the world to be only "seemingly complete"; and thus they need a conceptual apparatus that will allow them nothing less than to denounce the whole as untrue. They cannot achieve this aim by way of an immanent critique of science, because a conceptual apparatus that could satisfy their desiderata would still share the pretensions of the great philosophical tradition. But this tradition—and this is the Weberian thorn in the side of critical theory—cannot simply be renewed with its systematic pretensions; it has "outlived" its own claims; in any case, it cannot be renewed in the form of philosophy.[4]

The lesson Habermas draws from the self-annihilating critiques of Horkheimer and Adorno is that such a philosophy—critical of present society but unable to make any foundational claims in its own right—risks degenerating into a contentless, "empty exercise of a self-reflection."[5] According to Habermas, critical theory can avoid this fate only by turning its attention back to the field of concrete social praxis. No longer able to exclude itself from the contingent workings of everyday life, critical theory must locate itself *within* those workings, and must seek to identify the "kernel of rationality" that is both internal to the conduct of communicative action and constitutive of the possibility of rational criticism. Habermas's concept of "communicative rationality" is intended to capture this substantial, critical, and rational element implicit in all "communication aimed at understanding." This shift in focus—away from the critique of consciousness, which characterized the work of his Frankfurt School predecessors, and toward the development of a positive theory of communicative praxis grounded in the normative order of lifeworld relations—can be better understood against the backdrop of Habermas's reconstruction of Weber's theory of the rationalization of law in modern societies.[6]

Weber's conception of the rationalization of modern legal institutions is situated within his more general theory of the transition from traditional to posttraditional forms of social organization. Weber argues that this transition is characterized by ongoing processes of institutional differentiation and rationalization. On this view, areas of public life which in traditional societies arise out of the customary and practical social behavior of a people are, in the modern world, progressively differentiated into relatively autonomous spheres of activity—of art, science, and law. Each of these three spheres develops its own distinctive patterns of organization and rationality. In so doing, they become increasingly detached both from one another, and from the traditional patterns of organization typical of premodern social life. Hence, the prevailing trajectory of development of modern legal systems is toward the formalization of legal statutes and procedures in line with a mode of legal rationality that is increasingly specialized and technical, and so increasingly cut off from the traditional authority of practical (or "customary") moral life.

For this reason, Weber concludes that in modern societies the legitimacy of legal authority cannot be derived from principles of practical moral life, but rests instead on the legitimacy of forms of rationality—methods of codification, procedural requirements, standards of argument, and so on—that are "intrinsic to the form of law itself." Hence, for Weber, "any fusion of law and morality threatens the rationality of law and thus the basis of the legitimacy of legal domination."[7]

With the rise of the modern welfare state, however, we witness precisely this sort of interpenetration of law and morality as legal systems increasingly are called on to arbitrate between the competing claims of different sectors of society in line with ethically charged notions of equality, social justice, and the like. What Weber diagnosed as the "materialization of law" is the process by which the formal structure of the legal system is broken down by external demands for substantive justice, and by the revelation of the law's sensitivity (and hence, susceptibility) to the pressures of practical-moral disputes. According to Weber, this development threatens the autonomy of legal rationality, and with it, the viability of the legal system as a form of social control.

Weber's theory of the rationalization of law provides Habermas with a critical foil for advancing an alternative account of the socio-logical basis of legal-rational authority. According to Habermas, Weber's crucial mistake was that he conceived legal rationality too narrowly, without attending to the historically specific conditions that make the form of rationality peculiar to bourgeois formal law both plausible and legitimate.[8] Habermas first points out that Weber's conception of the "rational" is meant to exclude all moral valuations or so-called subjective value orientations. His conception of "legal rationality" thus carries with it overtones of a "pure" rationality in which practical-moral considerations are excluded *by definition* from the domain of rational dispute and deliberation.

It is at this point that Habermas makes his most compelling argument against the view that the legitimacy of modern legal systems is grounded in the autonomous rationality of positive law. What Weber overlooked, according to Habermas, was that the different modes of formal rationality—the procedural, the purposive, and the scientific—all rely on relatively informal, practical methods of moral reasoning. He thus failed to appreciate the degree to which practical reason, though concerned with the common moral life of the community, is nevertheless deeply woven into formal procedures of deliberation and adjudication, and further, that these practical methods of moral reasoning follow a procedural logic that is at core *rational*, in the classical sense of "being capable of formalization." Habermas then argues that an analytic distinction can be made between the value orientations that emerge in the course of practical moral discussion, which are contingent and particularistic, and the procedural (socio-)logic on which practical moral discourse is (ideally) based. As he concludes:

> Weber did not recognize [the] moral core of civil law because he qualified moral insights as subjective value orientations . . . He did not distinguish the preference for values which, within the limits of specific cultural life forms and traditions, *commend* themselves, so to speak, as superior to other values, on the one hand, from the moral oughtness of norms that *obligate* equally all whom they address, on the other. He did not separate the value judgments spread across the whole range of competing value contents from the formal aspect of the binding force or validity of norms, a validity that does not vary with the contents of the norms. In a word, he did not take ethical formalism seriously.[9]

Far from denying the profound effects of processes of rationalization, Habermas's strategy is to *extend* Weber's rationalization thesis by showing how a belief in the autonomous rationality of modern legal systems is itself historically situated and mythical in nature, and how the demand for rationality that is intrinsic to positive law forces a reliance on processes of argumentation that first appear outside the domain of legal discourse. While he agrees with Weber, for instance, that "[i]n positive law all norms have, at least in principle, lost their sheer customary validity,"[10] the consequence he draws from this is that the formal principles of positive law, and with them, the rationality and legitimacy of their exercise, have become increasingly subject to inspection and rational critique within the practical-moral discourse of the public sphere. Whereas for Weber, the autonomy of positive law is threatened by incursions from (an essentially irrational) public discourse, for Habermas, that "threat" signifies the development of a critical public discourse in which forms of practical-moral reasoning and argument that are basic to the exercise of legal authority increasingly are brought into view.

Once the burden of legitimation has been shifted from the autonomous rationality of positive law to the development of forms of critical public discourse, the question then becomes whether or not these critical discourses are themselves legitimate bearers of the concept of rationality (where "rationality" is construed in the positive sense of the methods by which a community expresses a reflexive grasp of the rights, duties, and principles of mutual recognition and respect that form the basis of enlightened forms of political association). Here Habermas argues that while rational disputes over the legitimacy of legal norms are conducted in terms that are suitable to the legal culture in which they arise—that is, in line with modes of legal argumentation—they must also inevitably appeal to "the internal constraints of a logic of argumentation for producing good reasons."[11] The upshot of this argument is that Weber's diagnosis concerning the threat to the autonomy of legal-rationality in posttraditional society was essentially correct, though for different reasons than he suspected. Processes of rationalization at work within posttraditional society bring with them a growing awareness that the claim of positive law to represent the moral will of a community stands in need of continual testing and discursive validation. These processes of testing and validation rely, in turn, on principles of argumentation and language use that are drawn from outside of legal culture proper. As Habermas puts it: "The legitimacy of legality is due to the interlocking of two types of procedures, namely, of legal processes with processes of moral argumentation that obey a procedural rationality of their own."[12]

The task Habermas sets for critical theory is to recover the rational basis, or "procedural rationality," underlying legitimate processes of practical reasoning and argumentation. In contrast to the writings of Horkheimer and Adorno, which grew increasingly pessimistic in their attempt to swim against the rising tide of Weberian rationalization, Habermas opts instead to enter fully and self-consciously into the very center of the stream. The theory of communicative action presupposes the rationalization of communication, and with it, of all practical-moral life.[13] The question is no longer whether or not processes of rationalization will win the day, but rather, what specific form the outcomes of those processes will take; how "rationality" will be defined and understood; or again, which pillars will stand at the center of a "rational society" and which will be consigned to its margins. We thus arrive at the strategy, so central to the theory of communicative action, of seeking a way around the rather grim implications of Weber's rationalization thesis via the elaboration of a positive conception of forms of rationality specific to communicative action.

This seemingly counterintuitive strategy—of opposing instrumental rationality by embracing processes of rationalization—makes sense once we adopt a longer view in which purposive-rationality is seen as a contingent moment within a more general and encompassing history of rationalization. Habermas's strategy is to reach back behind Weber in order to reconstruct a history of rationalization that extends in directions other than the narrow trajectory mapped by the concept of purposive-rationality; *an alternative history that traces the development of rational properties of practical-moral discourse.* This is what Habermas means when he accuses Weber of not having taken ethical formalism "seriously enough": that Weber failed to recognize *first,* that the mode of rationality specific to legal discourse trades on elements of practical reason and moral argumentation that shape the taken-for-granted discursive backdrop of everyday life in modern civil society; and *second,* that this practical-moral discourse has specifiable formal properties, and therefore is itself *rationalizable.*

In sum, the theory of communicative action aims to *deepen* Weber's claim regarding the progressive rationalization of the modern world by showing how, under conditions of modernity, processes of rationalization are implicated in the very constitution of the lifeworld, and hence, in the most basic structures of human experience and social relations. Of course, this trajectory of development is itself a contingent theoretical projection that remains to be realized through actual developments in social and political practice. In this regard, the concept of "communicative rationality" is, as Gunn points out:

> less . . . a panacea or guarantee than . . . a "wager": a wager in which reason and salvation are not gambled against each other, as in Pascal, but in which reason and salvation weigh together on the same side. This is so if, on the one hand, communication and theorizing as an instance of communication are seen as projecting—prefiguring—mutual recognition . . . and if, on the other, mutual recognition is seen as the medium in which theory and reason exist.[14]

Philosophy and social theory can become a "practical force" to the extent that they are able to locate themselves as a critical and redemptive moment within this history of the rationalization of society. The purpose of a critical theory of society is thus to elaborate concepts of "reason" and "understanding" that are sufficient to oppose the rationalizing effects of instrumental reason at the primordial level of everyday thought and practical social experience.

CRITICAL THEORY AND ORDINARY PRACTICE

In order to develop a concept of communicative rationality that resists the reduction of "what is reasonable" to "what is effective," Habermas needs to insist on a strong distinction between instrumental, or "purposive rationality," and the "substantive rationality of everyday life." Moreover, he needs to show that the latter is *in principle* irreducible to the former. At this point the relevance of practice-based inquiries for Habermas's project becomes clear: it is these traditions that have elaborated a methodologically consistent approach to the study of everyday life that neither reduces practical action to categories of formal analysis, nor forsakes the analytical issues associated with the classical problematics of reason, logic, and social order.

In the Introduction, I argued that Wittgenstein's remarks on rules and rule following were directed primarily against theoretical idealizations of the foundations of human behavior. In parallel fashion, ethnomethodological studies are founded on a radical critique of theoretical idealizations of practical action. It was this issue that exercised Garfinkel in his early critique of Parsons: namely, that those features of practical activities that constitute their organizational coherence—their reasonability, comprehensibility, order, and sense—are irreducible to the terms of "rational action" contemplated by constructive theorizing in general, and by Parsons's conception of the "unit act" in particular.[15] Parsons's "rational actor" was seen by Garfinkel as the theoretical product of professional sociology's preoccupation with formal-analytic theories of action: a "judgmental dope" who in principle would be incapable of functioning in the social world, much less of actively participating in its constitution.

Studies by Garfinkel and the first generation of ethnomethodologists[16] were aimed at exploring the diversity of methods of practical reasoning in order to demonstrate the staggering insufficiency of prevailing social scientific conceptions of rational action to the actual, concerted activities of social actors, and to begin to outline a set of alternatives for sociological investigations of the classical themes of reason, logic, and order.[17]

Unfortunately, this radical epistemological critique is often blunted by textbook interpretations of the ethnomethodological "classics." As Sharrock and Anderson have recently pointed out, while Garfinkel's famous "breaching experiments" were originally formulated as investigations of the practical limitations on specific modes of inquiry, and thus on particular species of rational action, textbook accounts routinely describe them as demonstrations of the fragility and contingency of social order.[18] For example, in one of these well-known exercises students were asked to engage people in casual conversation, and to insist at every opportunity on further clarification regarding the variously ambiguous, nonliteral, or indexical features of the other person's remarks. On Sharrock and Anderson's account, the demand for full-on semantic clarity—a requirement that has a home within the practices of scientific theorizing—is here being juxtaposed with the rational expectations of ordinary conversation. As might be expected, "[t]he implementation of that requirement [of semantic clarity] does not, however, result in better organized, more rationally conducted conversation but in the disruption, even destruction, of the conversation itself."[19] Thus, Garfinkel's experiment demonstrates not only the *difficulties* of making ordinary conversation accountable to the methods and practices of scientific inquiry, it shows the *impossibility* of doing so. As such, it provides *prima facie* evidence that the rational properties of practical activities are irreducible to any one standard or any single set of uniform criteria of rational action.

Like Wittgenstein, Garfinkel insists on the socio-logical integrity of ordinary speech and social activity, and on the sufficiency of endogenous methods of reasoning and acting to the task of organizing and comprehending everyday events. On this account, reason is not "abolished," but is respecified praxiologically as "the rational properties of practical activities that emerge in and as the course of those activities' orderly conduct." In contrast to Wittgenstein, however, Garfinkel envisions a program of empirical sociological inquiry that extends beyond the critique of philosophical method. This program seeks to recover socially organized methods of practical action such that the diverse species of "rationality-in-practice" come into plainer view.

Although the conception of rationality that emerges from Garfinkel's program of ethnomethodological studies contrasts markedly with the formal-analytic conception developed by Habermas—and indeed, takes its point of departure from a critique of systematic theory—there are nonetheless three areas of significant overlap between the two projects:

1. Both reject the standing model of "rational action" as an unwarranted reduction on the "rational properties of practical activities";
2. both maintain that a rejection of this narrow conception of rationality is a first step toward understanding how social activities are described, explained, argued about, and understood in situ; and

3. Both regard these practical methods of description, explanation, argument, and understanding as definitive of what it means for social activities to be capable of being "rationalized."

This general agreement on basic issues surrounding the rationality problematic provides initial grounds for a dialogue between ethnomethodology and the theory of communicative action.

A further warrant for presuming that practice-based inquiries have serious bearing for Habermas's project concerns the stated requirement that the formal criteria of communicative rationality be grounded in what Habermas terms "empirical pragmatic" analyses of communication. In order to demonstrate that the criteria of communicative rationality are foundational to the overall structure of the lifeworld, Habermas must find a way of linking the distinction between "purposive-rational action" and "communication aimed at understanding" to the basic conditions of everyday speech. However, by focusing exclusively on the linguistic determinants of order and meaning, the theory of communicative action leaves aside many of the most salient issues concerning the pragmatic organization of speech and social activity, issues to which ethnomethodologists and conversation analysts have closely attended in their empirically guided studies of language and social life.[20] By restricting his conception of pragmatics to the terms of formal linguistic analysis, Habermas is constrained to adopt a narrowly cognitivist approach to the pragmatics of understanding and agreement.

Habermas defines "communicative action" as communication aimed at understanding, and contrasts communicative action with purposive-rational action, or action aimed at producing some instrumental effect. The question of whether or not some utterance is "aimed at understanding," however, is, for Habermas, determined by reference to formal-pragmatic criteria of communicative rationality (truth, rightness, and sincerity). But these criteria refer, in turn, to determinations of whether or not that discourse, or any of its particulars, is "aimed at understanding," thus forcing a regress to the definition of communicative action. While this conceptual bootstrapping may be a useful for framing the central intuition of an ethics of communication grounded in the normative expectations of everyday speech, it is inadequate to the task of specifying what the procedural rationality of understanding and agreement comes down to in practice. In order to sustain the claim of having provided pragmatic criteria for distinguishing between communicative rationality and instrumental reason the theory of communicative action needs to be linked to material sites where that distinction is at issue, and to the actual methods by which relevant determinations of meaning and intent are made. Failing this, Habermas is forced to impute his conceptual machinery to communicative settings without regard for the ways in which the "rational properties of practical activities" emerge as accountable courses of social action. As long as the concept of communicative rationality lacks a referent in the practical life of social actors critical theory will remain incapable of overcoming the impasse posed by Horkheimer and Adorno: of the choice between authoritarian social science, on the one hand, or the collapse into relativism, on the other. An important consequence of this argument is that the need to provide formal justification (or "grounding") is, for Habermas, an internal requirement of the history of rationalization. This point serves as a corrective to the impression left by Rorty, among others, that Habermas's foundationalism is part of a kind of sentimental attachment to the worn-out demands of enlightenment metaphysics, and could be tossed off like an old coat. Here there appears to be a conceptual disagreement over the purpose and meaning of "philosophy."[21]

What the formal specification of the preconditions for "communication aimed at understanding" does, however, is to thematize understanding and agreement as possible topics for investigation of settings where the "ends" of discourse are routinely placed at issue, deliberated, and criticized. This opens up a rather deep inroad for ethnomethodological studies of social activities organized by and as a variety of deliberative, argumentative, and interpretive tasks.[22] So, for instance, the problem of resolving discrepant versions of past events can be studied from within the working context of persons who have this task as their professional charge.[23] Practice-based inquiries provide a working alternative to the definition of "the problematics of understanding and agreement" provided by the methodological discourse of the social sciences. In what follows I shall consider the consequences that an ethnomethodological reworking of these issues holds for the theory of communicative action.

THE PROBLEM OF UNDERSTANDING MEANING
IN THE SOCIAL SCIENCES

The argument to this point has been as follows: (1) that Habermas's turn toward communicative action is motivated by a concern to reconstruct the rationality problematic at the level of practical moral discourse; (2) that critical theory and practice-based inquiries share an interest in the foundational critique of standing conceptions of rational action; and (3) that Habermas's account of the key concepts of "communicative action" and "communicative rationality," though formally rigorous, is pragmatically empty. There thus exists a *prima facie* case for treating practice-based studies of language and social action as candidates for filling out the pragmatic level of the theory of communicative action. What follows is an attempt to clarify the relationship between Habermas's philosophical project and the empirical-analytic program of Wittgenstein-inspired ethnomethodology through a consideration of Habermas's reflections on the "problem of understanding meaning in the social sciences."[24]

This discussion recalls the second of Habermas's "three urgent tasks" for critical theory outlined above: namely, that critical theory must establish relations with methodological questions in the social sciences such that "the elaboration of adequate basic concepts for systems of communicative action [is] not hindered but promoted." To accomplish this Habermas needs to demonstrate the relevance of the concept of communicative rationality to the methodological self-understanding of the social sciences. His strategy is to identify the methodological position of the social scientific interpreter with the hermeneutic principle of translation that, he argues, is implicit in the general evolutionary structure of communicative action. On this view, the methodological discourse of the social sciences represents a special case in the development of hermeneutic self-understanding insofar as the social sciences adopt a self-consciously rationalized approach to the problematics of understanding and agreement. This history of methodological discussion, reflection, and critique thus provides critical theory with a form of disciplinary access to what Habermas terms the "rational infrastructure" of action oriented to reaching understanding.[25]

Habermas's reflections on the problem of understanding meaning in the social sciences are situated within his broader critique of positivism, and of the objectivistic self-understanding of the "empirical-analytic sciences of action." In this regard, his general argument has not changed much over the past three decades. Because they are concerned not merely with behavioral events, but with the *meanings* of those events and with the symbolic structure of their interpretation by members of a community, the social sciences are at essence a hermeneutic enterprise. Moreover, as a consequence of the observation that the meaning of events is dependent on the historical and cultural positioning of their symbolic interpretation, the discourse of the social sciences is forced by its internal rational structure continually to reflect on the epistemological foundations of its own inquiries. In short, the social sciences are understood by Habermas as *reflexively self-constituting sciences of action*. For this reason, they provide an historical site par excellence for the philosophical analysis of the transcendental preconditions of objectivating interpretive practice. As Habermas continues:

> What is at issue here is the transcendental conditions of the intersubjectivity of linguistically mediated systems of action as such, and thus the logical structure of the social lifeworld, which has a twofold status in research. On the one hand it is the object domain of research; in this respect a transcendental analysis yields infor-

mation about structures of reality that are prior to any empirical analysis. On the other hand, however, the social lifeworld is also the very basis of research; in this respect a transcendental investigation permits a self-reflection of the methods employed.[26]

The discourse of the social sciences is thus bound to reflect on the logical structure of the lifeworld in two ways: (1) at the level of the phenomena that comprise the material substrate of analysis, and (2) at the methodological level of the conditions that provide for the coherence of its own investigations. The investigation of the logical structure of the lifeworld thus requires both the empirical-analytic study of lifeworld relations—that is, of basic structures of language, experience, and practical action—and the critical-theoretic reflection on the contents, methods, and aims of those investigations as these are constituted *pretheoretically* within the cultural and historical horizon of the social scientific interpreter. Habermas identifies three intellectual traditions that prefigure the sort of transcendental investigation he has in mind: phenomenology, Wittgensteinian "linguistic" analysis, and philosophical hermeneutics.

In the third chapter of *On the Logic of the Social Sciences* Habermas discusses each of these approaches in order. Because I wish to argue that Habermas's readings of Wittgenstein and phenomenology are skewed to fit with his reflections on philosophical hermeneutics, I will invert the order of his discussion, and begin with a brief sketch of the background to the hermeneutic conception of language through which these other two traditions are being read.

Habermas's discussion of the *Verstehen* problematic is framed by a conception of understanding that emphasizes the *distance* between the author (of a text or action) and its interpreter, and places "understanding" as the *endpoint* of a process of fusing historical, cultural, and cognitive horizons. This approach is consistent with a line of argument initiated by Schleiermacher, Droysen, and Dilthey, and elaborated more recently in the work of Hans-Georg Gadamer.[27] The canonical move in this tradition is to treat the "problem of understanding" arising within the scholarly interpretation of historically and culturally "distant" texts as a *general precondition* of all communication. This conception of communicative activity is summarized in the Schleiermachian maxim that "misunderstanding, rather than understanding, arises of its own accord."[28] By generalizing the hermeneutic problem of understanding to all communicative settings the search for universally valid principles of rational interpretation is established as a central topic for metatheoretical reflection.

It is in this context that the historical development of the social sciences takes on special importance. According to Habermas, the principal task of the social scientific interpreter is to describe and understand cultural beliefs and practices in terms of the meaning, plausibility, and coherence they have for members. This means that social scientific interpretation must proceed from a position that is *internal* to the participants' culture and their methods for the symbolic constitution of meaning. This requirement raises the familiar methodological difficulty of reconciling native understandings with the assumptive grasp of actions, events, and their meanings that constitute the familiar world of the social scientific interpreter. The issue becomes more pronounced as the cultural and historical distance between the discourse of the social sciences and the lifeworld of the "native culture" is increased. Here the position of the social scientist begins to approximate the circumstance of classical hermeneutics, where cultural and linguistic differences are compounded by vast temporal distances between author and interpreter. On this view, both the social scientist and the hermeneutician operate on the cusp between horizons of meaning that are historically, linguistically, and culturally distinct. The significance of hermeneutic practice, according to Habermas, is that in the course of attempting to translate between alternative systems of meaning, the social scientific interpreter continually runs up against particularities of language and belief that constitute his or her own tradition of symbolic expression. The revelation that one's own language is in this sense limited in no way contradicts the possibility of the hermeneutic achievement. On the contrary, hermeneutics overcomes the "limits" of ordinary languages in and through the act of translation. Philosophical hermeneutics and interpretive social science merely appropriate a "tendency to self-transcendence" that is built into the structure of ordinary language. As Habermas continues:

> Languages themselves contain the potential for a rationality that, expressing itself in the particularity of a specific grammar, reflects the limits of that grammar and at the same time negates them in their specificity. Reason, which is always bound up with language, is also always beyond languages. Only by destroying the particularities of *languages*, which are the only way in which it is embodied, does reason live in *language*. . . . This mediating generality is attested to by the act of translation. Formally, it is reflected in the trait that all traditional languages have in common and that guarantees their transcendental unity, namely, the fact that in principle they can all be translated into one another.[29]

Habermas identifies the transcendental-pragmatic moment of critical theory with the position of the social scientific interpreter because he conceives the (ideal-typical) social scientist as the embodiment of a material engagement between cultures, mediated by a rational discourse oriented toward achieving understanding. For Habermas, interpretive understanding is a practical discursive achievement, and the methodological discourse of the social sciences is (or at least, ought to be) concerned at the most fundamental level with the epistemological status of that achievement.

A similar argument occurs in the first chapter of *The Theory of Communicative Action*.[30] Here, Habermas aligns the discussion of the *Verstehen* problematic with Giddens's formulation of the "double-hermeneutic" task of the social scientific interpreter.[31] On this account, the materials on which social scientists base their accounts are always already "symbolically prestructured" by the work of local practitioners. The "problem of understanding meaning" therefore consists in the difficulties of providing warrantable—that is, *rationally valid*—interpretations of an analytical substrate that is itself an assemblage of "first-order interpretations," the coherence and integrity of which is available only with reference to a native understanding:

> The *specific Verstehen problematic* lies in the fact that the social scientist cannot "use" this language "found" in the object domain as a neutral instrument. He cannot "enter into" this language without having recourse to the pretheoretical knowledge of a member of a lifeworld—indeed of his own—which he has intuitively mastered as a layman and now brings unanalyzed into every process of achieving understanding.[32]

The familiar consequence of the "double-hermeneutic" is that it places the social scientific interpreter between the competing demands of culture-specific understanding, on the one hand, and objectivating social science, on the other.[33] As Habermas continues:

> The *Verstehen* problematic can thus be expressed in the brief question: How can the *objectivity of understanding* be reconciled with the performative attitude of one who participates in a process of reaching understanding?[34]

The solution he proposes is to conceive the process of rational interpretation as involving a continual alternation between the "performative attitude" of one who participates in interaction and the "objectivating attitude" of the social scientific interpreter who reflects critically on the "pretheoretical knowledge" necessary for achieving a participant's understanding. This process of making explicit the "pretheoretical knowledge" of the social scientific interpreter reveals the core structure of communicative action; that is, the "rational infrastructure of communication aimed at understanding" which, by virtue of their specialist preoccupation with the problematics of understanding, has been developed and formalized to an extraordinary degree within the methodological discourse of the social sciences. For

Habermas, the social sciences therefore represent a special case of "communication aimed at understanding": A hermeneutically oriented discourse which, owing to its tradition of methodological reflection on the bases of communicative understanding, articulates the formal-pragmatic conditions of communicative action. By extending the formalization of social scientific methods in the direction of "communicative aimed at understanding" Habermas hopes to arrive at a concept of communicative rationality that is "encompassing and general" and "satisfies universalistic claims."[35]

In the previous chapter I briefly sketched how Habermas assimilates Wittgenstein to a conception of language use modeled on the principles of philosophical hermeneutics. It should be clear from this and the discussion above that Habermas is operating with an idealized conception of social scientific practice. It is, however, an idealization that finds support within the philosophy of the social sciences, and in particular, within the tradition of *verstehende* sociology culminating in the writings of Peter Winch.[36] It remains for the ethnomethodologists to provide the next step of the argument in which philosophical conceptions of interpretation, understanding, and agreement that rely on an idealized image of social scientific practice, are subjected to critical sociological scrutiny.

RESPECIFYING THE PROBLEM OF
UNDERSTANDING MEANING IN THE SOCIAL SCIENCES

Habermas's attempt to make contact with universal principles of communicative action via the intermediaries of hermeneutic philosophy and professional social science contrasts sharply with the strategy, common to the traditions of ethnomethodological and Wittgensteinian argument, of attempting to unravel the problems of philosophy and social theory by consulting perspicuous cases drawn from domains of ordinary practice. It is not surprising, then, that the two approaches should yield quite different appreciations of the problematics of interpretation, understanding, and agreement, and of their significance for the interpretive social sciences, as well as for sociological inquiries more generally construed.[37] In making the case for the ethnomethodological/Wittgensteinian alternative, I will be concerned to show not only how it differs from the approach adopted by Habermas, but more important, how it undermines the very terms in which Habermas's hermeneutically inspired conception of the "problem of understanding meaning" is framed.

An exceptionally clear treatment of these issues is provided by Sharrock and Anderson in their discussion of the relationship between ethnographic theory and the practices of ethnographic research.[38] Their argument centers on what they term "the inaccessibility problem" in contemporary ethnography.

According to Sharrock and Anderson, ethnographic theory has tended to presume that "cultures" represent uniformly discrete (i.e., "monolithic") systems of thought and action, and that "native understanding" consists in transparent and total access to a given cultural system. Hence, the vocabulary within which the discourse on ethnographic methods is conducted establishes a series of polarities—"native"/"nonnative," "us"/"them"— which organize persons "into standard types following standard patterns of behavior and, thereby, showing *their* culture."[39] It follows from this that ethnographers face the problem of gaining access to an entire way of life, and with it, an entire historical, cultural, and cognitive legacy, that is not only different from, but radically alternative to, their own. "The inaccessibility problem" consists in the theoretical impossibility of being at once both "inside" (as "native") and "outside" (as "ethnographer") the host culture. It is this conception of "culture as monolith" that frames the familiar theoretical puzzles surrounding the relativity of cultural knowledge and the so-called incommensurability thesis, or the general impossibility of achieving a "total" understanding of cultures other than one's own.[40]

As Sharrock and Anderson point out, however, this negative conclusion regarding the possibilities of doing ethnography is not based in any sort of fieldwork experience, but is instead arrived at a priori on the basis of the theoretical idealizations of "culture" and "native understanding." As they continue:

> The mapping of one set of cultural experiences onto another is not found to be impossible: it is assumed to be so. We are being invited to accept that if we meet a society of people who claim that they carry their souls around in boxes, or that paternity has nothing to do with reproduction, or that some people can inflict harm on others merely by wishing to do so, we are faced not merely with a translation problem which ought, in principle, to be soluble. Instead we have incomprehension which can never be resolved.[41]

At the center of these difficulties lies a conception of "understanding" that is at once too general and too narrow. It is too general insofar as it presumes that "the problem of understanding" is an invariant feature of cross-cultural discourse—that there is nothing, for instance, on which we and the Azande might possibly agree. At the same time, because actions and their meanings are depicted as either wholly transparent or entirely opaque, "native understanding" appears as a sort of "uniform content," with no middle ground accorded to commonly recognized pathways of acculturation and with little recognition of the diversity of practices that makes up what we commonly refer to as "a culture." Persons may, with respect to a specific practice, have differential knowledge or be at various stages in their training without having their membership in the culture thereby raised for question. The theoretical idealization of "native knowledge" leads us to overlook both that practical knowledge is unevenly distributed throughout human communities and that the so-called "natives" are ongoingly engaged in social and cultural inquiries of their own.

The overly general nature of this conception of "understanding" follows from its narrowness with respect to ordinary methods of expression and their situated comprehension. The "problem of understanding meaning" becomes a theoretical barrier to ethnographic research only when practical actions and their local interpretations appear as fundamentally incomprehensible expressions of an alien culture. But here we need to ask what criteria are being brought to bear on these actions and their interpretations such that "fundamental incomprehensibility" might emerge as their salient feature. Typically, this occurs where specific actions, reports, or descriptions are taken to be emblematic of an overarching cultural cosmology. They are then compared with a paired proposition drawn from the anthropologist's own (usually western scientific) belief system, the contradiction between the two serving as proof of the former's "fundamental incomprehensibility." Note that it is not necessary that one come down on one side or the other for this demonstration to succeed. All that is necessary is that one accepts the legitimacy of the rivalry between the paired statements.

This discussion recalls Gilbert Ryle's famous example of the undergraduate student and the college accountant.[42] The student is given access to the accountant's books, where he finds that for every matter associated with his daily life at the college, there is some sort of entry. Their are entries for the tuition that students pay, for the salaries their instructors receive, for rent on the buildings, and care of the grounds. As Ryle continues:

> At first the undergraduate is merely mildly interested . . . But then under the influence of the auditor's grave and sober voice he suddenly begins to wonder. Here everything in the life of the college is systematically marshaled and couched in terms which, though colorless, are precise, impersonal and susceptible of con-clusive checking. To every plus there corresponds an equal and opposite minus; the entries are classified; the origins and destina-tions of all payments are indicated. Moreover, a general conclusion is reached: the financial position of the college is exhibited and compared with its position in previous years. So is not this expert's way, perhaps, the right way in which to think of the life of the college, and the other muddled and emotionally charged ways to which he has been used the wrong ways?[43]

Ryle's aim is to show how deep the temptation can be to treat systematic descriptions as competitive with our everyday or commonsense accounts and understandings. At first the student is unimpressed, but as it gradually emerges that the accountant's books comprise a record of university life that is both systematic and complete, the student begins to doubt the merits of his own appreciation of "university life." It begins to look as if there is no room for alternatives to the accountant's ledger; that everything that needs to be said about the life of the college has been said, and that, in the words of the accountant, "the stories that you tell about it to your brothers and sisters are only picturesque travesties of the audited facts."[44] The confusion arises from our supposing "university life" to be a singular (and thus, singularly accountable) thing. "University life" is not a thing, but rather, it is a *concept* that takes on occasional relevance by virtue of its relationship to some sort of business, preoccupation, or task-at-hand.

Ryle illustrates this point with the example of library books. For the accountant, what is important about the book is that a receipt for its purchase is recorded. His records are, in this sense, complete when for each book in the library's possession there is a corresponding figure in his ledger. It is *not* a matter of accountant's interest what the subject matter of some book might be, who its author is, or where it can be found on the shelves. Neither is it the case, that the accountant's interest in the book is competitive with the student's, though there may be occasions on which the two interests might momentarily come together (e.g., if the book is lost and a reckoning of charges is required). The book has a different place in "university life" for both the accountant and the student in accordance with their different understandings of what "university life" comes down to in practice. We do not feel compelled, at this point, to figure out whose book—the accountant's or the student's—is the real book, since, in Ryle's words, "There are not two books, nor yet one real book, side by side with another bubble-book—the latter, queerly, being the one that is useful for examinations. There is just a book available for students, and an entry in the accounts specifying what the college paid for it."[45]

Recall the anthropologist's dilemma: Native accounts appear to contradict propositions fundamental to the anthropologist's own belief system. This circumstance is then taken as evidence for the "fundamental incomprehensibility" of "native understanding." The point of Ryle's argument, however, is to show that this dilemma is the result of a theoretical confusion concerning the nature of scientific accounts. Owing to their completeness, systematicity, standards of precision, and the like, scientific accounts may often seem to provide the "last word" on things, or more, to explain the world (or some dark corner of it) so fully as to leave no room for any other method of approach. But this is so only if we accede to an epistemic amnesia concerning the manifold nature of our own experience and the diversity of our ordinary linguistic practices. There is no *essential* rivalry between "native accounts" and the propositions of western science just because they are sometimes, strictly speaking, *incomparable*. A painted portrait and a mugshot offer quite different views of the same person, yet there is room in the world for both things. As Sharrock and Anderson continue:

> Many of the propositions to be found in other cultures turn out to be wrong or meaningless if they are measured against our standards of factuality. We know that paternity is necessary for human reproduction and that souls, if they exist, are not the kinds of things you can tote about in boxes. But are we not then in the same position as someone who claimed not to understand what was meant when it was said that one person had all the brains in the family, since experimental biology had conclusively demonstrated that cranial content varies among the human population?
>
> By casting the argument as one about facts and values, subjectivity and objectivity, and not the plausibility or otherwise of alternative translations, what is being discussed gets irretrievably stuck in the quagmire of the determinants of rationality, the existence of logical universals and the foundations of truth.[46]

This is not to say that *all* native accounts are metaphorical or that there are no conditions under which "native understandings" conflict with the values of western science and rationality. However, when such conflicts do arise, they are also recognized and disputed in terms of contextually specific matters of practice and belief. Indeed, the process of translation is itself a contextually *specific* achievement insofar as the criteria by which the adequacy of a specific translation is judged are tied in fundamental ways to the circumstances of its production.

A recent study by Bjelic provides a case in point.[47] Bjelic recounts a situation in which he served as a translator for a Bosnian woman whose son had been wounded when the Croation military had shelled their village near the city of Mostar. The young man was initially sent to a local hospital where he received only superficial treatment. He was then rescued by United Nations personnel and admitted into a U.S. military hospital in Split, Croatia. A U.S.-based aid organization called Veterans for Peace then had the mother and son brought to the United States to continue his treatment. Thus began their cultural odyssey.

Bjelic was asked by the local organizers of Veterans for Peace to accompany the boy and his mother from Andrews Air Force Base in Washington, D.C. to the U.S. military base in Lewiston, Maine, and to serve as a translator during their journey. Bjelic describes the mother as "a simple village woman with little or no cosmopolitan sensibility." In the context of her son's grave condition, she had been rushed by the U.S. military and the aid organization to leave her home and fly to the United States. She had little time to reflect on where she was going or what it would be like. As Bjelic continues: "She arrived with the help of the Pentagon, and the New World offered her quickly, instantly, her 'fifteen minutes of fame.' While listening and observing her intense anxieties, I found myself offering her not only linguistic, but also emotional and cultural support."[48] Upon their arrival at the military base in Lewiston they were met by a welcoming delegation, and the mother and Bjelic were escorted to an area in front of the plane where the local media had organized an impromptu news conference. They approached the microphones, and one of the reporters asked the mother, "What do you have to say about the trip?" Bjelic recounts the sequence of events that followed:

> I turned to her. She was hiding behind my back. I translated the question. She looked at me confused and in an unpleasant voice said, "I don't have anything to say," as though she were insulted by the spotlight. "Well, you have to say something," I insisted, "It will be very humiliating if you don't say anything." I was explaining to her not only the content of the question, but above all, the *context*. Cornered by my insistence, she finally made a concession. "Well," she said, "you say whatever you want." I turned around without anything to say and a license to say anything I wanted.[49]

Following is a transcript of a segment of the report that aired that evening on the local 6 o'clock news. Bjelic's brief speech comes immediately after the mother's utterance "Well . . . you say whatever you want" (which was not aired in the report):

> She says, thank you very much. She said as a mother, there are no words a- a- a- that can express her gratitude for the kind of help that her son is receiving from you. She is overwhelmed . . . (overwhelmed) with the good reception and the help from all sides . . .[50]

As Bjelic notes, the act of translation here involves bridging the cultural gap between the media's demand for the day's news and the mother's unwillingness or inability to provide them with what they need. The problem is *not* how literally to translate the meanings of words, but rather, how to recognize and moderate between competing contextualizations of the present events. In this case, the translator is called on to perform a kind of cultural arbitrage in which the authenticity of the mother's original utterance is sacrificed to the demands of providing a statement all parties to the exchange can live with. It is not just a revision of her words, but of the communicative intention with which they were uttered. If we nevertheless grant the adequacy—indeed, the "rightness" (in Habermas's sense)—of this translation, then we are faced with a picture of "meaning" unhinged both from the claim embedded in the original proposition ("I have nothing to say"), and from the logic of speaker's intentions.

The fact of the existence of these ordinary practices of translation, and the fact that, despite the apparent "endlessness" of the translator's task, these methods and procedures are adequate to the local contingencies of "rational interpretation," demonstrates the inadequacy of the "incommensurability thesis" as a general account of ethnographic practice. In contrast to philosophical accounts aimed at glossing the field of translation in the interest of a general account of hermeneutic practice, Sharrock and Anderson suggest that ethnographic research might better be served by a methodological discourse that elucidates methods of interpretation and translation in the particularity, richness, and variety with which they appear in practice. Bjelic's study provides one such example, but there are many others within the corpus of ethnomethodological work.[51]

CONCLUSION

The significance of this argument for the theory of communicative action is clear: The conception of communicative rationality that lies at the core of that project presupposes the "inaccessibility problem" as a general precondition of all communicative action. Indeed, the central idea of the interpretive achievement of "understanding" is explicitly framed in terms of a generalized opposition between "self" and "other," and is connected to processes of practical-moral development via the interplay between these two discrete positionings across a horizon of interpretation. In this, the linguistic and cultural monolith of "language-games" is not so much *overcome* as it is *displaced* by the moral-cognitive monolith of the rational "subject."

This argument also implies an alternative to Habermas's conception of the relationship between communicative action and the methodological discourse of the social sciences. Habermas's reliance on an idealized conception of the social scientific interpreter as the model of hermeneutic engagement fails to reckon with the range and nature of methods of interpretation available to the social scientist as a *practical actor*. He does not consider, for instance, that the fact that the "data" of the social world are symbolically prestructured raises some rather deep and abiding problems for "just anybody" trying to make their way through daily life, and that these problems include, among other things, the need to provide methodological clarifications and justifications for a variety of claims about the nature of the world they inhabit. In sum, the possibility that there is an indefinite number of practical-hermeneutic methods already at work in the social world, and that these are sufficient to tasks of interpretation, translation, and understanding—*indeed, that these are all we have*—seems to escape him. Were he to take this possibility seriously, it would allow him to exploit the objectivating features of everyday linguistic and social practices, rather than conceiving them as implicit operations that shadow the "objectivating attitude" cultivated within the methodological discourse of the social sciences.[52]

Ethnomethodological reflection on the problem of meaning in the social sciences begins from the proposal that social activities are available for study by sociologists insofar as they are produced by participants as (at least *potential*) objects of analysis. In this way, the "double-hermeneutic" is turned on its head: because all analysis operates within the "thick" field of culture- and context-specific practice, the cultural membership of the social scientist always operates in the first instance as an essential resource rather than as an impediment to analysis. This contrasts with Habermas's position, where the cultural membership of the social scientist is viewed as invariantly problematic since it is seen as limited by the sheer interiority of cultural belief and practice existing at a specific place and time. This conception of the limits of culture provides Habermas with the leverage he needs to establish critique and critical self-reflection as the *sine qua non* of discursive agreement. However, as I shall attempt to show in chapter 2, it also commits him to a conception of formal pragmatics that is too narrow to account for the pragmatic foundations of speech.

2

Formal Pragmatics and the Logic of Conversation

A central aim of the theory of communicative action is to explicate forms of procedural rationality that underlie and guide "communication aimed at understanding." Habermas conceives action aimed at reaching understanding (communicative action) and action aimed at exerting influence (strategic action) as mutually exclusive trajectories of everyday speech. This strong distinction is based on the conceptual argument that a "rationally motivated agreement" by definition is shaped without the imposition of force or outside influence, but is instead motivated by the force of *reasons* internal to the discussion at hand:

> From the perspective of the participants, an agreement cannot be imposed from without, cannot be foisted by one side upon the other—whether instrumentally, through direct intervention into the action situation, or strategically, through direct influence, again oriented only toward success, on the propositional attitudes of the other. Whatever manifestly comes to be through external influence (gratification or threat, suggestion or deception) cannot count inter-subjectively as an agreement; an intervention of this sort forfeits its effectiveness for coordinating action.[1]

Habermas argues that there exist different "mechanisms" by which "alter's plans and actions" can be "linked up with ego's plans and actions." In general, speakers distinguish between these coordinating mechanisms depending on whether the action they coordinate is oriented toward "reaching understanding" or "exerting influence." In this way, Habermas locates the distinction between communicative and strategic action in speakers' rational intuitions concerning the different coordinating mechanisms of speech. He thus conceives the critique of instrumental reason as

39

a kind of formal pragmatic potential built into the structure of everyday language as it is used and understood in actual speech situations.

This argument aligns the theory of communicative action with the tradition of practice-based inquiries in the following crucial respect: it identifies formal structures of language and social activity with their situated use and recognition. The concept of communicative rationality requires that participants understand, make use of, and are able to formulate the distinction between communicative and strategic action. Its coherence as a theoretical construct is thus tied to the objectivating possibilities of ordinary speech.

This argument resonates with the position developed by Garfinkel and Sacks in their classic study "On Formal Structures of Practical Action."[2] The main thrust of that paper was to show how social activities are ordered through a variety of formal methods and procedures used and understood by participants as devices for rendering those activities as orderly, accountable, managed courses of events. The core of this argument had already been elaborated in a series of remarkable lectures given in the mid-1960's and early-1970's by Sacks in which he outlined the basic analytical principles for the ethnomethodological study of conversation.[3] The discipline of "conversation analysis" is founded on the insight that ordinary speech is produced and recognized by participants as structured activity, and that actual courses of interaction are bound together by virtue of participants' situated analyses of that structure, and by their ability to produce analytically appropriate responses in their subsequent talk. Talk is, in this sense, *sequentially organized*. It is a produced order of utterances that is collaboratively fashioned, in its course, and on the basis of exceedingly local grammatical resources—most saliently, what was said just prior to the present utterance. The sequential organization of talk represents the central logical discovery of conversation analysis.

In this chapter I will argue that Habermas's conception of formal pragmatics is based in a doctrine of literal expression that defines the logical operations of everyday speech too narrowly. Because his conception of *logos* remains wedded to the assertoric force of the decontextualized proposition, Habermas fails to comprehend the significance that the conversation analytic elucidation of sequential logic has for formal pragmatics. If the goal is to develop a formal pragmatic theory that can account for the *procedural rationality* of actual speech, then it is necessary to understand how utterances are *bound together* into coherent, followable, orders of talk; or, in the language of the theory of communicative action, how the validity claims implicit in speech are expressed, managed, and understood over actual courses of talk and social interaction.[4] As an alternative to Habermas's position, I argue for an approach to formal analysis that conceives procedural rationality in terms of the sequential organization of actual instances of talk. I conclude with a summary of the consequences this approach holds for the theory of communicative action.

FORMAL PRAGMATICS

Habermas's approach to formal pragmatics is characterized by an assimilation of Searlean speech act theory to the sentential logic of truth-conditional semantics.[5] Sentences are understood and analyzed as the embodiment of context-free grammatical structure that expresses specific propositional content. This "content" is then given pragmatic "force" through a series of eight intermediate steps that serve to contextualize sentences, and turn them into utterances in actual situations of language use.[6] In this way, Habermas retains the a priori distinction between propositional content ("literal sentence meaning") and the pragmatic deployment of sentences in situ. This conception of formal pragmatics is given symbolic form in the so-called double structure of the speech act: a propositional content, (p), is deployed with specific illocutionary force, f, which yields a general pragmatic structure of utterances, f(p).[7] Although this distinction is central to Habermas's conception of communicative rationality, he pays for it with a greatly limited view of the logical structure of speech.

　　Habermas's central concern is that empirical investigations should not lose sight of the rationality problematic as a general point of orientation. This concern is tied in turn to the possibility of maintaining the strong distinction between strategic and communicative action as a fundamental precondition of human cognitive and moral development:

> The linguistic *demarcation of the levels of reality* of "play" and "seriousness," the linguistic construction of a fictive reality, wit and irony, transposed and paradoxical uses of language, allusions and the contradictory withdrawal of validity claims at a metacommunicative level—all these rest on intentionally confusing modalities of being. For clarifying the mechanisms of deception that a speaker has to master to do this, formal pragmatics can do more than even the most precise empirical description of the phenomena to be explained. With training in the basic modes of language use, the growing child gains the ability to demarcate the subjectivity of his own expressions from the objectivity of an external reality, from the normativity of society, and from the intersubjectivity of the medium of language itself . . . (h)e knows how one can master the confusions, produce de-differentiations intentionally, and employ them in fiction, wit, irony, and the like.[8]

This passage isolates Habermas's suspicions concerning the empirical organization of everyday language: that it is a disorganized, unwieldy, contradictory, and confusing array. It also reflects the relationship he envisions between formal pragmatics and actual speech. Formal pragmatics, in Habermas's view, serves as a beacon for making our way through the contingent entanglements of empirical speech situations. The three validity claims of truth, rightness, and sincerity correspond to the three formal world relations of subject to world, subject to others, and subject to self. They thus provide formal guidance for ego's moral development in and through its continual engagement in these relationships.[9]

Habermas pins his hopes of connecting the concept of "communicative rationality" with "ancient conceptions of *logos*" on the "communicative employment of propositional knowledge in assertions."[10] The "ideal speech situation," which represents the universal context of the principle of communicative rationality imminent in speech, is shaped out of the pragmatic tension between the "literalness of expression," on the one hand, and "mechanisms of deception," on the other.

Although Habermas acknowledges that the formal analysis of literal sentence meaning "cannot be explained at all independently of the standard conditions of its communicative employment,"[11] the implication he draws from that pragmatic insight is that the analysis of "conditions of communicative employment" can only take place against the backdrop of a theoretically robust conception of "standardized context." As he continues:

> To be sure, formal pragmatics must also take measures to see that in the standard case what is meant does not deviate from the literal meaning of what is said. For this reason, our analysis is limited to speech acts carried out *under standard conditions*. And this is intended to insure that the speaker means nothing else than the literal meaning of what he says.[12]

Following Searle, Habermas seeks to specify communicative action as a typology of speech acts in "standard form." "Standard form" refers to the model of speech acts mentioned earlier, where propositional contents, (p), are packaged in the form of different illocutions, f(p). So, for instance, Habermas analyzes the following three statements—"Peter's smoking a pipe," "I assert that Peter smokes a pipe," and "I beg of you (Peter) that you smoke a pipe"—as embodying the same propositional content, deployed for different illocutionary purposes (describing, asserting, offering/appealing, respectively).[13]

In general, Habermas's analytical method is to distinguish sharply between the formal model of the preconditions of "communicative action" and the empirical domain of utterances "in actual situations of language use," and to then seek to build the lifeworld back in, as it were, through an elaborate process of mediations. Through this process, the "pure types of linguistically mediated interaction" are brought into line with "the complexity of natural situations without sacrificing all theoretical perspectives for analyzing the coordination of interactions."[14] This strategy works only if utterance meaning is, in a formal sense, derivative of "the literal meaning of the linguistic expressions employed in standard speech acts." As Habermas concludes: "if formal pragmatics is not to lose its object, knowledge of the conditions under which speech acts may be accepted as valid cannot depend *completely* on contingent background knowledge."[15] For Habermas, "the literal meaning of the linguistic expressions employed in standard speech acts" comprises the abstractable grammatical structure around which a formal theory of meaning which realizes the rational potential of communicative action can be built.

THE LOGIC OF CONVERSATION

The point of departure for conversation analysis is, in many respects, exactly opposite to the approach Habermas takes to the formal analysis of speech. Where Habermas approaches the logical "core" of language through an analytical process of decontextualization, conversation analysts thematize the situated and situating properties of speech as internal to the (socio-)logical organization of natural languages. What, for Habermas is a troubling notion— that the meaning of an utterance is always and irremediably tied to the context of its production—is, for ethnomethodologists and conversation analysts, a resource for the analytical explication of the local conditions of practical action. Garfinkel and Sacks' radical application of the notion of "indexical expressions" is intended to capture the *irremediably* context-dependent, purpose-relative nature of social actions: that utterances and actions are produced with reference to, and in ways dependent on, their immediate surround, and are, in turn, constitutive of what that local surround consists in.[16] Coulter summarizes this position and its consequences for the kind of formal analysis that Habermas envisions:

> Garfinkel and Sacks . . . note that paraphrasings, idealizations and other formal methods for 'repairing' the contextual-dependency and purpose-relativity of sense and reference of indexical expressions only "preserve in specifics" the original problems, and they contend that, since *no* expression in a natural language can have *any* comprehensibility *without* a context (where semanticists' so-called 'zero contexts' . . . are simply rhetorical ways of tacitly assuming *some* particular context), this will include *also* 'formu-

lations' designed to repair the indexicality of expressions used or encountered. For 'formulations' of sense will themselves have indexical properties (context-dependence and purpose-relativity). There can be no real-worldly 'meaning-invariant and context-free' *praxis*.[17]

On this view, Habermas's derivation of "the literal meaning of the linguistic expressions employed in standard speech acts" represents a canonical move within the philosophical tradition of conceiving logic as a source of regimentation and rational supplement for what are, according to this tradition, the relatively chaotic and logically incomplete workings of ordinary linguistic and social practice. Coulter then contrasts this position with the conception of "logical standards" that emerges within ethnomethodology and conversation analysis:

> People manage to communicate effectively by any practical standards of comprehensibility and orderliness for the most part in their daily lives. Therefore, indexical expressions do not require "cleaning up" prior to analysis. Indeed, such efforts risk considerable distortion of the phenomena as they are produced and monitored by speakers and hearers, by practical reasoners. Rather, *analysis must begin with the actual, situated properties of communicative conduct itself*.[18]

Within the discipline of conversation analysis, the ethnomethodological approach to indexical expressions achieves the status of a methodological axiom. Conversation analysts follow a policy of employing only "resources intrinsic to the data themselves"[19] in explicating the sequential organization of any particular stretch of talk. This constraint is coupled with the claim that speakers' analyses of the meanings of utterances are displayed in and through the construction of turns-at-talk. This property of the sequential organization of speech not only provides a procedural foundation for participants engaged in talk, it also provides an ex post facto resource for professional analysts:

> Understandings of other turn's talk are displayed to co-participants, they are available as well to professional analysts, who are thereby afforded a proof criterion (and a search procedure) for the analysis of what a turn's talk is occupied with. Since it is the parties' understanding of prior turns that is relevant to their construction of next turns, it is *their* understandings that are wanted for analysis. The display of those understandings in the talk in subsequent turns affords a resource for the analysis of prior turns, and a proof procedure for professional analysis of prior turns, resources intrinsic to the data themselves.[20]

The approach to the analysis of conversation initiated by Sacks, Schegloff, and Jefferson extends Wittgenstein's critique of the calculus conception of logic by showing how, in actual cases, speakers' local analyses of one another's utterances constitute the rational basis for the order of activity in which they are engaged. As Coulter has argued, ethnomethodological studies of conversation are distinguished from other forms of linguistic analysis by virtue of their commitment to the explication of "an endogenous logic for practical reason."[21] This project contrasts with the attempt to derive standards of reasoning and logical regimentation that are exogenous to actual orders of speech and social interaction as they are oriented to, produced, and recognized by participants. As Coulter continues, "This accumulating body of work is designed to exhibit 'the work' for which the expression 'rationally-accountable communicative *praxis*' is a proper description, or 'gloss.'"[22]

The appeal of this position is that it locates the formal mechanisms of language within the details of its situated performance and comprehension. By according primacy to the locally displayed and managed competencies of social actors, conversation analysts have been extremely successful at recovering the endogenous logical orders of ordinary speech activity. Given the avowedly empirical and atheoretical posture of this discipline, the successes of conversation analysis stand in marked contrast to Habermas's assertion in *The Theory of Communicative Action* that, "an empirical pragmatics without a formal pragmatic point of departure would not have the conceptual instruments needed to recognize the rational basis of linguistic communication in the confusing complexity of the everyday scenes observed."[23]

Although it is clear that Habermas's formal pragmatics is intended to capture a pure type of rationality that is *immanent* in all "communicative action," it is less obvious how such a picture could be linked to the findings of empirical pragmatic investigations that take the rational organization of lifeworld relations as their phenomenon of interest. Habermas suggests that "(l)iteral meanings are . . . relative to a deep-seated, implicit knowledge, *about* which we normally know nothing, because it is simply unproblematic and does not pass the threshold of communicative utterances that can be valid or invalid,"[24] but he does not offer an argument that would link the literal meaning of utterances to this background of implicit knowledge in such a way that "literalness" could emerge as the decisive category in the situated production of intelligible utterances. His concern is to explain how literal sentence meaning—or what he calls "the semantic level"—is connected to "the accord relevant to the sequel of interaction"—or what he calls "the empirical level." This connection occurs, he argues, through a coordination of agreement which takes place at "the pragmatic level."[25] However, because he conceives sequential organization as having little consequence for the understanding of speech at the semantic level, Habermas is unable to comprehend the relationship between conversation analysis and the ongoing "coordination of agreement" that he identifies with the pragmatic function of language. Further, because he patterns the development of formal pragmatics after Searle's typology of speech acts, Habermas is forced into the logical absurdity of assigning the structures that conversation analysts have identified to a unique class of utterance-types, the so-called communicatives, which "serve *the organization of speech*," and are defined by "their *reflexive relation to the process of communication.*"[26]

In the remainder of this chapter I will defend a conception of sequential analysis that stands as an alternative to Habermas's disparaging view of the logical significance of "empirical pragmatic" investigations. Although in subsequent chapters this model of conversational organization will itself be the subject of critique, for now it is important to establish how the discoveries of conversation analysis could plausibly serve as a pragmatic complement to the theory of communicative action, and how they challenge the methodological and analytical assumptions of Habermas's formal pragmatic theory of meaning.

Following Coulter, I begin by arguing that the most significant findings in conversation analysis rest on a priori arguments which are tied to the self-explicating features of everyday speech. The upshot of this argument for Habermas is that the program of formal pragmatics as it currently stands conceives the objectivating possibilities of natural languages too narrowly. Thus, were it to become the touchstone for empirically guided analyses, it would serve more to attenuate our intuitions of natural language use than to illuminate them.

The argument that the results of conversation analysis represent *logical* findings leads to the more general conclusion that the distinction Habermas draws between formal and empirical pragmatics rests on a basic misunderstanding concerning the nature of empirical-analytic treatments of language use. This misunderstanding is traced in turn to Habermas's reduction of the preconditions of "comprehensibility" [verständlichkeit] to speakers' rational intuitions of grammatically well-formed sentences. In contrast, I argue, following Coulter, that "comprehensibility" is more fruitfully understood as the "combinatorial tolerances for illocutionary activities . . . and . . . concepts in a natural language."[27] I conclude with a brief summary of the consequences this argument holds for the theory of communicative action.

A PRIORI SEQUENTIAL STRUCTURES

In his essay, "Contingent and *a priori* structures in sequential analysis,"[28] Coulter presents a compelling argument for a program of formal analysis based on the conceptual analyses of ordinary language philosophy and conversation analytic studies of sequential organization. He begins by arguing that these two traditions are complementary insofar as they have a common interest in the "[*logical*] explication of our intuitions as natural-language users in actual situations of language use."[29] In order to advance the argument that these two traditions form branches of a common, logical enterprise, Coulter must first dispense with the claim, common to some regions of the discipline, that the results of conversation analysis represent inductively arrived at empirical findings.

Coulter distinguishes between two sorts of findings that have been advanced within the conversation analytic literature:

1. *A priori formulations*, which are abstract enough to admit a vast array of empirical cases, and for which claims to general-izability can be advanced with a high level of confidence; and
2. *Contingent formulations*, which specify "vernacularly defined sequence types," and for which claims to generalizability beyond the demonstrable local orderliness of the utterances in question are unwarrantable.

In the former case, claims for the conventionality of findings are founded on the *rational intuitions* of natural-language users vis-à-vis the combinatorial possibilities of the conversational object(s) in question; potentially confounding instances are treated as grounds for more abstract reformulations, or adjustments of initial formulations. In the latter case, claims to the generalizability of findings are arrived at inductively through the identification of other analytically identified "like instances." The extensibility of the conventional structures identified beyond the empirical instances in the developed collection is either denied or left unmentioned. In order to advance strong claims for the conventionality of findings analysts would either explicitly have to move beyond the developed collection aprioristically, or they would have to seek to extend the collection in the hope of gaining an inductive warrant for a more powerful claim to con-ventionality. This latter possibility, however, is closed off by the recognition that the logic of empirical distribution is incommensurate with the logic of conventionality. As Coulter argues:

> The sense in which these abstract structures are logical rather than contingent becomes clearer when one considers the first structure, the "adjacency pair." This constitutes a very basic organizational unit, not on distributional grounds, but on the grounds that each first pair-part (question, offer, request, invitation, summons, etc.) is given meaning only by reference to its appropriate second pair-parts

(answer, accept/reject, grant/deny, accept/reject, answer, etc.). You cannot specify the concept of a "question" independently of any reference to an "answer," and the same holds for all of the concepts of utterance-types with transitive properties. It is not that answers invariantly follow questions, or that they follow with a probability of o.*n* or in *N*% of cases. Rather, they follow *conventionally*.[30]

Moreover, inductive attempts at establishing the conventionality of findings must treat potentially confounding instances either as limits on the general-izability of findings, or as falsifications of analytical hypotheses. Where potentially confounding instances are seen as limits on generalizability, findings can be said to be weak. Where potentially confounding instances are seen as falsifications, findings can be said to be incorrect or mis-formulated, and thus, as standing in need of reformulation in more abstract aprioristic terms. On this account, it is not that a priori arguments are *preferable* to "weak inductive evidence" in making claims concerning the conventionality of conversational structures, it is that they are *inevitable*. The main thrust of the distinction between contingent and a priori formula-tions is thus to redesignate arguments concerning the conventionality of conversational structures as intrinsically *logical* (as against distributional) and *normative* (as against empirical).

In his subsequent remarks, Coulter makes a more programmatic set of claims for a priori formulations. He argues that a priori sequential structures constitute basic elements of "the overall logical structure of conversational organization," and that they can be further distinguished from *contingent* formulations insofar as they are founded in our rational intuitions as speakers of a natural language:

> Although the original formulation of an *a priori* sequential struc-ture may involve a great deal of study of actual transcribed materials, once it is rationally intuited and argued for it becomes *incorrigible* with respect to further instances; indeed, incorrigible *a priori* structures such as adjacency-pairs, pre-expansions, repair sequences and the rest may be relied on as bases for locating *new* sequential phenomena. Here lies the key connection between the "logic" of sequential analyses and the study of logical grammar: in neither enterprise are claims for conventionality supported or subverted by arguments predicated on a distribution of occurrence, except in the most mundane sense in which one speaks of "com-mon" or "normal" occurrence. In logical grammar, for example, no matter how many instances one may perversely collect in which speakers appear to employ the term "mistake" to mean "accident" . . . we would still not be inclined to revise our beliefs about the

distinctions between them and their combinatorial tolerances for other concepts. We should more readily query the competence of the speakers in the "sample," or try to find some specific perlocutionary effect or figurative intention to ascribe to them.[31]

It is this *incorrigibility* with respect to potentially confounding instances which Coulter takes to be the earmark of a priori sequential structures. Both the derivation and the demonstration of conversation analytic findings relies on the practical certainty of "our rational intuitions as natural language users." It is in this sense that the findings of conversation analysis represent logical explications that extend our understanding of what we mean by "grammar."

Coulter's respecification of conversation analytic findings as intrinsically logical and linked to a program of logico-grammatical investigations serves to broaden the scope of empirically guided analyses while at the same time placing them on more solid analytical footing. The recognition that the warrant for analysts' claims concerning the conventionality of their findings is strictly noninductive discharges the need for a formal pragmatic complement for abstract formulations of sequential orderliness without sacrificing the analytic power necessary to illuminate our intuitions as natural language users.

FORMAL AND EMPIRICAL PRAGMATICS REVISITED

This argument has profound consequences for Habermas's distinction between formal and empirical pragmatics. As mentioned earlier, Habermas's central contention is that empirical investigations which lack an explicit grounding in a formal pragmatic theory of meaning will be inadequate to the task of recognizing "the rational basis of linguistic communication in the confusing complexity of the everyday scenes observed."[32] Clearly Habermas is operating with a conception of empirical pragmatics as constrained by inductivist and empiricist methodologies that prevent the leap to logical analysis. This is the position he takes, for instance, in his remarks on Kreckel's schema for the classification of speech-acts:

> The advantage of this and similar classifications consists in the fact that they provide us with a guideline for ethnolinguistic and sociolinguistic descriptive systems and are more of a match for the complexity of natural scenes than are typologies that start from illocutionary points and purposes rather than from features of situations. But they pay for this advantage by relinquishing the intuitive evidence of classifications that link up with semantic analyses and take account of the elementary functions of language (such as the representation of states of affairs, the expression of

experiences, and the establishment of interpersonal relations). The classes of speech acts that are arrived at inductively and constructed in accordance with pragmatic indicators do not consolidate into intuitive types; they lack the theoretical power to illuminate our intuitions.[33]

On Coulter's account, however, as with any other empirically derived formulations of illocutionary activities, "classes of speech acts" are arrived at strictly *noninductively*. Moreover, where such formulations succeed aprioristically, they have already demonstrated "the theoretical power to illuminate our intuitions." To the extent that conversation analytic findings faithfully reproduce participants' situated resources for sense-making, these results are logically equivalent to the local operations of "the rational basis of linguistic communication."

To contend in this case that empirical pragmatic approaches to the analysis of natural language are generally inadequate to the task of recognizing "the rational basis of linguistic communication" is to contend that the situated resources of natural language users are likewise inadequate to this task, and therefore that participants' understandings are likewise in need of a formal pragmatic supplement. By virtue of his espoused intention of reconstructing the pragmatic competencies of natural language users (in line with a stipulated version of "the rational basis of linguistic communication"), Habermas is forced to impute his formal pragmatic framework to the assigned knowledges of communicative participants without at the same time being able to show the procedures by which such formal pragmatic elements become relevant for participants in situ. The only plausible theoretical solution to this problem is to postulate the existence of a communicative *context in general*, and to then propose a series of mediations for building participants' realizations of contingent contexts back into the theory of "standardized context." But this vindication of formal pragmatics is bought at the price of a rigorous empirical-analytic counterpart: without an account of the procedures by which participants invoke "context in general" in the form of the *locally relevant* "rational basis of linguistic communication," we have no way of knowing how—or by what standards—some specific course of activity is organized.

In a related discussion, Schegloff articulates this problem as it appears to the analyst:

> The set of ways of describing any setting is indefinitely expandable. Consequently the correctness of any particular characterization is by itself not adequate warrant for its use; some kind of "relevance rule" or "relevancing procedure" must be given to warrant a particular characterization.

He then offers the following as a possible methodological solution:

> Here I must vastly oversimplify by suggesting that there are two
> main types of solution. One is the positivistic one (in one of the
> many contemporary uses of that term): Any description the
> investigator chooses is warranted if it yields "results," statistically
> significant or otherwise, with the further possible proviso that these
> results be theoretically interpretable. The second type of solution
> requires for the relevance of some characterization *by the investi-*
> *gator* some evidence of its *relevance to the participants* in the
> setting characterized; that is, reference is made to the intrinsic or
> internal ordering and relevance assertedly involved with sentient,
> intentional actors. We are operating with the second of these
> positions, and it is therefore required that we be able to warrant
> any characterization of the parties or setting by showing that it is
> relevant to the parties, and relevant to them at the time of the
> occurrence of what we are claiming is related to them or con-
> tingent on them.[34]

We thus need to distinguish between the formal pragmatic stipulation of
context in general (Habermas's project) and the empirical-analytic recovery
of the *relevant context* of practical action; the critical issue being that a
formal pragmatics that does not begin with a close attention to the latter will
be left without a warrant for its own analytical statements.

A central confusion in Habermas's argument stems from the fact that he
uses the terminology "empirical pragmatics" to designate a domain of
professional practices rather than as a gloss for the situated practices of
competent language users. That is to say, if it is the case that speakers
monitor one another's talk for its locally relevant features of order, structure,
comprehensibility, and the rest, then it is the sum total of *these* practices for
which "empirical pragmatics" stands as an appropriate gloss. If analytical
findings can be anchored within a domain of communicative relations that
precede other more discrete forms of discourse, then claims regarding the
conventionality of findings can be warranted intuitively: "mistake" cannot
mean "accident" any more than "cat mat sat on the" can be considered a
well-formed sentence. Both involve errors in grammar. At the same time, this
conception of the logic of language as consisting in conventional orders of
grammar that are "incorrigible" seems to confound Habermas's proposal for
a concept of "communicative rationality," which places both the substance
and the procedures of communication continually "at issue." It is to this
tension—between the practical foundations of everyday speech and the discursive redemption of Habermasian validity claims—that we now turn.

RATIONAL INTERPRETATION AND RATIONAL INTUITIONS

Habermas's "disquieting thesis" that "(c)ommunicative actions always require an interpretation that is rational in approach"[35] appears to challenge the assumption of a stable foundation of cultural and linguistic relations that stand outside the process of rational discussion. Among the most general features of ordinary speech is the ongoing and contingent production of *discursive closure*. Participants are willing and able to formulate, reason about, dispute, or attempt to ground their communicative activities only in certain contextually relevant ways, and only up to a certain point. What we might call the "bottoming out" of commonsense knowledge consists in the fact that interlocutors can be pushed only so far in giving reasons for their conduct, and that, at the point where the critical process ends, they may—and characteristically do—question the motives behind the process of "asking for further reasons." While the possibility of "communication aimed at understanding" involves practices aimed at remedying the characteristic fragility and situatedness of commonsense knowledge, this same possibility rests heavily on the presumed practical adequacy of situated accounting procedures, and this practical adequacy is in turn marked by the fact that no further reasons are forthcoming.[36] From this, it would appear that modeling a "formal pragmatics" after the limit case of translation undercuts the communicative bases it sought to provide for in the first place.

Habermas accounts for the tension between the demands of rational interpretation and the stability of grammatical convention by situating the theory of formal pragmatics outside of the "implicit" and "holistically structured knowledge" of the lifeworld. This allows him to formulate conditions of "communicative rationality" in the absence of a full-blown account of participants' prehermeneutic rational commitments to the terms and alignments of their natural language.

I have attempted to show, however, that the possibility of articulating nonarbitrary standards of rationality rests on suppositions of commonality that are logically prior to the possibility of raising and assessing validity claims. Or again, that the comprehensibility of utterances depends on participants' mutually displayed alignments to a natural language. From the standpoint of professional analysis, this means that the analyzability of any particular stretch of interaction relies on a normative-rational congruence between analysts' intuitions and the order exhibited in the text under analysis. As in Habermas's account, the meaning of the text can only be approached from within, but now the claim is even stronger: the only checks available on "pretheoretic know-how" are the rational intuitions that analysts possess as speakers of a natural language. Coulter's argument that "no matter how many times someone used 'mistake' to mean 'accident' we would still not be inclined to revise our beliefs about the distinctions between them and their combina-torial tolerances for other concepts" carries the full weight of the intui-tionist's methodological burden: there is an implicit appeal to the analyst's competence in the natural language in question, and this competence cannot be vouchsafed by further arguments. Rather, competence is anchored in the same sort of practical certainty that any speaker would have when confronted with an anomalous usage, and it carries the same results. We are not inclined to revise our beliefs concerning the basic terms of the language on the basis of anomalies, since it is our alignment with the basic terms of a language that provides for the recognition of certain utterances, usages, and so on, as variously anomalous and (at least potentially) in need of interpre-tation in the first place. In contrast to Habermas's focus on the "meta-hermeneutical" task of the reconstructive sciences, the program of logical analysis advocated by Coulter attempts to exploit speakers' and analysts' *prehermeneutic* understandings of the more or less inviolable conventions of speech. The full epistemological weight of a priori formulations of sequential structures rests on this sort of claim concerning the practical certainty of our grammatical intuitions.

In sum, while it must be accepted that the explication of utterances involves the imputation of some form of "immanent rationality" to those utterances[37], this does not by itself force an appeal to criteria of *philosophical rationality*. The alternative suggested here is that the imputation of "imma-nent rationality" is, in the first instance, identified with what Habermas terms "the claim to comprehensibility," and that the "redemption" of this "claim" proceeds from the same *practical certainty* that participants routinely display in producing orderly, intelligible talk.

One of the central issues of contention in the dialogue between practice-based inquiries and critical theory is whether analyses of natural language use can be grounded in analysts' rational intuitions, or conversely, whether our intuitive grasp of grammar is not itself undermined by the vision of a lifeworld increasingly under siege from forces of communicative distortion. For Habermas, the task is to demonstrate the existence of forms of ration-ality that logically precede the possibility of using language for instrumental ends, and that function as a linguistic and cultural medium for the development of a mutually recognitive social, political, and cultural life. At the same time, consistency demands that the forms of procedural rationality that project "the unconstrained, unifying, consensus-bringing force of argumentative speech"[38] are also at least potentially open to criticism. At this point, the theory of communicative action appears to have reached a performative impasse: the concept of communicative rationality requires *both* that procedures for the conduct of open, critical discussion be con-sidered *foundational* to the structure of communication, and that they adumbrate a critical discussion in which any and all conditions of discourse—including those procedures—are in principle subject to critique, and thus, withdrawal. Benhabib attempts to address this issue through a pragmatic defense of what might be termed "the preference for dialogue" (as opposed to force):

> The presuppositions of the moral conversation can be challenged within the conversation itself, but if they are altogether suspended or violated then might violence, coercion, and suppression follow? One thus avoids the charge of circularity: by allowing that the presuppositions of the moral conversation can be challenged within the conversation itself, they are placed within the purview of questioning. But insofar as they are pragmatic rules necessary to keep the moral conversation going, we can only bracket them in order to challenge them but we cannot suspend them altogether.[39]

The philosophical concept of communicative rationality thus yields a model of ideal discourse in which any and all of the procedural relations are, in principle, open to systematic reflection and discursive justification. This contrasts with the position articulated by Wittgenstein throughout his later work in which basic grammatical understandings are "procedural," in the sense that they provide the grounding conditions for the deployment of language in practice, and yet, their "basic-ness" consists precisely in the fact that they are not susceptible to the kind of justificatory challenge that the model of ideal discourse projects. This is what Wittgenstein means when he writes that people do not ordinarily dispute whether the rules of language have been obeyed or not. He then continues:

> "So you are saying that human agreement decides what is true and what is false?"—It is what human beings say that is true and false; and they agree in the *language* they use. This is not agreement in opinions but in form of life.[40]

Thus, to characterize speakers' mutual alignment to the language they use as "consensual" misses the point: the concept of "rational agreement" implies the existence of alternatives, but here there are none. It is not that we agree about the basic principles of the language that we use, but rather, "agreement" is a possible rational relation achievable in language. What, for Wittgenstein, is the spade-turning "bedrock" of social existence—a conventional, necessary, yet essentially arbitrary set of alignments—is, for Habermas, a matter of historical contingency subject at every point to the self-reflective, self-defining moral discourse of the species.

This theme of salvation is absent in Wittgenstein. For Wittgenstein, the basic operations of language are, with respect to *philosophical* criteria of rationality, beyond the pale. Though philosophy seeks at every turn to extend the terms of its own practice to the workings of language in general, it is itself a kind of language-game which, in the end, "leaves everything as it is."[41]

While there exist certain affinities between Coulter's attempt at assimilating sequential analysis to the "[logical] explication of our intuitions as natural-language users in actual situations of language use" and Habermas's program aimed at reconstructing the universal validity basis of speech, their positions concerning the rational basis of speech are at odds, the result being two quite different methodological stances toward the task of providing analytically for the possibility of intersubjective understanding. Given the apparent lack of fit between these traditions, we might question whether further dialogue is worth pursuing.

This dialogue is defensible on at least three counts. First, both analytic programs are concerned to connect the pragmatic analysis of utterances with broader conceptions of *logos*. Although Coulter does not share Habermas's view that this connection is to be sought in the pure-type of "the communicative employment of propositional knowledge in assertions"—a position which is motivated primarily by Habermas's strong distinction between "communicative" and "strategic" modes of language use—they share the common concern of demonstrating the connections between logical form and social practice.

Second, Habermas needs to establish a link between his formal pragmatic theory, which is concerned with "the rational reconstruction of isolated, highly idealized speech acts," and forms of empirical analyses that are sufficiently abstract to grasp "our [rational] intuitions as natural-language users *in actual situations of language use*." Although to date the imagination of the theory of communicative action has been captured by the formal typologies of speech act theory, Habermas is nonetheless concerned to have his model vouchsafed by the empirical work of conversation analysts, sociolinguists, and the like. Of the current work being done, conversation analysis offers one of the most promising cases of empirical-analytic investigations that are abstract enough to link up with formal pragmatic considerations.

Finally, Habermas's concept of "communicative rationality" is, as I have attempted to show, essentially procedural in nature, and is connected, at the pragmatic level, to the specification of structures of discourse that provide for the recognition and maintenance of agreements over the course of interaction. Although Habermas has not always been clear about what these basic procedural conditions might be, Benhabib has argued that they are essentially two:

(1) that we recognize the right of all beings capable of speech and action to be participants in the moral conversation-I will call this *the principle of universal moral respect*; (2) . . . that within such conversations each has the same symmetrical rights to various speech acts, to initiate new topics, to ask for reflection about the presuppositions of the conversation, etc. Let me call this *the principle of egalitarian reciprocity*.[42]

Both of these principles address the organizational auspices of conversation, and the second—the principle of egalitarian reciprocity—is concerned essentially with principles for the sequential allocation of turns-at-talk. Conversation analysis is alone in having investigated and formally described the conditions of procedural rationality that underlie the model of ideal discourse. This connection between the theory of communicative action and the logic of sequential organization will be explored in greater detail in subsequent chapters.

CONCLUSION

If the strong thesis of "communicative rationality" is to be maintained in its present form, Habermas must demonstrate that the "literalness of expression" is a context-free and basic possibility available (at least implicitly) *for participants* in every concrete speech-situation. This requires in turn that "literalness of expression" must be connected to the procedural conditions underlying the fourth and somewhat forgotten validity claim of "comprehensibility" [verständlichkeit]. However, Habermas has so far conceived "comprehensibility" as a context-independent outcome of sentential grammar.[43] Thus, the claim to comprehensibility, while *presupposed* in every concrete speech-situation, does not enter into formal pragmatic considerations since it attaches to the prehermeneutic production of grammatically valid or invalid sentences. In this way, Habermas secures a domain for the "literalness of expression" without thereby embedding the claim to comprehensibility within the formal pragmatic theory of "communicative action."

If, alternatively, "comprehensibility"—and hence, what we mean by "grammar"—was respecified in line with practice-based analyses of the "combinatorial tolerances for illocutionary activities . . . and . . . concepts in a natural language," then the "literalness of expression" would appear as a situated and contingent production that may arise out of conditions of comprehensibility, but does not determine them. Here "comprehensibility" becomes a technical marker for the concrete precondition of any meaningful utterance: that it be hearable as an expression in a natural language participants assume that they share in common. With this respecification of "comprehensibility," the narrowing effects of Habermas's formalism come into plain view: the formal pragmatic reliance on the grammatically well-formed sentence as the seat of comprehensibility operates as an unnecessary constraint on empirical arguments vis-à-vis our rational intuitions as natural-language users. In the interest of defending the "literalness of expression" as a basic mode of language use, formal pragmatics opts for an attenuated conception of rational intuitions; a conception that ignores the concrete modalities of our rational intuitions in actual situations of language use.

From the perspective of practice-based inquiries, "a concept of the lifeworld that is complementary to the concept of communicative action"[44] could only emerge if the theory of communicative action took the ethno-methodological approach to context seriously. This would mean a shift in focus away from sentential grammar and the specification of a communicative context in general, and toward the situated production of comprehensible utterances as a matter of participants' relevant contextualizations.

3

The Doctrine of Literal Expression
and the Theory of Speech Acts

In the previous chapter I argued that Habermas's theory of communicative action relies on a doctrine of literal expression that is inadequate to the task of reconstructing "the competence that directly underlies speaking and understanding a language."[1] In this chapter, I want to extend this argument by considering the place occupied by the doctrine of literal expression in Searle's theory of speech acts.[2] If it can be shown that this doctrine is formally incoherent in Searle, then further progress will have been made toward a critique of Habermas's program of "formal pragmatics" insofar as this initiative takes Searle-inspired analyses of illocutionary activities as its working method.[3]

My criticisms of Searle focus on the explanatory weight he accords to "the principle of expressibility," and to the fact that the accomplishment of speech activities may involve the use of vernacular activity-categories (e.g., "promising," "requesting," "offering") in the first-person indicative mode ("I promise . . . ," "I request . . . ," "I offer . . . ," and so on).

I then consider some of the troubles these criticisms raise for Searle's well known attempt at "deriving 'ought' from 'is.'" It is in this context that the difficulties caused by Habermas's reliance on the theory of speech acts become most acute, for unless it can be shown that there are general standards by which linguistic form is related to social obligations, it makes little sense to claim that the "binding force" of communicative action can be secured theoretically via an inspection of speech acts in standard form.

Against both Searle and Habermas, I argue that the problem of relating linguistic form to social obligations is not, in the first instance, a philosophical task, and that it therefore should not be conceived in terms of philosophically derived standards of descriptive and inferential adequacy.

As an alternative, and on the basis of work done in the areas of ethno-methodology and conversation analysis, I suggest that pragmatic relations between linguistic form and social obligations operate as occasional resources for the situated production of intelligible utterances and activities—as "tools" rather than "rules." Conceived in this way, relations between linguistic form and social obligations constitute a vast, heterogeneous, and largely unstudied field of social phenomena that cannot be captured by the formal typology of the theory of speech acts.

THE THEORY OF SPEECH ACTS AS POSITIVE PHILOSOPHY

Searle begins his discussion of the theory of speech acts with an account of the difference between "linguistic philosophy" and "the philosophy of language." "Linguistic philosophy," he argues, "is the attempt to solve particular problems by attending to the ordinary use of particular words or other elements in a particular language." "The philosophy of language," by contrast, attempts to give

> philosophically illuminating descriptions of certain general features of language, such as reference, truth, meaning, and necessity; and it is concerned only incidentally with particular elements in a partic-ular language; though its method of investigation, where empirical and rational rather than a priori and speculative will naturally force it to pay strict attention to the facts of actual natural languages.
> . . . The "data" of the philosophy of language usually come from natural human languages, but many of the conclusions about, e.g., what it is to be true or to be a statement or a promise, if valid, should hold for any possible language capable of producing truths or statements or promises. In that sense this essay is not about languages, French, English or Swahili, but is about language.[4]

Searle's distinction between "linguistic philosophy" and "the philosophy of language" marks the difference between forms of conceptual analysis that address philosophical problems through explications and criticisms of philo-sophical usage (e.g. in Wittgenstein and Ryle), and his own, more systematic aim of reconstructing the formal requirements of a pragmatic theory of meaning. Inspired by a formalist reading of Austin's seminal lectures on the logic of speech acts,[5] Searle seeks an account of language use that, while *informed* by the methodological critiques initiated by Wittgenstein and the ordinary language philosophers, is capable of saying something *in general* about the logical preconditions of meaningful speech.[6] For this to be pos-sible, the theory of speech acts must locate itself within the production/

recognition machinery of actual speech while at the same time preserving standards of meaning that extend beyond—and are invariant with respect to—the local and contingent determinations of utterance meaning.[7] The distinction Searle implies between an analytic method that is "empirical and rational" as opposed to "*a priori* and speculative" suggests just such a point of (methodologically secure) contact between the theory of speech acts and the object domain of "natural languages as they are actually used."

In his appeal to the conditional-universal, "for any possible language capable of producing truths or statements or promises," we can already discern the importance of the notion of "language-games" and the affiliated concept of "constitutive rules" for Searle's analytic method. By connecting the claim that a game is the sum total of (the application of) its rules to the claim that the activities of language—"promising," "requesting," "ordering," and so on—have gamelike properties, Searle maps out a unique domain of linguistic phenomena for formal analysis: namely, *the analytically recoverable orders of rules for the (felicitous) production of speech acts.*

Construed in this fashion, the theory of speech acts appears to hold forth the promise of advancing beyond the mostly negative effects of Wittgenstein's philosophy for the project of *explaining* language *philosophically.*[8] It will be my argument, however, that it can do so only by disregarding the deep connection, evidenced in Wittgenstein, between the methods of "linguistic philosophy" and the findings of "the philosophy of language." In what follows I will consider an area in the theory of speech acts where this disregard is most pronounced: Searle's formulation of "the principle of expressibility." Although I have chosen initially to restrict my remarks to this single case, further inspection of Searle's text will show that the critique of "the principle of expressibility" ramifies across the entire range of his arguments.

THE PRINCIPLE OF EXPRESSIBILITY

Searle defines "the principle of expressibility" as follows:

> For any meaning X and any speaker S whenever S means (intends to convey, wishes to communicate in an utterance, etc.) X then it is possible that there is some expression E such that E is an exact expression of or formulation of X.[9]

In order to make sense of this assertion we need first of all to understand the kinds of theoretical troubles "the principle of expressibility" is designed to avoid. If, as Searle claims, the theory of speech acts addresses language per se, then it should not turn out that its formulations are dependent for their sense on locally contingent features of their production and recognition. In short, some method or standard for *stabilizing* "context" must be found in order that the pure, ideal-typical forms of "linguistically mediated" communication might emerge. "The principle of expressibility" accomplishes this task by placing a determinate standard of "exact expression" (the literal expression of the intended speech act) at the heart of any possible communicative activity. As such, "the principle of expressibility" amounts to the assertion that for any conceivable speech act there is a characteristic, literal, sentential paraphrase that would, *under standard conditions*, count as the utterance of that speech act. The immediate consequence of this view is that it provides a way of closing the gap between analytically derived rules of linguistic communication, on the one hand, and the actual production and recognition of meaningful speech in situ, on the other:

> [The principle of expressibility] enables us to equate rules for performing speech acts with rules for uttering certain linguistic elements, since for any possible speech act there is a possible linguistic element the meaning of which (given the context of the utterance) is sufficient to determine that its literal utterance is a performance of precisely that speech act. To study the speech acts of promising or apologizing we need only study sentences whose literal and correct utterance would constitute making a promise or issuing an apology.[10]

Of course, it is precisely the "context of the utterance" that his critics will not simply "give" to Searle. Baker and Hacker argue, for instance, that the distinction on which the doctrine of literal paraphrase is predicated—between an utterance's propositional "sense" and its illocutionary "force"—is conceptually inconsistent and confused,[11] while Derrida makes the more diabolical suggestion that Austin himself can be mustered in defense of the context-dependency of "context" and the contingency of speakers' intentions.[12]

A second thing to notice about "the principle of expressibility" is that it defines the meaning of any utterance as, at least in principle, reducible to a single, unequivocal speech act. That is, it treats all utterances as more or less monological instantiations of one and only one "exact expression."[13] In the face of the obvious objection that speakers may do several things at once in and through a single utterance,[14] Searle argues that it is nevertheless possible *analytically* to isolate the literal meaning of an utterance (as a singular speech act) from the manifold effects that an utterance may produce in situ. On Searle's account, such effects are parasitic on the basic form of linguistic communication—the deployment of a singular, literal proposition in the performance of an illocutionary act—and are therefore of secondary importance to the theory of speech acts. As he continues:

> [The principle of expressibility] has the consequence that cases where the speaker does not say exactly what he means—the principle kinds of cases of which are nonliteralness, vagueness, ambiguity, and incompleteness—are not theoretically essential to linguistic communication.[15]

Although there are compelling reasons for rejecting the general distinction implied above between "what a speaker says" and "what he means,"[16] at present it is more important to see how the doctrine of "exact, literal, and singular expression" works to further stabilize a formal object domain for the theory of speech acts.

Unless it can be claimed that there exists a class of utterances that have certain specifiable semantic features in common, and for which some vernacular activity-gloss ("promising," "requesting," "ordering," etc.) stands as an appropriate categorical index, there would be no possibility of developing a *systematic* connection between semantic indicators and illocutionary activities.

The third important feature of "the principle of expressibility" is that it proposes a method for remedying the indexical properties of situated utterances in terms of their formal-semantic (i.e., literal-propositional) features.[17] Searle argues, for instance, that for any situated utterance-activity that might reasonably count as "promising," the formula "I (hereby) promise (you, to, that) . . . X" stands as a meaning-adequate, sentential paraphrase for that utterance-activity. Thus, for Searle, the analysis of "promising" consists in (and only in) the analysis of the rational-linguistic presuppositions of the sentence-type "I (hereby) promise (you, to, that) . . . X." Or again, the "deep structure" of "promising" is identical to the rules for generating the meaningful sentence "I (hereby) promise (you, to, that) . . . X." In this, the connection between semantic content and pragmatic effect is achieved by identifying illocutionary force with canonical semantic indicators. (Note, however, the argumentative weight being placed on the lexical curiosity that one method for promising involves the use of the word "promise" in a sentence.)

Even if it is accepted that vernacular categories of illocutionary activity can be adequately paraphrased in terms of their formal-semantic, sentential equivalents, this does not in itself prove that the rules for producing those sentences govern, constitute, or are even relevant to, the ways in which activities such as "promising," "requesting," and "ordering" get done in practice. Searle's injunction that "the 'data' of the philosophy of language usually come from natural human languages" commits him to the view that the rules recovered by the theory of speech acts are analytical equivalents to the rules for the production and recognition of intelligible speech in situ.

Without some method for showing that the formal rules for producing unequivocal and discrete speech acts are presupposed in the actual production and recognition of meaningful speech, the theory of speech acts would have to give up its positive aspiration to explain language "extra-philosophically."[18]

The fourth important claim made on behalf of "the principle of expressibility" is that this principle can be located concretely within the practical methods of actual speech. As Searle argues:

> I might say "I'll come" and mean it as a promise to come, i.e., mean it as I would mean "I promise that I will come," if I were uttering that sentence and meaning literally what I say.[19]

We often have occasion in everyday talk to repeat, correct, formulate, paraphrase, and so forth something that we or somebody else has said, and we do this, among other reasons, in order to clarify what was said and/or what was thereby meant. For Searle, the canonical form of "saying in so many words what was meant" is the sentential expansion of contextually dependent, indexical expressions in terms of the "exact expression" of the illocutionary act that the speaker intended. In this way, the possibility of offering an "exact expression" of what was meant in terms of a literal, illocutionary type-sentence becomes the transcendental condition of any meaningful utterance.[20] At the same moment, an analytic space is opened up between "what is said" ("I'll come") and "what is meant" ("I promise that I will come") that can only be filled, on Searle's account, by the production/recognition rules elaborated in the theory of speech acts.

The argument I have been making so far can be summarized by saying that Searle's "principle of expressibility" acts to stabilize the indexical properties of speech in line with a model of the exact, literal, sentential expression of speech acts. This accomplishment is, in turn, tied to three related claims:

1. that there is, at least in principle, a one-to-one correspondence between any single utterance and the speech act it instantiates;
2. that formal characterizations that identify speech acts with their "typical" sentential correlates are meaning-adequate to the vernacular activity-types they are designed to capture; and
3. that these formal characterizations operate as practical linguistic resources wherever and whenever the "meaning of what is said" becomes problematic in actual situations of natural language use.

In what follows I shall raise two objections which, if they are correct, have devastating consequences for "the principle of expressibility." The first contests the claim that the canon of literal, sentential expression can serve as the invariant measure of an utterance's "exact expression." This claim, I will argue, is based on the mistaken idea that indexicality is a *logically residual feature of communication*, and hence, that indexical expressions represent incomplete, ambiguous or elliptical references to some literal meaning that stands "behind" utterances, prior to their deployment in actual situations of language use. The second objection addresses Searle's failure to appreciate fully the implications of his own argument that "[p]ropositional acts cannot occur alone; that is, one cannot *just* refer and predicate without making an assertion or asking a question or performing some other illocutionary act."[21] As a consequence of this argument, the expression or formulation of an utterance's "exact meaning" must *itself* involve a discrete illocutionary act (e.g., "formulating," "reporting," "describing," "correcting," or "emphasizing"), and this means that *no* expression or formulation of an utterance's "exact meaning" is intelligible apart from the illocutionary (perlocutionary, etc.) purposes to which it is put in situ. Although this second objection ramifies throughout the theory of speech acts, its most relevant consequence for the present discussion is that it undermines the terms of Searle's famous argument for "the derivation of 'ought' from 'is.'"

THE INTERACTIONAL PRECISION OF INDEXICAL EXPRESSIONS

As was noted above, the theory of speech acts begins from the supposition that indexical expressions—unlike their literal, sentential correlates—are incomplete expressions of speakers' intended meanings. That is to say, for any indexical expression it is left up to recipients of the utterance to figure out, guess, disambiguate, or otherwise complete the sense of the utterance via an inspection of the locally relevant, contingent, circumstances of its expression. Thus, for the theory of speech acts, indexical expressions stand in constant need of remedy both *formally* and *practically*. And if the theory of speech acts is to have a point, that remedy must consist in the possibility of bringing formal clarity to the as yet unspecified mass of background assumptions and conventions going into the intelligible conduct of indexical speech. Cast in this way, the "incompleteness" of indexical expressions means a lot of work for ordinary language users and professional analysts alike.

A radically different picture is obtained if we give up on the idea that indexical expressions are merely vague or elliptical methods for "saying in so many words" what is (literally) meant, and ask instead how it is that what is actually said operates (indexically) as a way of saying what is meant *exactly*.

Now, as Wittgenstein first pointed out, questions of the "exactness" or "inexactness" (of expressions, measures, calculations, directions, and so forth) invoke standards of precision relative to some purpose:

"Inexact" is really a reproach, and "exact" is praise. And that is to say what is inexact attains its goal less perfectly than what is more exact. Thus the point here is what we call "the goal." Am I inexact when I do not give our distance from the sun to the nearest foot, or tell a joiner the width of a table to the nearest thousandth of an inch?

No *single* idea of exactness has been laid down; we do not know what we should be supposed to imagine under this head—unless you yourself lay down what is to be so called. But you will find it difficult to hit on such a convention; at least any that satisfies you.[22]

To say, for instance, that it is "almost ten" is a rather imprecise formulation of the current time when measured against the standard of atomic clocks, but to say that it is "almost ten" as a preface to "so we should probably continue this argument in next week's class" is a perfectly intelligible and contextually precise formulation of the current time in its relevance to the present course of activity. Indeed, even in the wake of digital watches, to adjourn an argument by saying that it is "nine-fifty-eight and thirty seconds" might legitimately occasion questions concerning speaker's motives, mental make-up, or fetishistic relation to "exact time." The point here is that the preface "almost ten" is logically tied to its consequence "so we should probably continue this argument in next week's class" in a way that "nine-fifty-eight and thirty seconds" is not, even though "nine-fifty-eight and thirty seconds" might, in some sense, be a perfectly correct formulation of the current time.

At one point in his Fall 1967 Lectures, Sacks expands on this point with reference to the following utterance-pair:[23]

Q: When did you have the cast taken off?
A: Tuesday.

Sacks begins his discussion of this fragment by noting that, in this case, "Tuesday" is a perfectly appropriate answer to the question "When did you have the cast taken off?," and in part, it is the unremarkable "fit" between the question and its response that accounts for what Sacks terms the "fabulously bland" character of this exchange. The point of interest, however, is that for such a thing as "When did you get your cast off?" there are a number of answers that might be factually correct ("November eleventh," "The eleventh," "November eleventh, ninety sixty seven," and so on), but which, as Sacks puts it, "are altogether wrong, inappropriate, sometimes even crazy."[24] And this means that the method involved in producing such an answer cannot be merely that of selecting from among some list of factually correct equivalents, but on the contrary, that the "correctness" of the answer, its clarity, simplicity, and so forth, hinges on its providing the order of response being sought by the question. As Sacks continues:

> The criteriality of such little items is enormous. People will make an enormous amount of what you might consider to be a minor failing, such that, e.g., it's a most routine thing in psychiatric hospitals when, say, a doctor is going around in the morning after a weekend in which people have been picked up, to decide whether they should be committed, kept, let go, for the whole procedure to take place by the exchange of one question-answer sequence. He'll come in and say "What day is it?" Some answers are enough to have him walk out and say "Keep that guy."[25]

The upshot of these remarks is that the meaning-adequacy of an utterance refers, in the first instance, to its location within some local context of interaction, and most important to what has come just before. Hence, the logical "precision" of an utterance cannot be judged by standards obtained outside of its situated occurrence, but refers instead to its adequacy as a means of reckoning with local contextual considerations.

This argument can readily be extended to the use of pronouns and referring expressions in everyday talk. Sacks's discussion of the sequential organization of referring expressions provides a case in point.[26] He begins by criticizing the conventional view that pronouns ("I," "you," "she," "he," "we," "they") operate primarily as substitutes for nouns. As an initial consideration, Sacks notes that pronouns are routinely used as terms of address or self-reference. So, for instance, "'I' is the way I refer to myself in talk, not 'Harvey saw it,' 'Harvey did,' etc. You don't use your own name in the first instance, and a pronoun is not a substitute for it."[27] He then continues:

> Furthermore, if you're doing directed talk, then you can hardly do it with just the name of the addressed person. You have to do it with the name of the addressed person and 'you,' most likely: "Ken, face it, you're a poor little rich kid." Not: "Ken, face it, Ken's a poor little rich kid."[28]

One significant interactional consequence of the use of pronouns is that speaker selection (who will speak next) can often be seen to turn on the selection of a specific pronoun. For instance, the use of "she" (rather than "you") in referring to someone who is copresent may serve as an indication that the party so formulated is specifically *not* being selected as next speaker (although, as Sacks notes, neither is that person being specifically excluded). That is to say, there is an array of methods for selecting next speaker *specifically,*[29] among them the use of the second-person singular form of address ("you"), but less often, and only under some rather peculiar circumstances, the use of the third-person singular ("she"/"he"), such that the use of the third-person where the first-person might otherwise do will be a *recognizable* use; and this means, simply, that it will be heard and appreciated by participants for its interactional consequences, and among these, that the person so formulated has not been specifically selected to speak next.[30] On the basis of these considerations, Sacks argues that the use of referring expressions is indexically tied to participants' display and management of the illocutionary activities in which they are engaged. For participants, the meaning-adequate use of referring expressions is a matter of when, where, and with what interactional consequences some referring expression is being used. That is to say, it depends in fundamental ways on its *sequential location*. Although Searle's argument that "one cannot *just* refer and predicate without making an assertion or asking a question or performing some other illocutionary act" attempts to capture this feature of referring expressions, he nonetheless maintains the distinction between the "raw" propositional content of the speech act (its "sense") and the various illocutionary purposes to which that content may be put (its "force"). In Sacks, by contrast, this priority is reversed: rather than construing reference and predication as context-free resources for discerning the illocutionary upshot of utterances, Sacks argues that who or what is being talked about (and how) is the contextually contingent result of participants' attending to their own and others' talk for, *inter alia*, the illocutionary upshot of utterances in terms of their sequential location within an ongoing course of activity.

Sacks notes, for instance, that speakers sometimes invoke forms of "intentional misaddress" in responding to an immediately prior utterance. He discusses this phenomenon with reference to the following fragments:

A: Ken, face it you're a poor little rich kid.
B: Yes, Mommy, thank you.
A: Yer not old enough. Leave the room.
B: Yeh, Daddy.[31]

In these examples, the terms of reference in second turn ("Mommy," "Daddy") relevance an ironic hearing of the preceding utterance's illocutionary upshot. Though initial speakers' "intended meanings" may figure in subsequent talk about these utterances, they can in no way determine their local sense, but can only enter incidentally (as explanations, clarifications, apologies, and the like); that is, on the same level as other topical matters in the continued conduct of the interaction-at-hand. Sacks argues that in these as well as in an array of other cases,[32] the formal linguistic machinery that regards referring expressions as, at essence, names for things cannot account for the intelligibility of referring expressions as they are used in practice:

> You could imagine that for some set of parties to a conversation, if a given name was used in an address position in an utterance, then the parties scrutinize the set of persons to find who it was that has that name. If they find the person who has that name, then that's the person being named. If they don't find such a person, then they can find that, say, an error was done, or they can look around in puzzlement. What would be operating there is that the known meaning of the term is used to find the person being referred to by it.[33]

On Sacks's account, this is the conventional view of the method by which participant's determine how, and to what, referring expressions refer. It is a conception that "seems obviously applicable in the case of objects" and "would also seem obviously applicable in the case of named persons."[34] The trouble Sacks has with this picture is that it cannot account, among other things, for cases of intentional misaddress; that is, instances of actual, continuous, relatively unproblematic speech, where "referring" is being adequately done and recognized, but for which there exists no standard "search procedure" for pairing references with persons.

The solution Sacks suggests is that we look to where such utterances characteristically occur within a stream of talk: that, for instance, cases of intentional misaddress tend to follow immediately after insults, commands, requests, and so on. He then suggests that the sequential sense of an utterance as "a second in a pair" will, at times, be a methodic feature for determining who that utterance refers to:

> It may be that the detectability of the addressee turns on the fact that if the person who has been the recipient of, e.g., the insult, talks, and does what could be a return-insult, then treat the name he uses as one way of making an insult to the person who has done it to him.[35]

And he then continues:

> What that seems to mean is that, at least to some extent and in some places, such a thing as sequencing pairs operate—as you might say—prior to the use of reference considerations in locating a person. One looks to who it is that may be addressed by the given utterance, and sees how the name used serves as a possible return to the prior utterance. And in that regard, then, one can see how there is no initial puzzle, there is no initial search, given, e.g.,

"Yes, Mommy," "Yes, Boss," "Yes, Teacher," and things like that; and that furthermore, not only can terms be used that have specific recipients in general, i.e., there are mommies, bosses and teachers in the world, but various terms which have no proper recipients: "dope," "clod," etc.[36]

Searle's response to this kind of argument is that these cases merely demonstrate that once a speaker has mastered the *basic terms* of reference and predication, it may then be possible to produce utterances (such as those above) and have them understood, but these are variously ironic, vague, nonliteral, or incomplete expressions that are *parasitic on* the stable unity of literal usage. There are at least two problems with this position.

The first is that, as was argued above, the standard of literal usage is derived from the internal constraints of the theory of speech acts, and has no demonstrative basis in the actual operations of natural language use. But this objection merely says that the doctrine of literal and exact expression is, at base, a theoretical idealization; a claim that Searle might fully accept given his espoused concern to "explain the possibility of, not to provide evidence for, linguistic characterizations."[37] However, if it can be shown that this idealization lacks the power to come to terms with certain meaning-constitutive features of natural language use that are also (arguably) basic to the organized, orderly conduct of actual speech, then that idealization must be seen to be impoverished with respect to its self-prescribed mission of identifying the constitutive rules for the production and recognition of intersubjectively meaningful utterances.

We have already considered two kinds of argument in support of this second objection. The first is that standards of exactness are themselves context-dependent and purpose-relative. The second is that the analytic machinery for translating indexical expressions into their exact and literal correlates requires a theory of reference that cannot account for the inter-actional precision of indexical expressions as they are routinely used and understood. By beginning from the perspective of intentionalist semantics, the theory of speech acts commits itself to a monological account of meaning-adequate expression, thereby ignoring entirely the constitutive role of contextual considerations in the situated production and recognition of intelligible utterances.

The failure of the doctrine of literal and exact expression is perhaps clearest in cases where indexical expressions are formulated in situ as referentially inadequate or incomplete (as in the following exchange):

A: Mr. Wilkes, will you please inform the other students that the exam will begin in one-half hour.

B: Yes.
A: Yes what?
B: Yes sir!

Here speaker B's "yes" in second turn is taken-up in A's subsequent utterance as incomplete. An alternative might be to hear A's "Yes what?" as targeting B's "Yes" as an overly elliptical response to A's initial request. Thus B might opt for a "literal" hearing: "Yes I will inform the other students that the exam will begin in one-half hour." Such minor insurrections are often constructed with an ear toward the "literal and exact" hearing of some preceding utterance, but the important point here is that the hearing that A's "Yes what?" gets (in turn four) is that B's response to A's request was referentially incomplete, and this is because (as it turns out) it was no request at all, but was instead an order. In this, we begin to see the ways in which an order of referential particulars interlaces with an order of illocutionary activities to produce a stretch of mutually intelligible talk. The nature of that intelligibility cannot be recovered, however, apart from the analysis of these particulars and activities as a step-by-step and orderly movement across turns-at-talk.

This argument can be generalized by saying that, for participants, "literal and exact" formulations of indexical expressions may figure in their talk, but only as *contingent* and *sequentially relevant* features of the talk in which they are embedded.

We are now in a position to tackle one residual issue raised in the preceding section. The issue concerns Searle's undue reliance on the fact that there are circumstances in which the accomplishment of certain speech acts (e.g., "promising," "requesting," "ordering") involves the indicative use of a lexical item that is, superficially at least, identical with the action being done. It is possible, for instance, to utter "I promise that I will come," and to have thereby promised something. The question is: "What significance does this fact have for a pragmatic theory of meaning?" The answer I propose is: "Not much." Why I think this is so may already be obvious, but it is worth considering the issue in a bit more detail if only to clarify why such an incidental lexical relation cannot possibly shoulder the heavy explanatory burden assigned by Searle.

To briefly recall the earlier discussion: It was argued that unless it can be claimed that there exists a class of utterances with certain specifiable features in common, and for which a vernacularly defined activity-type (e.g., "promising") stands as an appropriate gloss, all hopes of developing a systematic connection between semantic indicators and illocutionary activities would evaporate. For Searle, the claim that whenever speakers sincerely and nondefectively "promise" they are (literally and exactly) saying "I (hereby) promise (to, that) . . . X" works to solidify the connection between semantic indicators and illocutionary activities—that is, to solidify precisely that connection which any "formal pragmatic" theory of meaning needs in order to salvage its object domain. There are several problems with this claim.

One is that speakers ordinarily utter, or are asked to utter, for example, "I (hereby) promise (to, that) . . . X," only when some question concerning their intentions, the reliability of their word, the extraordinary nature of the present circumstances, and so on, is being raised. That is to say, "literal and exact" expressions have their own rather specialized uses. So, for instance, if I say to my child, "I promise to take you to the zoo tomorrow," it is constitutive of the sense of "promising" here—and of using the word *promise* to do it—that we are not going to the zoo today, even though I may have earlier said (promised?) that we would, and this has to do with the conventional and specialized uses we make of such "literal and exact" formulations of our own activities (as, for instance, *emphatic assurances* that, though we have just broken a promise, we will not do so again). Thus, it might be said, "promising" by way of "I (hereby) promise (to, that) . . . X" is not rightly thought of as the canonical (literal and exact) standard of "promising" (against which all other cases might be measured), but is instead intelligible only with reference to those situations where a person's intention or ability to carry through on a promise in other, less remarkable ways is somehow being brought into question.

A second problem with the idea that when a speaker does some speech activity (sincerely, nondefectively, etc.) he means the (literal and exact) sentential paraphrase of that activity, is that it misconstrues the relation between vernacularly defined activity-glosses and the activities they gloss. For one thing, from the use of "I promise," "I order," "I request," and so on in doing some utterance-activity it does not follow that the appropriate gloss for that activity would be "promising," "ordering," or "requesting." We have already seen that the use of the lexically identical item may very well shade meaning in a much different direction, and, at any rate, the use of "I promise," "I order," "I request" in some initial utterance could only serve as *evidence* for the claim that some "promising," "ordering," or "requesting" had been done, but could not be its defining feature.

Taking up the particular case of paraphrasing, Sacks points out that the relation between paraphrases and the activities they gloss ordinarily involves a variety of grammatical transformations (of tense, what was said, who said what, etc.) that preserve the sense of "what was said" precisely by departing from its original wording:

> It is regularly the case that when someone is proposedly para-
> phrasing something that another said . . . that they will include not

only some version of what that person said, but if that person's utterance is tied, or is, e.g., the second member of a pair, they will also include features of the utterance to which it is tied, to which it is a second. For example: A says, "Do you agree?," B says, "Yes." Later on, C may refer to that by saying, "But you said you agreed," to B, where what B had said was "Yes" . . . the fact that paraphrases normatively have this feature, so that you can't routinely say "I didn't say I agreed, I said 'yes,'" is one way in which things like utterance pairs and various sorts of tying are treated as natural phenomena by those who deal with them.

. . . And it's then of interest that the notion of 'paraphrase' does not routinely involve some operation on a given utterance only, but some operation on an utterance environment—an utterance and another utterance. So it's not, e.g., "You and John said X," it's "You said X." The notion 'paraphrase of an utterance' involves then, paraphrase of an utterance and other things as well; other utterances perhaps.[38]

In contrast to Searle's attempt at maintaining a context-free standard of "literal and exact" paraphrase, Sacks elaborates a conception of paraphrasing that is consonant with the methods by which this relation is brought off in practice: namely, as an analysis of an utterance in some context, and (minimally) as an analysis of an utterance and one other utterance with which it is being paired.

The study of utterances as sequential phenomena is a manifestly *sociological* enterprise. As such, it does not conceive the intelligibility of utterances as a product of linguistic form. On the contrary, sequential analysis shows that situated utterances display a characteristic autonomy with respect to stipulative versions of linguistic form of the sort provided, for instance, by Searle's doctrine of "literal and exact" expression.

So far I have attempted to show that the narrowness of Searle's doctrine consists in its fetishizing of one, rather incidental, lexical relation to the neglect of other, rather obvious, sociological considerations. In the following section, I want to extend this critique to Searle's discussion of the relation between descriptive and evaluative statements. As one important consequence of these criticisms, it will then be argued that Habermas's conception of the "binding force" of communicative action cannot be secured via an inspection of speech acts in standard linguistic form.

DERIVING "OUGHT" FROM "IS"

Searle's attempt at deriving "ought" from "is" is aimed, in the first instance, at disrupting that "picture of the way words relate to the world" that accepts a "rigid distinction" between descriptive and evaluative expressions.[39] Insofar as he is successful, the value of his argument as a counterpoint to empiricist conceptions of descriptivism can hardly be ignored. When we move to consider how this "proof" is brought off, however, we are immediately confronted with a series of misleading characterizations and internal inconsistencies. Central among these are Searle's equivocal use of the concept of "meaning," and his ill-founded assumption that activities characterizable as "uttering words" represent "brute facts" of language. It is necessary to consider briefly the different elements of his argument in order to isolate where the stepwise movement from description to evaluation miscarries.

Searle begins his analysis by asking us to consider the following series of statements:

1. Jones uttered the words "I hereby promise to pay you, Smith, five dollars."
2. Jones promised to pay Smith five dollars.
3. Jones placed himself under (undertook) an obligation to pay Smith five dollars.
4. Jones is under an obligation to pay Smith five dollars.
5. Jones ought to pay Smith five dollars.

He then continues:

> I shall argue concerning this list that the relation between any statement and its successor, while not in every case one of entailment, is nonetheless not just an accidental or completely contingent relation; and the additional statements and certain other adjustments necessary to make the relationship one of entailment do not need to involve any evaluative statements, moral principles or anything of the sort.[40]

Rather than considering the proof in its entirety, I will argue that the idea that statement 1 entails statement 2 is based on an incoherent conceptualization of 1 as a statement of "brute fact." This conceptualization can, in turn, be shown to be an artifact of "the principle of expressibility."

Now there are a variety of circumstances under which to do one activity carries conventional obligations for doing another. So, for instance, if I order eggs for breakfast, and if I do this in a restaurant, and if I am not one of the people that work there, and have never been extended credit by the management, and so on, then (it might be said) I *ought* to pay for them before I leave. Moreover, ordering eggs (successfully and nondefectively) may, on occasion, involve the uttering of some words, such as "I'd like to order some eggs," or "Eggs please," though to do so immediately on entering a restaurant, to another customer, to a waiter at another table, or at the top of my lungs while using the bathroom will more likely be taken as a sign of belligerence, confusion, or mental incapacity than as a successful and nondefective request for some breakfast. And it is important that this is so irrespective of the words chosen or the syntactic form in which they are delivered.

Now, of course, Searle is not interested in all of the contingencies involved in ordering eggs and being thereby obligated to pay for them. Rather, he is concerned with such formal matters as "ordering," "requesting," and "promising" per se, for which, it is proposed (though wholly implicitly), the relation between, for example, uttering the words "I hereby promise to pay you, Smith, five dollars" and what one is thereby obligated to do is somehow less a matter of circumstantial contingency and more a matter of linguistic form than is the relation between ordering eggs for breakfast and (thereby) being obligated to pay for them.

Whatever is significant about Searle's proof must be happening in statements 1 and 2, for everything after that is analogous to our example of ordering eggs and paying for them. The question then is: What is the relation between some bundle of words that someone has apparently uttered and the characterization of that activity (of uttering those words) as, for instance, "having promised someone something?" So Searle:

> How is 1 related to 2? In certain circumstances, uttering the words in quotation marks in 1 is the act of making a promise. And it is a part of or a consequence of the meaning of the words in 1 that in those circumstances uttering them is promising. "I hereby promise" is a paradigm device in English for performing the act identified in 2, promising.[41]

What is most interesting about this passage is that the prefatory clause, "Jones uttered the words . . . ," has already dropped out of the account of statement 1. This curious sleight-of-hand proves crucial to Searle's subsequent analysis of the entailment relation between statements 1 and 2.

For Searle, statement 1 ("Jones uttered the words 'I hereby promise to pay you, Smith, five dollars'") is a sentence describing a brute linguistic fact: certain words were uttered by a specific person to another person, and those words were, "I hereby promise to pay you, Smith, five dollars."[42] And indeed, when we consider circumstances under which sentences of the sort, "X uttered the words . . . ,'" might ordinarily be deployed, we find that one of their central uses is to describe, report, quote, or in other ways assert that "whatever occurs between the quotation marks is a brute linguistic fact." So, for example, there are circumstances under which people disagree as to whether someone actually promised to do something, and one kind of argument that can be used in such circumstances is, "Well you said (uttered the words) 'I promise (to, that) . . . X.'" It should also be clear, however, that arguments about whether or not someone actually promised something rarely begin or end with such statements of brute linguistic fact. That is to say, although assertions, descriptions, quotations, reports, and so forth of brute linguistic facts may *figure* in the determination of what someone actually said, whether or not they thereby "promised (to, that) . . . X," and so on, such assertions are, in turn, open to challenges concerning their accuracy, completeness, or relevance to some present circumstance.

In a sense, this argument merely represents a consistent application of Searle's own proposal that "(p)ropositional acts cannot occur alone; that is, one cannot just refer and predicate without making an assertion or asking a question or performing some other illocutionary act." Returning to the analogy of language-games, this proposal means that utterances, activities, statements, and so on, are only intelligible against the backdrop of some collection of constitutive rules that make for their production and recognition as, in Garfinkel's words, "game-possible actions."

> The basic [i.e., constitutive] rules provide the solution to the problem of jurisdiction by providing themselves the meaning of "adequate recognition" of actual appearances as recognized appearances-of-the-object. In that the basic rules specify the domain of game-possible actions, they define the domain of "game-possible actions" to which the variable of "mere behaviors" can be assigned. Basic rules frame the set of possible events of play that observed behaviors can signify.[43]

There is no such thing as "mere behavior" subsisting, as it were, in a field of meaning-neutral observation. Rather, the "adequate recognition" of meaningful action consists in attending to its potentially game-relevant features with respect to some present course of activity. As Garfinkel continues:

> Bridge players respond to each other's actions as bridge events, not behavioral events. They do not treat the fact that the other player withdraws a card from his hand and places it on the table as the event "putting down a pasteboard" or "effecting a translation of position of a card." Instead, through the translation of the card's position the player signalizes that "he has played the ace of spades as the first card of the trick." From the player's point of view the question "What can really happen?" is for him correctly decided in terms of basic rules.[44]

These remarks suggest that the language of "mere behavior" (as in, for instance, "Jones uttered the words . . .") cannot serve as a uniform standard of descriptive adequacy. Or again, since the meaning-adequacy of any activity or description consists in its observability as a "game-possible action," no single standard of descriptive adequacy can claim independent legislative authority over other possible, game-relevant and game-decidable, descriptive criteria. It is not that "effecting a translation of position of a card" is a stripped down, or empirically basic description of "play[ing] the ace of spades as the first card of the trick." Rather, it is the kind of description that might be offered where, for instance, someone is not yet familiar with—does not yet *understand*—the game of bridge.[45]

It is the empiricist rhetoric of "Jones uttered the words . . ." that makes statement 1 look like a technical description of some natural fact (as against, say, a conventional and defeasible method for asserting that "whatever occurs between the quotation marks is a brute linguistic fact"). It is also this rhetoric that allows the absenting of "Jones uttered the words . . ." in Searle's subsequent analysis of the relation between statements 1 and 2, for it is only on an empiricist reading of "Jones uttered the words . . ." that statement 1 can be conceived as a transparent statement of fact; or again, as a sentence that simply refers and predicates.[46]

As I have already argued, sentences of the sort "Jones said (uttered the words) . . .'" are conventionally used to ascribe the saying of certain words to a specific person. Such descriptions, reports, quotations, or what have you, are intelligible by virtue of the fact that they are done at certain times, in certain places, for specific purposes at hand. With respect to Searle's immediate purpose—the attribution to Jones that in saying something, he thereby "promised (to, that) . . . X"—the sentence "Jones uttered the words 'I hereby promise to pay you, Smith, five dollars,'" may, in certain circumstances, serve as *evidence* for the claim that "Jones promised to pay Smith five dollars," but cannot, in any general sense, be said to *entail* that claim.[47] Thus, a consistent application of Searle's own argument—namely, that the idea of pure reference and predication is formally incoherent—means that the relation between statements 1 and 2 cannot be one of entailment.

I want now briefly to spell out a few of the consequences this argument holds for Searle's analysis of the relation between descriptive and evaluative statements. In order to do this, I need first to make clear one kind of consequence that I do *not* think can be drawn from these criticisms.[48]

I do not, by this argument, mean to imply that Searle's "proof" miscarries because he fails to recognize that statement 1 is shot through with value commitments, or again, that what he has really shown is merely that certain evaluative statements (e.g., "Jones uttered the words 'I hereby promise to pay you, Smith, five dollars'") may conventionally entail other evaluative statements (e.g., "Jones ought to pay Smith five dollars"), and thus, things being what they are, we can never move (formally) from "is" to "ought" since every descriptive statement can be reduced to an evaluative statement.

There are at least two reasons for rejecting this kind of argument. First, although this criticism targets the "literalist fallacy" in Searle, the solution it offers merely supplants an objectionable theoretical stipulation with the far more reductionist and praxiologically insensitive doctrine of blanket skepticism. At core, this doctrine represents a wholesale capitulation to the terms of the classical dilemma that Searle's analysis is designed to avoid. In order to claim that there are no such things as descriptive statements that are not also evaluative statements, the skeptic must assume that there are (or can be) general and invariant standards for deciding whether or not some statement counts as purely descriptive. It is not a question of denying these standards, but rather, of assuming them in and through showing that they are standards against which no statement can possibly measure up.

The second problem with the skepticist reading is that it inevitably treats all descriptive statements *ironically*, as (mere) rhetorical posturings in the ongoing, foundationless movement from one evaluative statement to the next. While the skepticist position affords the analyst the initial theoretical privilege of exposing the evaluative presuppositions involved in (would-be) statements of "brute fact," this critical advantage is quickly discharged through the reflexive application of this treatment to the skeptic's own analytic claims. The well-known consequence is that *all* analytic claims get leveled. And this means simply that the choice between (foundationless) statements of "brute fact" and the skeptic's own (equally foundationless) ironic reformulations is rendered formally undecidable.

As an alternative to the skepticist position, I propose to treat distinctions between descriptive and evaluative statements as locally contingent, nonarbitrary methods for specifying, *inter alia*, certain "facts-of-the-matter" and their interactional or argumentative consequences. What this proposal means is that the specification of standards for distinguishing between descriptive and evaluative statements is not, in the first instance, a philosophical task, and should not be treated as such. Rather, the recommendation is that such distinctions be conceived as eminently *practical* demarcations, and hence, as subject to the vicissitudes of their situated deployment.

This proposal is no less unsettling for the philosophical skeptic than it is for Searle. Against Searle it is argued that the possibility of deriving obligations from descriptions is contingent on local determinations of what count as "facts-of-the-matter," and how (i.e., with what "force") these facts are produced and recognized as such. As a consequence of this, Searle's "proof" demonstrates only that it is *possible* to move from statement 1 to statement 5, but not that it is a *logical necessity*.

The skepticist position interprets this lack of philosophical foundations as grounds for a principled rejection of *any* rigorous distinction between descriptive and evaluative statements. In this, the skeptical position reveals its commitment to philosophically derived standards of logical necessity. For the skeptic, any movement from description to evaluation that cannot be accommodated by the model of strict entailment is somehow suspect. And since (taken out of context) all movements from description to evaluation can be shown to require additional premises, no rigorous distinction between descriptive and evaluative statements can be drawn. This reduction of praxiological rigor to the terms of logical necessity becomes untenable once we begin to examine how distinctions between "brute facts" and statements predicated on those facts figure in ordinary usage.

"BRUTE FACTS" AS DEFEASIBLE BASES OF INFERENCE

So far I have argued that Searle's attempt at deriving "ought" from "is" is inconsistent with respect to his own proposal that no meaningful statement can just refer and predicate. It has also been argued, however, that this does not mean that Searle's "proof" requires a skeptical rereading. Both of these positions assume that without decontextualized criteria for determining whether or not some description is indeed a description of some "brute fact," no *formally valid* warrant can be found for the movement from description to evaluation. But this assumption, as the example of bridge has shown, neglects the possibility that the meaning-adequacy of descriptive statements is internally related to their deployment in actual situations of use. The assumption that descriptions must appeal to decontextualized criteria of "brute facticity" is predicated on the deep philosophical prejudice that regards "the world of things" and "the world of values" as discrete entities (i.e., as "worlds"), and conceives the task of philosophy as the construction of formally valid procedures for crossing the gaps between and integrating "worlds." This philosophical picture ignores the possibility that "brute facts," evaluations based on those facts, and the reasonable procedures that provide for the movement from factual to evaluative statements are, under ordinary circumstances, organized as methodic elements and procedures for determining, for instance, what happened where and when, how someone came to know something, what are the "brute facts," and so on.

As an example of how such an alternative program might proceed, I want briefly to consider Pomerantz's analysis of routine methods for constructing and displaying inferences as "inferences with a basis."[49] The following extracts are taken from that analysis:

> E: I- You had Ea:rl down.
> L: Yeah.
> → E. Ya:h I saw his car last °( )°
> E: How's Earl
> L: Well he le:ft today
> → E: I was thinking about it. Yeah I didn't see his car

Pomerantz argues that utterances of the sort "Ya:h I saw his car last °( )°" or "I didn't see his car" formulate features of past events as objective features that provide for further inferences concerning the significance of those events. Pomerantz refers to such formulations as "raw data" or "no-inference reports." The significance of such formulations is not merely that they trade on the possibility of distinguishing between "what was witnessed" and "what was inferred," but more important, that they *enact* that distinction as relevant to the interaction-at-hand. As she continues:

> By virtue of producing a "raw data" report, what is seeably excluded are *inferences*. The way in which "raw data" stand as manifestations or evidence or clues for a now proposedly inferable state of affairs is through a member's use of his knowledge of the relatedness of particular artifacts or experiences with a particular state of affairs. A known social organization of the facts described in the "raw data" report provides for a determination of an inferred state of affairs.[50]

As a further illustration of this phenomenon, Pomerantz considers the following fragment taken from a standing area on a train (A and B are conversing; C is listening in):

> A (to B): Leamington is the next stop
> C: I think it's the second stop
> ((A looks at C))
> → C: I was told it's the second stop

In this case C offers a correction to A's utterance, "Leamington is the next stop." The correction is neither accepted nor ratified by A, but gets instead a simple return of attention. At this point C "cites a source" (i.e., gives the basis for) her previous utterance. The preface "I think . . ." in C's initial utterance provides, in part, for the intelligibility of her next utterance by providing for the possibility that "it's the second stop" may be a kind of secondhand knowledge, and not a matter of firsthand experience. In light of her subsequent utterance, C's first utterance is revealed as an inference concerning some fact—a possibility that was prefigured by the preface "I think"—where the "raw data" for that inference becomes "that someone told her that . . . X."[51] It is then left up to the ensuing conversation, A's further inquiries, or the markers at the next station to determine whether or not C's assertion counts as a correct formulation of the "facts-of-the-matter."

If "raw data" operate as occasional warrants for inferences concerning certain "facts-of-the-matter," then it follows that one way of defeating claims concerning those facts would be to show how (would-be) "no-inference reports" in fact turn out to be inference-laden. This point can be clarified by considering the following extract:

> [Los Angeles *Times*, February 22, 1969]
> (R. F. Kennedy assassination inquest; testimony of a bystander who was shot)
> "I felt someone kick me," said Stroll, adding that *he didn't know at first* that he had been shot. "*Then I noticed*—because I had on blue pants—that one of my legs was red."[52]

In this example, the distinction between "what was witnessed" and "what was inferred" is enacted with specific dramatic consequences for the event in question, in and as that event's recountable features. That is, the witness's report includes, first of all, an account of his or her initial and immediate experience of the event ("I felt someone kick me")—just the kind of account that might otherwise, under less extraordinary circumstances, have stood as a "no-inference report" of some witnessable occurrence. However, given the witness's subsequent appreciation of other features relevant to that account ("one of my legs was red"), that initial experience turns out *not* to have been merely an *experience*, but is instead formulated as having been an inference-laden *account of an experience*; an account that— though not without a basis (the witness indeed felt *something*)—turned out to be incorrect (it was a gunshot and not a kick). This example not only points up how "raw data" or "no-inference reports" are circumstantially open to defeat, but furthermore, how questions of the routine or extra-ordinary nature of events, or of a person's competency as a witness of such events, might turn on the subsequent appreciation that those events were, in the first instance, witnessed incorrectly.

The "at first . . . then . . ." formulation is one of a family of devices for reporting on the extraordinary character of witnessed events. The "bystander" is in a particularly good position to experience and report on these events as "out of the ordinary" just because he is not (like, say, the bodyguard) specially trained to observe such scenes for their possibly extraordinary character. By marking the temporal lag between his initial experience and the subsequent appreciation that that experience was incorrect, the bystander displays both the revelatory nature of his experience of "witnessing" and the basis on which an ordinary observation might become a revelation; namely, via the subsequent appreciation that the "naked experience" was already clothed in conventional expectations. It is important to see in this that the issue for the bystander is *not* that he should have been a better witness—for example, that he should have felt the "kick" as just "a pain in the leg"—but rather, that *for anyone*, and *under similar circumstances*, to feel a gunshot as a kick in the leg is a perfectly appropriate, meaning-adequate experience to have.[53] That is to say, the determination of the "facts-of-the-matter" has as much to do with the meaning of his initial experience (as a natural and appropriate experience to have), as with the fact that it turned out to be incorrect.

CONCLUSION

Even on this schematic account of Pomerantz's analysis, it is apparent that the distinction between a scene's *objective features* and its *inferable sense* has routine occasions of use, and that *enactments* of the distinction between "what was witnessed" and "what was inferred" carry manifold consequences for the situated specification of what may come to count as a statement's "descriptive adequacy."

The "rigor" of these procedures has little to do, however, with formal requirements of philosophically derived standards of logical necessity, cogency, completeness, etc. On the contrary, their rigor consists in *using* the distinction between "facts" and "inferences" as a method for displaying just how it is that some inferential movement is being done. Given the immense variety of ways in which speakers routinely "give a basis" or "cite a source" for their inferences, the relation between "brute facts" and what is inferable on the basis of those facts is irreducible to the narrow terms of logical entailment.

This does not mean, however (*pace* the skeptical reading), that these methods are somehow logically defective or invariably open to an ironic or even critical treatment. Just because there is no *single standard* for distinguishing between legitimate irony or criticism and open belligerence (or even lunacy) does not mean that such distinctions are never made, nor, when they are, that they are hopelessly debased.

Here the difference between Searle and the skeptic is a difference in kind but not consequence. Where Searle needs to argue that "effecting a translation of position of a card" is an empirically basic description of "play[ing] the ace of spades as the first card of the trick," the skeptic needs to argue that either description will do equally well (or poorly), since *no* description can defend itself as *uniquely adequate* to the activity it seeks to describe. In either case we are left without methods for the adequate description (or playing!) of bridge.

4

The Organization of Talk

To this point, I have been concerned to demonstrate that the pragmatic foundations of the theory of communicative action are based in a conception of utterance-meaning that fails adequately to grasp how "lived" speech is organized. It thus fails to comprehend the significance of conversational organization for our understanding of "grammar" and "logic." Throughout this discussion, the discipline of conversation analysis has served as a counterpoint to Habermas's pragmatic theory of meaning. Where Habermas seeks to strip away the contingencies of local context in order to identify the formal-pragmatic "core" of speech activities, conversation analysts take the "contextualizing work" of participants as the primary object of analysis. In line with the methodological policies of ethnomethodology, conversation analysts treat the empirical settings under consideration as self-organizing and self-explicating orders of practical conduct and reasoning. Hence, analysts' competencies as speakers of natural languages are conceived as resources for comprehending the logical texture of actual utterances and actions *in situ*. This contrasts with Habermas's methodological discussions in which empirical-analytic investigations are seen as necessarily limited in the absence of a formal theory of how languages operate in general.

In this chapter I will pursue a line of argument in which criticisms developed in the context of this earlier discussion are applied to the discipline of conversation analysis itself. From the standpoint of practice-based inquiries, this discussion involves a reflexive methodological critique in which the standards of practice within a discipline "close to home" are subjected to review and critical assessment. This internal critique follows from a consistent application of the antiformalist position developed in this book: through its discovery and demonstration of the sequential organization of everyday talk, conversation analysis provides a radical alternative to prevailing conceptions of logic and formal analysis. At the same time, over the history of its development, the discipline has come to rely on a set of idealizations concerning the nature of conversation and its foundational role within the overall organization of speech and social activity. Through an analysis of the nature of proof and demonstration in conversation analytic texts, I aim to explore the practical methods by which, as a feature of those arguments, logical structure is conjoined to empirical instances of talk. Those developments that epitomize the foundational aspirations of conversation analysis are collected by the gloss, "the organization of talk," and form the central topic of this chapter.

This discussion follows a line of argument begun by Anderson and Sharrock in their study of the organization of conversational data.[1] The strategy developed there was to pursue an analysis of conversation analytic practice based in ethnomethodological studies of work and practical reasoning; in short, to study one brand of ethnomethodological research from the perspective of another. The idea of treating sciences as organized complexes of practical activity has a long history within ethnomethodological research. It is already present in Garfinkel's radical proposals for treating social scientific and other kinds of formal analysis as species of commonsense reasoning, and has more recently been extended in a series of ethnomethodological investigations of work and scientific practice.[2] The novelty of Sharrock and Anderson's approach is that they articulate the difference between the two enterprises—the conversation analytic and the ethnomethodological—with reference to the question of how each might address the other's work as the outcome of particular courses of practical reasoning and activity.

Throughout this discussion, the discipline of conversation analysis will be treated primarily as an order of textual and literary practice. I will be concerned to show how arguments are made and fragments of empirical data are mobilized in the context of the academic writings that constitute the core findings of that field. Insofar as it takes as its subject matter those conventional and unremarkable features of a science that give it its sense, adequacy, and discipline, this argument affiliates to the tradition of ethnomethodological studies of work and scientific practice mentioned above. Insofar as it treats the science of conversation analysis primarily in terms of a specific set of textual and literary technologies, it diverges from this tradition, moving instead in the direction of studies of the literary technologies of science.[3]

Initially I consider how Sacks's seminal idea that everyday, tape-recorded talk could be analyzed in such ways as to yield, in his words, a "technology of conversation"[4] has come to be identified with a foundational interest in elaborating "conversation" as the generic substrate of language and social life. The subsequent discussion attempts to specify techniques by which the foundational nature of "conversation" is made a recoverable feature of the conversation analytic text.

The analysis will center throughout on a paper by Emanuel Schegloff that was written in the late-1980s, and was based on materials taken from the 1987 pre-election interview between Dan Rather and then vice-president George Bush.[5] There are a number of reasons for organizing this discussion around this particular paper. First, Schegloff is one of the people who helped to invent conversation analysis and he has, over the past two decades, remained one of its foremost practitioners. A second reason for centering the analysis on this particular paper is that Schegloff uses these materials to make a number of more general theoretical points concerning those features of conversation analysis that distinguish it from other approaches to the study of communication as well as from its kindred discipline of ethnomethodology. As such, it brings many of the programmatic commitments of the field of conversation analysis to a head. Finally, this study represents a rare attempt by Schegloff to address materials of obvious popular interest and repute. It is largely in and through his recasting of these "dramatic" materials in terms amenable to conversation analytic technique that the working conventions of that technique come into plain view.

SCHEGLOFF'S REPLY TO SHILS'S COMPLAINT: CONVERSATION AS FORM OF LIFE

In a 1989 essay on antifoundationalism, Stanley Fish argues that the establishment of a modern linguistic science typically involves the organization of some specifiable phenomenal field in terms of its "foundational," or basic elements, on the one hand, and its secondary or derivative phenomena, on the other.[6] Basic elements are then contrasted with secondary elements, and a series of structural transformations are devised to explain how secondary elements can be derived from the set of basic structures. Though Fish's arguments are inspired primarily by Chomsky's efforts at establishing a science of transformational grammar, recent developments in conversation analysis closely parallel his conception of "foundational inquiry."

It is the unique achievement of conversation analysis to have shown that "conversation" comprises a collection of discrete phenomena, and to have made a persuasive, empirical case that conversational activities are basic to the conduct of all other, more specialized forms of social activity.[7] At the same time, and as part of the work of managing this achievement, the foundational picture of "conversation" has, in recent years, begun to be identified with a classical interest in social structure.

Consider, for instance, the following argument from the theoretical preface to Schegloff's analysis of the Bush/Rather interview:

There is a danger in dealing with dramatic material . . . that there will be a sense that the analysis should "live up" to what is being analyzed. Something dramatic should get a "monumental" analysis, one "proportional" to the drama being addressed. And the analysis may be expected to shed light on just what makes the event dramatic or of interest.

. . . In a variant of the old methodological saw that constants cannot explain variation, it may be felt that dramatic occurrences cannot be understood by reference to mundane considerations. . . . On the other hand, sometimes a coup may be achieved by showing how some spectacular outcome is the product precisely of a slippage in the society's mundane underpinnings . . .

. . . But one might ask, is it not a proper task to deal precisely with what marks the data as special? Is that not a proper task for analysis? Echoing Garfinkel's argument, and, as he reports . . . Shils to have asked Bales in the Chicago jury study: the issue is not what makes it a small group, but what makes it a jury?

To that it may be argued: it surely *does* matter what makes it a small group. In the context of the focus of the present analysis, whatever the source of the political notoriety of the event here examined, it had in the first instance to be conducted as talk-in-interaction, and talk of a particular sort.

. . . [B]efore addressing what is unique, analysis must specify what is the generic domain within which that uniqueness is located.

And so this analysis will look to this "special" event with mundane colored glasses, and try to turn a topically transient occurrence into a source of longer lasting analytic resources.[8]

The effect of these remarks is to isolate the unique subject matter of conversation analysis by outlining the conditions under which a widely available, politically noteworthy occurrence can sustain a specialized interest in talk's own organization. The "danger of dramatic material," as Schegloff sees it, is that an appreciation of the event *as dramatic* will tend to obscure its more humble and generic features as a mundane instance of talk-in-interaction.

What this makes clear is that, for Schegloff, a *technical* interest in certain events (or certain of their features) is, in a very specific sense, incompatible with their "*ordinary*" appreciation. In fact, ordinary interests may often interfere with the analytic-task-at-hand. Ordinary interests attend to variation, uniqueness, notoriety, and the like. A technical interest, by contrast, attends to the discoverable constants of "society's mundane underpinnings," disclosing the generic, "mundane-colored" clothing beneath the captivating vestments of the public spectacle.

Hence, Schegloff's interest in "dramatic materials" is first of all that they provide a rhetorical lever for aligning "Shils's complaint" with an ordinary (and analytically debased) appreciation of the "topically transient" features of interactional organization.[9] Wherever it can be shown that ethnomethodology's long-standing interest in the singularity, strangeness, and integrity of practical activities' sense and conduct is of a piece with a (merely) ordinary fascination, a place will have been created for a vision more stable and penetrating than "what one ordinarily sees." Schegloff's response to "Shils's complaint"—that it "surely does matter what makes it a small group"—summarizes this position nicely: it matters because, on this view, in order for something to be a "jury" ("interview," "public spectacle") it must *first* be constituted as a "small group," or better, as a "small group in conversation."

Schegloff's "mundane colored glasses" provide a distinctly *leveling* vision of social life. Far from banishing the dramatic from analysis, he uses what is "special" about the event to enact a technically informed counterdrama that dissolves the public notoriety of these events in a celebration of "the mundane." Through this sustained assault on our ordinary fascination with the live public spectacle, the dramatic entitlements of "the Bush/Rather encounter" are transferred to a technical specification of that event as yet another instance of "talk-in-interaction." In this way, a dramatic space is created for analyses which are at once orthogonal to and authorized by "mundane considerations."

From this point on, wherever and in just the way that conversation analysis can mobilize actual instances of interaction to demonstrate the relevance of sequential issues to "mundane considerations," *those* demonstrations and *those* results will be taken as definitive of just what "the mundane" could, in the end, amount to. In and through its deceleration of the public spectacle, Schegloff's "discourse of the mundane" constructs a system of *countersignificancies* that establishes sequential analysis as proxy for those structures that organize practical activities, but are absent to an ordinary appreciation of those activities' sense and significance.

To briefly summarize: I have argued that the distinction between "ordinary conversation," and other variously constrained or specialized, interactional settings is basic to the establishment of the foundational enterprise of conversation analysis. In practice, this distinction is derived from the observed *presence* of certain contingencies, problems, and remedial practices in instances of the former that are specifically and significantly *absent* in instances of the latter. The prevailing analytic strategy, then, is something like the following: show that certain, routinely recurrent contingencies, problems, and remedial practices of "ordinary conversation" are absent to some other institutional order (e.g., "news interviews"); then show how the structure of the institutional setting in question involves or relies on a set of basic rules that "obviates" those contingencies and problems in advance of their (otherwise probable) occurrence.[10] In this, the answer to the classical question, "How is social order possible?," becomes an empirical issue of specifying how it is that any particular institutional setting is recognizably *not* an ordinary conversation, and thus, how it is in one sense or another a *standard variation* on the "base structure(s)" of talk-in-interaction.

What remains to be shown is how this is done in any particular case; how "instances" are transcribed, cited, analyzed, and reiterated such that they testify to the inescapable relevance of mundane conversational structures to the conduct of some particular stretch of talk; and how, as a result of such demonstrations, sequential properties of talk emerge as natural, foundational elements of language and social life.

Again, the attempt will be to remain as close to the text as possible. By conceiving Schegloff's analysis as something that unfolds for a reader, in specific ways, over the course of a predominantly line-by-line reading, it is hoped that the unremarked on, dramatic elements of those arguments and claims will be brought into plainer view. I will be taking things, then, in the order in which they appear in the original, beginning with the transcript of two janitors having a conversation.

CULTIVATING AN INTEREST IN "JUST PLAIN TALK": THE ANATOMY OF AN INSTANCE

Consider the following extract from a preliminary section of Schegloff's analysis of the Bush/Rather interview:

> Consider, for example, the following exchange . . . between two janitors, one of whom—Vic—has swept up a mess of broken glass at the building of the other—James. Now Vic wants his garbage pail (which he had left at James's building) back, as well as a little credit for the good turn he has done James:

(1) *US: 45–46*

```
1 → V:   The pail is in yuh hallway, [ (uh,)
  J:                                 [ I know it hu(hh)h!
1 → V:   The-the- I didn' have a broom wit] me, if I adduh
         hadda [ broom I'd uh swept [ up.
  2 → J:        [ e(hh)h!            [ That's alright.
    V:   so [ (dat's, right on).
```

```
2 → J:        [ That's a'ri'-Somebody—[ got it up, I don't now who
   V:                                 [ (Look). But do me a favr-
3 → V:   Do, me, one fa:vuh, I [ cleaned it up!
   J:                         [ Yeh hh
   J:   Yeh right. I-ih-deh ca:n, (I- brought de) can (I'll) set it dehr
        own the sidewalk. [ Izzat ehkay=
   V:                     [ No.
   J:   =[ No.
   V:    [ Didjeh [ sweep up duh rest a' duh me[ ss.
   J:            [ ( )                          [ NO I didn'
        sweep up nothin!
   V:   Well o[ kay well that's why I left the can[ innuh hallway
   J:         [ Leave ih deh.               [ I'll do it
        (early) [ innuh maw:ning.
   V:          [ -so if you hadda br[ oo:m then you c'd=
   J:                               [ Yeh right.
   V:   =sweep up duh dust [ ( )-
   J:                      [ Very, uh very good I [ appreesh- °hhh
   V:                                            [ -the glass,
   J:   I apprecia[ te that Victuh,
   V:             [ Tomorruh I-
4 → V:   No. [ Tomorruh I want my pail back. Dass a[ ll.
   J:        [ E(hh)h yeh.                         [ Ye(hh)h!
   J:   I don'know I may keep dat pail.¹¹
```

Perhaps the most salient feature of this extract is that for anyone ac-
quainted with conversation analytic writing it is unquestionably an actual case
of an ordinary conversation. Schegloff's subsequent analysis of the "Bush/Rather
encounter" is deeply colored by the juxtaposition of the (apparent) "drama" of
the public spectacle with the contingent yet familiar detail of "ordinary
conversation." It is therefore worth considering in further detail how the genre
"ordinary conversation" is made an evident product of Schegloff's text. The
question is: How does this piece of text accomplish its actuality and ordinari-
ness, particularly given the at-first-sight strangeness of its notational scheme?

Both the prefatory remarks and the transcript radiate a mood of utter
mundaneity, though the manner in which this is accomplished differs
markedly between the two. For this reason, they are best conceived as *distinct*
textual devices that are nonetheless *complementary*; that is, as a complementary literary pairing.

Consider first the introductory remarks. The language is relaxed and
folksy: an off-hand summary of just plain folks, involved in just plain
doings.¹² These remarks enlist two janitors, Vic and James, in the service of

"ordinary conversation." It is the kind of situation with which, on thinking about it, we are all densely familiar: a paramount, practical reality that in its spontaneous, relaxed and monotonous familiarity, stands in sharp relief to the monumental tensions of, say, the public spectacle of a nationally televised news interview. The story of Vic and James thus forms a kind of analytic preface to the analysis of the Bush/Rather interview not unlike the dramatic position occupied by the gardeners, gravediggers, and other "low born" characters in Shakespearean drama whose "mundane" exchanges provide a point of allegorical contrast and comic relief for the more "refined" doings of the central characters.

Now consider the transcript. We are presented with a technically precise rendering of some actual event. To the untrained eye, however, the transcript is scarcely recognizable as the kind of thing an "ordinary conversation" is. How, then, do we come to see this transcript as a good and adequate record of an actual event, and to understand that event as having been an "ordinary conversation"?

Transcripts are a pervasive and elementary feature of conversation analytic practice. One learns that practice in and through learning to transcribe. Whenever findings are presented, analysts proffer transcripts and then instruct readers in methodic, often ingenious ways of reading them as evidentiary support for their arguments. It is in this sense that transcription comprises a primitive literary technology of conversation analysis. Clearly the transcript contributes *something* to the arguments and demonstrations of conversation analysts, though what *specifically* it contributes remains unclear. The suggestion here will be that the transcript functions as a literary genre, the business of which is to establish the *actuality* of the events in question. What the transcript contributes to analysis is not the real events, but the literary analogue of the real events—what real events *are*, or *must be*. That is, the transcript lends to the analysis what Barthes has termed a "realistic effect."[13]

At one point in his study of "narrative mood," Genette discusses this effect with respect of the contrast between Homeric epic narrative, or the "narrative of events," and its Platonic counterpart, or the "narrative of words." He first considers the following passage from the Homeric original:

> So said he, and the old man was afraid and obeyed his word, and fared silently along the shore of the loud-sounding sea. Then went that aged man apart and prayed aloud to king Apollo, whom Leto of the fair locks bare.[14]

He then contrasts the Platonic translation of the same passage:

> And the old man on hearing this was frightened and departed in silence, and having gone apart from the camp he prayed at length to Apollo.[15]

As Genette notes, the most obvious difference between these two versions is that the second is quite a bit shorter than the first. The issue that most interests him, however, is how this condensation is achieved and how it alters the prevailing mood of the epic narrative's voicing. As he continues:

> Plato achieves this condensation by eliminating redundant information ("so said he," "obeyed," "whom Leto bare"), and also by eliminating circumstantial and "picturesque" indicators: "of the fair locks," and especially "along the shore of the loud-sounding sea." This *shore of the loud-sounding sea . . .* serves no purpose other than to let us understand that the narrative mentions it only because *it is there*, and because the narrator, abdicating his function of choosing and directing the narrative, allows himself to be governed by "reality," by the presence of what is there and what demands to be "shown." A useless and contingent detail, it is the medium par excellence of the referential illusion, and therefore of the mimetic effect: it is a *connotator of mimesis*.[16]

The modern transcript is suffused with a mimetic principle that parallels the realist mood at work within the epic narrative. In line with its ancient counterpart, the authenticity of the transcribed "instance" is never to be found in some overt claim concerning, for instance, that "these events *really* did take place," but is instead an evidential property of the transcript's composition. In its cryptic citation of a larger, virtual collection ("(1) *US: 45–46*"), the odd spellings, the vertical interference of oversized brackets, parenthetical accounts of probable utterances, the extraordinary attention to false starts, partial utterances, breathing patterns, and the like, the conversation analytic transcript is a running citation of the actuality of events it means to capture. Notice too that this level of detail is always, unavoidably *excessive* with respect to any particular analytic point being made. (What difference does it make, after all, whether Vic, in his initial utterance, said "The pail is in yuh hallway" or "The pail is in your hallway"?) In the same way that the "shore of the loud-sounding sea" collapses the distance between "narrator" and "event," and thereby recovers the "event" as a *witnessed* order of activities, the transcript secures the authenticity of the "instance" in and as the transparent availability of talk's *surplus detail*. The "realistic effect" of the transcript consists in its giving itself over to the contingent and otherwise uninteresting details of "what was there to be seen or heard," and in its textual recovery of what therefore "demands to be shown."

There is, however, a crucial difference between the descriptive "excesses" of the Homeric narrative and the mimetic principle at work in the conversation analytic "instance." This difference becomes clear when we consider certain obvious limits on the descriptive adequacy of epic narrative. As Genette continues:

> The narrative of events . . . whatever its mode, is always narrative, that is, a transcription of the (supposed) non-verbal into the verbal. Its mimesis will thus never be anything more than an illusion of mimesis, depending like every illusion on a highly variable relationship between the sender and the receiver. It goes without saying, for example, that the same text can be received by one reader as intensely mimetic and by another as an only slightly "expressive" account.[17]

In contrast to the ancient "narrative of events," the dominant movement in the modern transcript is from the *verbal* to the *nonverbal*. Because it is unimaginable that such a density of detail could be recovered independent of an electromagnetic record, the transcript's technical excesses serve both as testimony to the existence of that other record and as an index to that record's analytic salience. In this, the electromagnetic record serves as an intermediate moment between the "event" and its transcription. Its voice is neither Homeric nor Platonic, but is instead the disembodied soundings of a monitored acoustic environment; a mode of "witnessing" that *collapses* all descriptive and mnemonic elements into an array of equally trivial acoustic details.[18] Hence, the mimetic principle at work in the electromagnetic record is, in a very specific sense, opposite to that of the Homeric epic. Where the latter depended on the *hyper*signification of otherwise insignificant details, the former enacts a methodic *de*signification of the event-in-question, swallowing-up all that is "memorable," "dramatic," "expressive," and so on, in a sea of endless detail.

In its evident reliance on the electromagnetic record, the modern transcript constitutes itself as a second-order account of "what was (acoustically) there to be heard," or (video-graphically) "there to be seen." At the same time, however, it revolutionizes the criteria by which the adequacy of the transcript will be judged. The modern transcript no longer pretends to describe events at all. Rather, the job of the transcript is to provide an orthographic "emplotment" of the relevant acoustic and videographic phenomena.[19] This respecification of the transcript's work dissolves the classical question of "descriptive adequacy" by transferring the duties and entitlements of descriptive representation to the electromagnetic record.[20]

At the same time, the modern transcript engages an array of technical issues arising out of the difficulties of translating from one textual medium to another. The question of the transcript's *descriptive* adequacy is displaced by the problem of obtaining a transcript that is *notationally* adequate to the details of the "original" record. Since there is in principle no limit on the amount of detail available for notational representation, this displacement accounts for the transcript's strange appearance. The task of analysis, then, is to respecify that hyperabundance of transcriptual detail such that what emerges as salient for analysis will turn out to be what is significant about the actual event.

The account Schegloff gives immediately following the transcript of the talk between Vic and James is aimed, in the first instance, at affiliating an initial reading of the transcript to the terms of some mundane problem-at-hand:

> For Vic, as we come to see in the sequel at arrow #4, the talk at the start of the sequence (at the arrows numbered 1) is leading up to a request for the return of his pail. But James hears it as said in its own right, and, far from giving Vic credit for a favor done, he understands Vic to have apologized, accepts the apology and credits some anonymous person for cleaning up the glass (at the arrows numbered 2).[21]

Schegloff then proposes that the *analytic solution* to the problem faced by Vic and James is *demonstrably* the solution they deployed in situ.[22] As he continues:

> So, "leading up" to something, or doing talk prefatory to some-thing else, can pose problems of sequential organization for the participants in ordinary conversation. And, indeed, by virtue of the structurally recurrent character of this possibility, there are specific practices of talking in interaction that are addressed to it.[23]

The demonstration of the adequacy of the analytic solution to the problem faced by Vic and James consists in a set of reader's instructions (in order of appearance: "at arrow #4," "at the arrows numbered 1," "at the arrows numbered 2," "at arrow 3") that direct a reading that moves back-and-forth between transcriptional materials and analytic commentary. These instructions provide a temporal order that contrasts with that of the actual event: unlike Vic and James, we have the entire interaction in hand from the very outset, and are instructed, first of all, to review the transcript from "arrow #4," or the point of Vic's eventual request for his pail. We are then instructed to work back through the transcript, as a way of seeing how Vic and James arrived at a position where Vic's request for his pail made sense. It is by virtue of this retrospection that the transcript first becomes readable in its technical significance: that is, as a conversation that is "leading up to something," and hence, as a perspicuous instance for a sequentially based account of how "leading up to something" gets done.

The next step in Schegloff's argument is to use the canonically "mun-dane" instance as an exemplar of a field of contingencies that can then be affiliated to the generic domain of "ordinary conversation." He begins the argument with the observation that speakers in ordinary conversation often need to do preliminary work in order to secure turn-space for the accomplishment of some specific speech activity (such as a "question" or "request"), and for getting their coparticipant(s) to hear their utterances as felicitous executions of that particular speech-act. In "interview" situations, by contrast, the availability of turn-space for certain parties to ask questions and others to answer them is, according to Schegloff, a relied-on feature of "doing" that interaction as an "interview." Therefore, what it means for interactants to cease to treat some present situation as a "news interview" is (at least in part) that they cease to treat their present circumstance as a turn-taking system that pre-allocates turn-space and speaker identities in line with a "simplest model for interrogative organization": namely, that one party asks questions and the other party answers them in next turn.[24] As a general matter, then, the *presence* of the model for interrogative organization is made evident by the *absence* of demands, problems, and remedies associated with "ordinary conversation."

In line with this conception of the relation between the conversational substrate and other forms of talk, Schegloff's analysis of the Bush/Rather interview seeks to isolate structural elements of "ordinary conversation" that are significantly absent in "news interviews." Vic wants his garbage pail back, and so needs to construct his talk in order that what is said will at some point be heard by James as a reasonable request to have his pail returned. The problem, as Schegloff's analytic commentary reveals, is that Vic's initial utterances (at the arrows numbered 1) are taken by James (in subsequent turn) as apologies for having left the pail in James' hallway, and *not* as preliminaries to Vic's eventual request (at arrow #4) to have his pail returned. What Schegloff proposes is that conversationalists attend to—that is, monitor their activities for—the mundane possibility that "leading up to something"[25] may raise various interactional problems. Such problems are, in his terms, "structurally recurrent possibilities" which, by reason of their patterned repetition, tend to occasion routine and specific remedial practices, or "dedicated solutions,"[26] to the problem-at-hand. Problems and solutions take on a reciprocal relation: the occurrence of some problem occasions a routine and specific remedy, while the use of that remedy retrospectively constructs the problem as *just* the kind of routine problem that it *was* for participants, and hence, as *just* the kind of patterned problem that the remedy is designed to treat.

In this case, the problem-at-hand—namely, that James heard Vic's initial utterances as part of a developing apology sequence and not as preliminary to a request—is remedied via Vic's use of what Schegloff terms a "pre-pre," or "an utterance which marks what directly follows it as said not in its own right, but as preliminary to something which will follow."[27] Here it is worth quoting Schegloff at greater length, since the analytic recovery of this specific structural component in Vic's and James' talk is central to his later analysis of the "Bush/Rather encounter":

> One way of doing a "pre-pre," for example, is to formulate in advance the type of utterance or action being led up to, and that is done by an "action projection" such as "Can I ask you a question?" In Vic's dealing with James, he follows the "misunderstood" talk with such an action projection (at arrow 3: "Do me one favor"), after which his preliminaries get heard as preliminaries, and his request gets registered as a request.[28]

In sum, the drama and eventfulness of Schegloff's analysis is built on the identification of the at-first-sight strangeness and opacity of the transcript with the analytic phenomenon's opacity for participants. We, like Vic and James, are initially placed in the position of figuring out where all this is leading. Unlike Vic and James, however, who simply do "where all this is leading," we already have *their work* of "doing 'where all this is leading'" in hand at the start of the analysis. We should distinguish, therefore, between two senses of "where all this is leading": the first, the opacity in situ of "where all this is leading," and the second, the opacity of participants' work of "doing 'where all this is leading'" as a feature of the transcript's emergent intelligibility.

By providing readers with a transcript that is recognizably mundane yet analytically obscure, Schegloff creates a space in which the interactional troubles faced by Vic and James become the readers' own. We, like Vic and James, must claw our way through a wilderness of surplus detail, with only the ensuing analysis as our guide through the "mundane" excesses of the transcript. A set of signposts (arrows) directs our attention to what is significant about the transcript (in this case, Vic's apt and efficacious use of the "pre-pre"), and those features are then located within a larger field of structural relevancies by subsequent analytic commentary. In this way, "doing 'where all this is leading'" becomes a technical highlight in the plot structure of Schegloff's analysis.

VENTRILOQUIST STRUCTURALISM

A central theme of the preceding discussion has been that the distinction between "ordinary conversation" and other more specialized interactional settings is basic to the foundational enterprise of conversation analysis. Further, it has been argued that in practice this distinction is derived from the observed *presence* of certain contingencies, problems, and remedial practices in instances of the former that are specifically and significantly *absent* in instances of the latter. To this point we have only been provided with the "ordinary" phenomenon: the use of the "pre-pre" in "leading up" to a request. The central task for the second phase of Schegloff's analysis is thus to demonstrate: 1. that the contingencies which the "pre-pre" is designed to handle tend not to arise in "news interviews," and 2. that the absence of these contingencies is a *significant* absence—that is, that their absence is a constitutive feature of doing activities as recognizably the "doings" of a "news interview."

The following is the first extract from the Bush/Rather interview that Schegloff discusses:

```
(2)  Bush/Rather, 00:00
        Rather:    . . . Today, Donald Gregg still works inside the White
                   House as Vice President Bush's trusted advisor.
                   ((End of feature; start of live broadcast.))
000                (1.0)
001  Rather:    °hh Mister Vice President, tha:nk you for being
002                with us toni:ght, °hh Donald Gregg sti:ll serves
003                as y'r tru:sted advi#sor, =he w'z dee:ply involved
004                in running arms t'the Contras an' he didn' inform
005                you.=
006                { (0.5)}
007  Rather:    {=°hhhh} + Now when President Rea:gan's, (0.2)
008                trusted advisor: Admiral Poindexter: (0.6) failed
009                to inform hi:m, (0.8) the President- (0.2)
010                fired'im.hh
011                (0.5)
012  Rather:    Why is Mister Gregg still: (°) inside the White
013                Hou@se'n still a trusted advisor.=
014  Bush:      =Becuz I have confidence in im, (0.3) en becuz
015                this matter, Dan, . . .
          #        Bush brings hands together and mouth opens
          +        Bush spearates hands
          @        Bush's lips part[29]
```

The exchange begins at the end of a prepared videotaped feature and is the first exchange of the interview. Leaving aside for now the more detailed aspects of Schegloff's analysis, his general argument at this point is that this exchange bears witness to participants' orientations to the structural arrangements, obligations, prerogatives, and so on, of "news interviews." This exchange, then, is seen to be occupied with activities analogous to the opening moves of a game:

Here, in this first turn of the occasion, we see Bush and Rather orienting to the constitutive properties of "interview," and organizing their conduct to produce them. It is by virtue of such orientation and conduct that they collaborate here to produce an exchange, a potential statistical "case" if you will, in which one asks a question and the other answers.[30]

In this case, Schegloff focuses on the sequential implicativeness of Rather's game-initial question which, together with Bush's bodily receipt of that utterance, serves as evidence for the claim that the two participants are collaboratively "doing" a recognizable-observable (i.e., accountable) "news interview" in the canonical form of "one party asks questions and the other party answers them in next turn."

Central to Schegloff's analysis is the observation that Bush's bodily movements—his bringing his hands together, separating them once again and then, shortly thereafter, parting his lips—occur in and around what, for "ordinary conversation," are potential turn-transition relevance places. Hence, on Schegloff's account, the first and the second of these movements (lines 003 and 007) evidence Bush's monitoring of the talk for its "ordinary" structural features,[31] and doing, in and through these movements, a physical display of "this is not an ordinary conversation"; doing, that is, "where I might have spoken (ordinarily), I now withhold my (potential) right to speak in deference to 'news interview' and the specific turn-taking machinery which is, at least in part, constitutive of its auspices."

The elegance of this argument is that it locates structure's efficacy, which to this point had been theorized as the *absence* of "ordinary" conversational practices, as palpably present to the interaction in and as the observed movements of Bush's body. In the transcript, over the course of Rather's game-initial utterance, the "structural joints"[32] of "ordinary conversation" are inscribed by the articulating joints of Bush's hands and jawbone.

This is the crucial move in Schegloff's argument, and the key to what might well be termed his "ventriloquist structuralism."[33] On the one hand, he offers constant reminders concerning the fundamentally situated nature of social activities; for example, that "participants constitute—do—the context which might otherwise be thought of, indeed is often described as, 'supplying' the setting for their talk."[34] On the other hand, his analytic story-line requires that participants be shown to be continually monitoring talk for "that we are not doing 'ordinary conversation'," "that we are now, for all practical purposes, diverging from the foundational organization of 'ordinary conversation'," and hence, "that whatever we are now doing, it is being done in respect of what we always might otherwise be doing: namely, having an 'ordinary conversation.'" Hence, even where the activities in which participants are engaged seem far from "conversational" in nature, their talk is nonetheless shown to be oriented at every turn to the underlying technical structure of ordinary conversation.

TALK'S TECHNICIANS

The overall orientation of talk to its conversational foundations requires a specific kind of social agent. In an earlier paper aimed at clarifying some consequences conversation analysis holds for the philosophy of language, Schegloff registers the following objection to theories, such as Searle's theory of speech acts, that treat vernacular categories of speech activities as stable objects of formal-analytic interest:

> If the mere presence of lexical items such as "I promise," "I bet," "I guarantee" can be taken as invoking the possible membership of the sentence in which they appropriately appear in a class such as "promises" or "bets," how much more powerful is the appeal of syntactic forms such as "question" or "injunction." A ready bridge is apparently before us to cross from language to social behavior, in which, it might appear, syntax will bear the load. . . . Now I think that such a view is, or would be, as misleading with regard to questions . . . as it is in the case of promises. The general point is that it is misleading to start to account for such categories of action as questions, promises, and so on as the analytic objects of interest. They are commonsense, not technical, categories and should be treated accordingly.[35]

At first sight this argument would appear to support a position in accord with the view, most commonly associated with the work of the later Wittgenstein, that the vernacular uses of language do not require technical supplement, or as Hunter puts it, that "the words themselves are quite sufficient" and so "we do not need to translate an expression into another expression . . . we do not need to guess, or interpret, or apply rules: we understand language just as it stands."[36]

Schegloff is not interested, however, in pressing this tine of the argument through to its post-analytic consequences. Rather, his aim is to respecify "commonsense categories" in terms of a machinery for the situated production and recognition of structurally recurrent phenomena. The move here is to equip *participants* with a detailed sensitivity to categories of sequential analysis such that treating activity-types *sequentially* becomes definitive of what it means to treat commonsense categories "accordingly."[37] With the case of "questions," for instance, Schegloff argues that:

Even where an utterance is in the linguistic form of a question, and seems to be doing questioning, the latter cannot adequately be accounted for by the former. For if the question form can be used for actions other than questions, then a relevant problem can be posed not only about how a question does something other than questioning, but about how it does questioning; not only about how questioning is done by nonquestion forms, but about how it gets accomplished by question forms.[38]

Thus, an analysis of linguistic form can neither account for the praxiological variety of "questions," nor the linguistic heterogeneity of "questioning forms." Rather than abandoning the project of giving formal specification to vernacular activity-types, however, Schegloff introduces an alternative technique which, it is argued, is identical with the technique that participants use in producing and recognizing their own activities as "typical" and "typifiable": namely, the methodic monitoring of practical activities as, in the first instance, sequentially located and locatable phenomena. Rather than stipulating commonsense categories in terms of some set of technical analogues, Schegloff makes the opposite and far more ingenious move of construing competent language users as conversational—that is, sequential—*technicians-in-residence*.

This conception of social agency locates practical activities within a minimalist ecology of "what came immediately before" and "what follows immediately after." Hence, the fundamental unit of analysis (both professional and lay) becomes the recognizable "pairings" of commonsense activity-types. On this account, "questions" and "answers" are, for instance, conceived as mutually implicative comembers of a question-answer adjacency pair. This respecification of "questions" and "answers" sensitizes the formal machinery by making the determination of "what a turn's talk is occupied with" dependent on an utterance's local production characteristics (where "local" refers to the utterance's *immediate sequential environment*).

Elsewhere, Schegloff and Sacks propose the following as "a basic rule of adjacency pair operation":

> [G]iven the recognizable production of a first pair part, on its first possible completion its speaker should stop and a next speaker should start and produce a second pair part from the pair type of which the first is recognizably a member.[39]

This basic rule not only provides for the production and recognition of talk's sequential components, it also links that production/recognition machinery to a principle of social obligation: that on the completion of a first pair part, current speaker *should then and there* provide for, and next speaker *should then and there* accept, the rights and duties associated with the production and recognition of the second part of the pair. I will term this normative principle the "immediacy principle" of coordinated activities.

The "immediacy principle" does heavy service in Schegloff's analysis of Bush's "withholding." Again, what Schegloff seeks to demonstrate is that where Bush might *ordinarily* speak, he does not do so, and in addition, he *displays* that he is not doing so such that what he *is* doing is a display of "withholding speech," a display which is maintained until just that point where the canonical form of "news interview" occasions a response.

The witnessable character of Bush's "withholding" turns on the assumption that, in Schegloff's words, "Bush clearly 'could have' talked earlier."[40] The reason that "*could have*" is doubly marked in Schegloff's text—that is, both placed in quotation marks *and* italicized—is that it represents a *technically*, as against commonsensically, derived sense of what "could have" occurred. Feeling unduly insulted by the subject matter and presentation of the initial video-clip, Bush *could have* gotten up and left the studio before the interview began, but he did not. Clearly the range of possibility Schegloff has in mind concerning what "could have" happened is more constrained than this. "Conversationally speaking,"[41] Bush "*could have*" spoken earlier than he did (on the basis of the immediacy principle), and even though he did not do so, his "not speaking" was done *articulately*: that is, with movements of his hands and lips just where he might have spoken. On Schegloff's account, this "nondoing" is linked internally to the structural constraints that "news interviews" places on "ordinary conversation."

In sum, Bush's bodily movements not only figure in the initial constitution of the interaction as "news interview," more importantly for Schegloff's purposes, they also articulate "withholding" as a system of embodied citations of "ordinary conversation." In this way, the organization of "news interview" is made demonstrably parasitic on "ordinary conversation." The "spectacular" features of *this* event are overwhelmed by its generic features as but one more instance of "talk-in-interaction."

SOME CONTINGENCIES OF SEQUENTIAL ORDER

The aim of the foregoing has been to identify the structure of argument in a canonical example of conversation analysis in terms of a set of literary "working methods" by which logical structure is conjoined to empirical instances of talk. It was argued that this argumentative structure is based in the foundationalist assumption that ordinary conversation provides talk's mundane and natural organization, and that other forms of speech and social activity represent orderly transformations off of conversation's base sequential structures. In addition, the following were identified as features of the analytic demonstration of talk's foundational organization:

1. the transference of the dramatic entitlements of "live" events to analytic specifications of their generic and mundane "underpinnings."

2. the use of the modern transcript as a documentary basis of conversation analytic investigations in and as:
   a. the "realistic effect" of its strange and technically prolix notation, and
   b. the emergent sense of its instructed reading(s);

3. the material demonstration that talk's mundane organization operates ongoingly over the course of any interaction whatsoever in and through the body's orientation and attention to its typical features even—and perhaps *especially*—in their absence.

So far, the aim has been to explicate the disciplinary organization of conversation analysis and its associated phenomenal field without regard for the validity of its findings. The disciplined practices that "conversation analysis" collects have been treated as unique and plausible ways of doing, and instructing others in the ways of doing, empirical social science.

The remainder of this chapter will be more critical in focus. On the basis of materials from a comparable and contemporaneous public event— the 1987 testimony of Oliver North before Joint Committees of Congress—a series of analytic claims will be advanced that challenge the foundationalist assumptions of Schegloff's analysis. The thrust of the argument is that "sequentiality" can itself be shown to be a contingent, at times, contentious and equivocal product of practical activities' situated conduct. It will be argued that these examples lead to a reformulation of Schegloff's findings as *contingent formulations* of the situated "sense" of Bush's bodily movements.

The examples below are taken from a much more comprehensive study of the Iran-Contra Hearings, which were held in the Summer of 1987.[42] In the course of that study, we arrived at the following, rather unsettling conclusion concerning the nature of the activities we were investigating: that their sequential order was not only a matter of "what had come just before" and "what came immediately after," but that "what had come just before" and "what came immediately after" was itself, at times, the subject of live disputes concerning the conduct, legitimacy, propriety, and so on of the actual event in the actual course of its conduct.

In order to comprehend this feature of the hearings, we needed to develop resources that would account for participants' activities as oriented at least in part to contentions over, arguments about, and formulations of the event's "sense" and "reasonability" as a mutually agreed on, continuous course of conduct in the first place.

One such resource was to begin to identify where and how the canonical order of interrogatory organization figured explicitly in these proceedings. It was thus with more than a passing interest that we listened to the Chairman of the Senate Select Committees (Sen. Inouye) when, very early on, he made explicit mention of the following, basic rule for these proceedings:

> Inouye: unless the Committee determines otherwise, a witness who
>   appears before the Committee under a grant of immunity
>   shall not be permitted to make a statement or testify except to
>   respond directly to questions posed by Committee members
>   or Committee staff.[43]

In this case, the problem of understanding the "basic rules" has primarily to do with determining how the *mention* of the rule is fitted to its application (or applications) in situ. To solve this problem we must consider *where specifically* the citation of the rule occurs, and not merely in terms of its *sequential* location, but also, where it is located rhetorically within a series of disputes-in-progress over the organization and legitimacy of the hearings themselves, and over the ways in which specific "turns-at-talk" are to be allocated, taken, and used in these proceedings.

These preliminary disputes are carried out primarily between North's attorney (Brendan Sullivan) and Chairman Inouye. They occur early in the morning of the first day of testimony, prior to the onset of questioning. Inouye's citation of the rule quoted above occurs within a larger stretch of talk in which Inouye first reads a letter from North's attorney, after which he gives a response to that letter. The letter, as read by Inouye, runs as follows:

> Inouye: . . . and I wish to read this letter. It is addressed to the chair
>   and to Mr. Lyman. "Dear chairman Inouye, Lt. Col. North
>   would like to give an opening statement in the event he
>   testifies tomorrow morning. We request that rule five point
>   three be waved and that as an immunized witness he be
>   permitted to make the statement. In view of the extraordinary
>   vilification and the many comments by Committee members
>   regarding Lt. Col. North's conduct and his credibility, fairness
>   warrants a wave of the rule. We have not been able to review
>   the massive quantities of documents which you provided to us
>   under severe restrictions over the course of the last six days.
>   Moreover we were advised this afternoon that seven hours of

tape-recordings were located today as a result of our persistent requests. We simply do not have the time to review that information and large quantities of other material prior to the scheduled start of testimony on July seventh, nineteen eighty seven at nine a.m. As you know there are many documents and slides which we have requested but which have not been forthcoming. These factors have severely hampered Lt. Col. North's preparation for interrogation by numerous counsel and twenty-six members of the Committee. We appreciate your cooperation. Respectfully yours, Brendan B. Sullivan Jr."[44]

Inouye's response focuses initially on the letter's claim that North and his attorney have not had time for adequate preparation. Inouye notes that the "record will show" that the hearing date of July 7, 1987, was requested by North and his attorney, and was "reluctantly" agreed to by the Committee despite their "strong encouragement" that the hearings be postponed until later in the month. He then summarizes the point by saying that "therefore . . . if counsel is having troubles, it is not because of our doings."[45]

Following this, Inouye takes up the letter's request that rule 5.3 be suspended in order that North might give an opening statement:

Inouye: . . . secondly (.) as to the opening statement (1.5) I wish to read (..) the pertinent parts of the rule. (0.5) ((looking up and directly at Sullivan)) and I'm certain that counsel (0.8) ((shifting his gaze to North)) and witness (1.5) ((returning his eyes to the papers before him)) have studied the hearing rules (..) very carefully (0.5) and I'm certain they-they know what they stand for. (0.8) *five point three* (.) says the following:
→   ((North licks lips)) (..) any witness desiring to make an introductory statement shall file twenty copies of the statement (.) with the Chairman or Chief Clerk (.) forty-eight hours in advance of the appearance (1.5) ((looking up at Sullivan and North)) the opening statement was filed with this Committee forty-five minutes ago (1.0) ((looking down again)) unless the Chairman determines that there is good cause for witness's failure to do so. (0.8) a witness may be required to summarize a prepared statement if it exceeds ten minutes. (0.5) unless the Committee determines otherwise, a witness who appears before the Committee under a grant of immunity (0.4) shall *not* be permitted to make a statement or testify except to respond directly (..) to questions posed by

Committee members or Committee staff. (2.0) ((looking up at Sullivan and North)) we have been here (0.4) sitting for several weeks(..) and we will continue to do so, to receive testimony, (..) and consider one thing above others (..) the *rule* of *law*. (1.5) here once again (.) the witness (.) is asking us to bend the law (1.0) and to suggest that he may be *above* the law. (1.0) we will abide with his wishes (..) however we will insist on following the rule of law (..) and if the colonel wishes to make the opening statement he may do so Thursday morning. (1.5) which is forty-eight hours from this date. (2.0) mister Nields please proceed.

Thus situated, it becomes clear that the specific application of the rule in question is that it provides a legal basis for Inouye's rejection of the letter's request. Whether or not and how that rule will be brought to bear on what witness might later have to say is subject to the limitations implied by this local usage. That is to say, while the rule may indeed be invoked as a reason for rejecting North's plea to give an opening statement—or any utterance of sufficient length and organization that it looks like an opening statement—it does not preclude the possibility that witness may, on occasion, interject, query the questioner, digress, reformulate questioner's questions, and so on. The rule works to close down a very specific sort of turn-option. It does not foreclose the possibility that, for instance, all of the materials that were prepared for the opening statement might well be decomposed, restructured, spliced, and fitted to legitimate turn-options elsewhere in the questioning. Seen this way, the rule that witnesses ought to "respond directly to questions posed" has a *particular* use and sense, and therefore could not be a singular, generic bit of legislation that organizes the conduct of these hearings.

Indeed, just a little while later, and under the auspices of "questioning," we get the following exchange:

Nields: Thee American:: (.) people (0.4) were told by this government that ou::r government had nothing to do (0.4) with the Hassenfus airplane. (0.6) °hh And that was false. And it is a: principal purpose (0.4) of these hearings°hhhh to replac:e (1.0) secrecy and deception (0.5) with disclosure and truth. And that's one of the reasons we have called you here sir. (0.5) °hh And one question the American people would like to know the answer to (0.5) °(tch)° is what did the President know (0.4) about the diversion (0.4) of the proceeds of Iranian arms sales (..) to the contras. Can you tell us what you know about that, sir.

North   You just took a long leap from mister Hassenfus's airplane.
          (3.5)

North: As I told this committee (..) several days ago, (0.4) and if you
          will indulge me counsel in a: (..) brief summary of what I said,
          (2.0) I never personally discussed (.) the use of (0.6) the
          residuals or (0.5) profits from the sale of U.S. weapons to Iran
          (1.2) for the purpose of supporting the Nicaraguan resistance
          (0.6) with the President. (1.0) I never raised it with *him* (0.6) at
          the National Security Counsel (0.6) I assumed that the Presi-
          dent was aware of what I was doing (0.8) and had through my
          superiors approved it. (1.0) I sought approval of my superiors
          fer every (.) one (.) of my actions, and it is well documented.
          (2.0) I assumed (1.0) when I (..) had approval to proceed from
          either (1.4) Judge Clark, Bud MacFarlane, (1.0) or Admiral
          Poindexter, (0.5) that they had indeed solicited and obtained
          the approval of the President. (2.0) To my recollection,
          Admiral Poindexter never told me (..) that he met with the
          President on thee issue of using residuals (..) from the Iranian
          (.) sales, to support the Nicaraguan resistance. °hh Or that he
          go:t the President's specific approval. (1.0) Nor did he tell me
          that the President had appro::ved (0.4) such a transaction.
          (0.8) But again I wish to reiterate that throughout (0.4) I
          believed that the President had indeed authorized such activity.
          (1.5) *No other person* (1.0) with whom I was in contact with
          (..)during my tenure at the White House (..) told me that he::
          or she (..) ever discussed the issue (.) of the residuals or profits
          (0.4) with the President.°hhhh (0.6) In late November, (0.4)
          two other things occurred (0.4) which relate to this issue. (0.8)
          On or about Friday, November twenty-first (0.5) I asked
          Admiral Poindexter (0.4) directly (..) *does* (.) *the President* (.)
          know. He told me (0.2) he did not. (0.6) And on November
          twenty-fifth (0.6) the day I was reassigned back to the United
          States Marine Corps for service,°hhhh the President of the
          United States called me. (1.0) In the course of that call, the
          President said to me (1.0) words to the effect that (0.6) "I just
          (.)didn't (.) know." (1.8) Those are the facts as I know them
          mister Nields, I was gla:d that when you (0.6) introduced this
          you- said that you wanted to hear the truth. (0.5) I came here
          to tell you the truth, (0.6) the goo:d (0.5) the bad'n the ugly,
          (0.6) I'm here to tell it *a::ll* (0.5) pleasant and unpleasant, (0.6)
          and I'm here to accept responsibility for that which I did, (0.8)
          I will not accept responsibility for that which I did not do.

```
        (1.0)
Inouye:  Before proceeding, may I make an inquiry of the witness?
         (0.4) Was that respons:e from a written text?
         (0.8)
North:   ih Those are from notes that I made in preparation for this::
         (.) session, sir.
         (0.5)
Inouye:  't is not a verbatim tex:t.
North:   No sir it is not
         (2.6)
Inouye:  Mister Nields.
```

What this fragment makes particularly clear is how limited the effects of the rule cited by Inouye are with respect to the shape of a witness's turn. Here we have an extended monologue, parts of which go to the (rather generic) substance of the question, and other parts of which are clearly rhetorical flourish. What Inouye concerns himself with, however, is whether or not the monologue is taken verbatim from a written text, in which case it would violate his ruling. This example shows how the sense and scope of any rule is tied to some concrete context of its application while at the same time pointing up the rather subtle connection between "rules" and "rulings."[46]

The point to be drawn from this discussion is that any talk of "rules" in the absence of some such concrete specification of where, when and how some particular rule is being applied is, by definition, talk *in general*, and usually of a legislative variety. What the generic conception of "rules" either misses or must attempt to mask is that "rule-talk" is but one of many practical methods for describing, bringing about, accounting for, codifying, justifying, explaining, theorizing, and so forth, observably patterned behavior as reasonable activity.[47] Moreover, "rule-talk" is not limited to, nor ordinarily much interested in, describing activities *in detail*. Rather, the application of a rule to some activity involves taking that activity as a case for the relevant application(s) of the rule, and this means simply that any feature or account of that activity not relevanced by the application(s) of the rule will inevitably appear as trivial.

The example above also raises the following issue for Schegloff's analysis of Bush's "withholding." Toward the end of Inouye's monologue, at just that point where he has finished a series of preliminary remarks and admonishments in preparation for the actual reading of the rule, and just before he begins that reading, North licks his lips (see ➔). Clearly the occurrence of this lip-lick *just there* would seem to indicate, as with Bush, some monitoring on North's part of the "structural joints" of Inouye's talk, but here there is nothing that would indicate an orientation to that spot as a turn-transition relevance place, much less a bodily notation of a potential turn that is here being "withheld."

What North's lip-lick suggests is that an evident orientation to the "structural joints" of a coparticipant's speech cannot, *of itself*, warrant the claim that such movements are done only—or even primarily—with an attention to potential turn-transitions, let alone that they articulate the sequential possibilities of "ordinary conversation."

It would be a misrepresentation of Schegloff's argument, however, to say that it turns on the general claim that a displayed orientation to the "structural joints" of speech is always and everywhere identical with an attention to potential turn-transitions. For his argument to succeed he only needs to demonstrate that this is so in this particular instance.

As noted above, this demonstration relies in part on a quasi-hydraulic reading of the emergence of Bush's first utterance relative to the marked, "ordinary conversational" turn-options displayed in Rather's game-initial turn. But the more important background to Schegloff's argument comes from the example of the two janitors, Vic and James, who—in going about their negotiations for the return of Vic's bucket—display a certain adeptness in the use of the "pre-pre." Recalling for the moment that, for Schegloff, the signal feature of Rather's first turn is that it continues until a point where a specific question has been asked, and that it does so *without recourse to preliminaries* (despite the fact that some preliminaries would otherwise— that is, "conversationally speaking"—be called for here), it becomes clear that Bush's bodily movements are conceived by Schegloff as standing proxy for the institutionally specific absence of preliminaries. On this conception, the movements of Bush's hands, lips, and jaw-bone are, as it were, given over to the work of accounting for the lack of preliminaries; his body becoming the physical point of contact between "ordinary conversation" and "news interview," and the physical site for the resolution of the structural tensions between the two.

As an alternative, I want to suggest that this analysis proceeds from the mistaken assumption that the transcript provides a basis for the claim that this initial exchange was carried out in the absence of "preliminaries." What we do not get from this transcript is any idea of what went into the production of the Bush/Rather "encounter" prior to the beginning of their on-camera performances. We can easily imagine, for instance, that as a preliminary matter, Bush may have been given some explanation of the way in which the interview was to proceed: "there will be a short video-clip that we have prepared, then Dan will summarize that clip and ask his first question, after which you will have a chance to respond," or something of that sort, in which case, Bush's failure to interject where he clearly "could have" spoken would be analyzable as directly related to the off-camera preliminaries. It is only because we are not given access to what came before the transcript that we are consigned to speculation on these matters.

In the case of the North testimony, however, we are provided ample opportunity to observe the transition from "preliminaries" to the actual, recognizable onset of "questioning," and it is in and through a careful attention to this comparative case that certain shortcomings of Schegloff's rigorous attention to the turn-by-turn construction of talk become most apparent.

Consider, for instance, the extended transcript of the first exchange of the North testimony noted earlier:

```
001   Sullivan:   =°right.° would you consider sir (.) ah permitting
002               him to give his opening statement ah during the
003               lunch break (0.5) to day: (.) ah u-utilizing this
004               room after the committee adjourns.
005               (1.0)
006   Inouye:     you may not sir. (1.5) Mr. Nields
007               (..)
008   Nields:     Colonel North were you invol::ved (0.4) in the use
009               (.) of the proceeds of sales of weapons to Iran
010               (..) for the purpose (..) of assisting (..) the n-
011               Contras in Nicaragua.
012               (5.0)
013   North:      counsel on ah (.) advice of counsel I respectfully
014               decline to answer the question based on my
015               Constitutional Fifth Amendment rights.
016               (2.0)
017   Inouye:     Colonel North you're appearing here today
018               pursuant to subpoenas issued on behalf of the
019               Senate and House Select Committees (0.5) I hereby
020               communicate to you orders issued by the United
021               States District Court (0.6) for the District of
022               Columbia at the request of the Committees (0.3)
023               providing that you may not refu:se to provide any
024               evidence to these Committees on the basis of your
025               privilege against self-incrimination (..) and
026               providing further that no evidence or other
027               information obtained under the oath (.) or any
028               information directly or indirectly derived from
029               such evidence (.) may be used against you in any
030               criminal proceeding. I therefore (..) pursuant to
```

```
031                     such orders (..) direct you to answer the questions
032                     put to you.
033                     (0.4)
034    Hamilton:        Colonel North ah:: I communicate a similar order
035                     obtained by the House Select Committee (.) ah:
036                     which is also (.) at the witness table (.) and I
037                     too direct you to answer the questions put to you.
038                     (2.0)
039    Sullivan:        We understand that Colonel North is here pursuant
040                     to compulsion of subpoenas issued by both the
041                     House and Senate. is 'at correct sir?
042                     (.)
043    Inouye:          You are correct sir (.) Mr. Nields, proceed.
044                     (1.5)
045    Nields:          Colonel North, you were involved in *two*: (0.8)
046                     operations of this government (.) of great
047                     significance to the people of this country, is
048                     that correct?
049                     (1.0)
050    North:           At least two. yessir=
051    Nields:          =And one of them (.) in*volv*ed the support of the
052                     contras (.) during the time the Boland Amendment
053                     was in effect, (0.4) and another one involved the
054                     sale of arms to Iran. (2.0) is 'at correct?
055                     (0.8)
056    North:           Yes, (ih) it also involved support for:: the
057                     democratic outcome in Nicaragua both before an:d
058                     *aft*er the Boland Amendment was in effect.
```

Perhaps the most obvious thing to say about this stretch of talk is that it accomplishes the transition from "preliminary matters" to the actual onset of "interrogation." Up to the time of this excerpt, neither the principal questioner (Nields) nor the principal answerer (North) have spoken. The movement from a discussion of preliminaries (concerning the legitimacy, organization, etc., of these proceedings) to Nields' first question is accomplished by Chairman Inouye's utterance [at line 006], "You may not sir. (0.8) Mr. Nields." This utterance works both to seal off a line of preliminary questioning on the part of North's attorney, and to select the principal questioner as next speaker. And indeed, Nields's subsequent utterance [lines 008–011] is occupied with a question that proposes an interactional organization of the sort we find at the end of the excerpt: namely, one questioner (Nields) asks questions, and one answerer (North) responds to those questions in next turn. Nields thus treats Inouye's utterance as having, *at least in principle*, directed the onset of "interrogation" as an interactional order of questions and answers.

What Nields's (would-be) game-initial question receives, however, is an utterance that explicitly formulates "this response is not an answer to the prior question," and hence, "the game has not yet begun." North's invocation of his Fifth Amendment rights against self-incrimination [at lines 013–015] momentarily suspends the question/answer protocol of "interrogation" by constructing the possibility that "questioning's beginning" may legitimately be superseded by his own unwillingness to enter into play (by virtue of his privilege against self-incrimination). Given that the preliminaries-thus-far have failed to mention this potential conflict, North's initial utterance takes the opportunity to display, in detail, how his "willingness to play" is presupposed in Nields' initial question.

This attention to the (logically prior) issue of "players' willingness to play" points up the radical possibility that a game's play may be terminated at any point owing to one or another participant's unwillingness to continue. It also shows that "the willingness to play" is, at times, irreducible to the terms of some silent and untextured set of "fundamental agreements." On the contrary, the citation here of North's unwillingness to play is, among other things, a method for placing "on the record" the specific arrangements, interests, and compulsions, by which the eventual game's conduct has been realized; in this case, by orders of the Senate and House Select Committees that override a witness's privilege against self-incrimination.

The ensuing talk transitions rather unproblematically from North's Fifth Amendment plea, to Inouye's "communication" of the order to testify, to Hamilton's communication of a similar order, to Sullivan's question, and back to Inouye's reply to Sullivan and his repeat of the direction to Nields [at line 43], "You are correct sir. Mr. Nields, proceed." The unproblematic, almost fluid movement through these exchanges indicates that the Fifth Amendment plea was an expected, even highly ritualized, pregame maneuver.

As such, and given that the talk beginning at Nields's *second* utterance orients powerfully to the question/answer order of "interrogation," we can characterize Nields's (would-be) game initial question [at lines 008–011] as having *instead* initiated the *final preliminaries leading up to* the actual, recognizable onset of "interrogation." The onset of "interrogation" then, is, an outcome of the transition from final preliminaries to the protocol of "one questioner asking questions; one answerer answering questions in next turn," and the simultaneous appreciation that all preliminaries have ended.

In sum, the onset of "interrogation" has, in this case, the following general features:

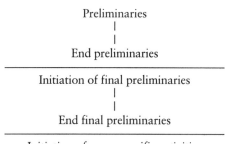

Preliminaries
|
|
End preliminaries
_____

Initiation of final preliminaries
|
|
End final preliminaries
_____

Initiation of game-specific activities

Much of what has been said so far seems to accord with Schegloff's picture of the rule-orientation of "questioning," and indeed, the present analysis abides by certain aspects of that picture. It is assumed, for instance, that if the hearings are to be conducted as an order of questions and answers, then it is up to participants to see that they are done that way, and to see that anything that they might say is fitted to a place within that order. Thus, if the witness is going to try and provide for an alternative version of the events-in-question, then he needs to do so under the constraints and privileges accorded him as a respondent to questioner's "lead" utterances. However, I also want to argue that *just what* those constraints and privileges will be remains, in no small part, to be established in and through the conduct of these initial rounds of questioning. It is therefore worth looking to these initial exchanges for the ways in which they place the rights, duties, obligations and enablements of "questioning" at issue for participants.

Following Schegloff's lead, I would agree that a detailed inspection of these and other "spectacular" proceedings can yield findings of generic importance for the study of natural language use; and, in this case, for our understanding of what an analytic object like "an order of questions and answers" might possibly be. Against Schegloff, however, I am also concerned to demonstrate how a detailed analysis of an event of this kind will show us something of the *unique* properties of that event that lend to it its *special* character, and make of it, among other things, an item of dense and immediate popular interest.

One way of accounting for the dramatic import of the North testimony is to recognize that although the entirety of its organization was "coproduced," and in this sense, involved the cooperation of the parties involved, much of what was done and said was done, *agonistically*, and with an attention to the rhetorical weight of participants' utterances as variously adept or inept moves within a testimonial struggle.

In line with an agonistic conception of these proceedings, it is worth considering these initial exchanges as the first moves in an interactive game (or joust), where participants are both "feeling one another out," and seeking to establish the *particular* rules by which the game will be played, and in such a way so that they may secure maximum advantage for their position while possibly scoring some initial points.

As Pollner argues in his study of traffic courts,[48] wherever the game-features of a performance are ambiguous or open to ambiguation, margins of free-play appear in which the rules of the game and the criteria for their successful application can be contested, established, or modified. What Pollner terms "explicative transactions" are those precedential or "liminal" moments in which the rules of the game are given texture and shape.

For our purposes, an adept performance is a performance that recognizes and exploits these liminal moments, trading off of threads of intelligibility to procure advantage and produce an audience for the appreciative reception of its activities. And since sequential organization is (at least in part) responsible for the intelligibility of utterances and activities, sequentiality figures as both a major resource for, and malleable product of, this sort of discursive play.[49]

Conversation analytic studies of law courts, occupational interviews, classroom interaction, and the like, have tended to take-for-granted that the protocol "one party asks questions and another party answers them" tends to favor the questioner vis-à-vis the determination of the interaction's course and outcomes. That is, where "questions" can be used to open up topics, generate new information, build accusations, and the like, the canonical "task" of an answer is to merely respond to its immediately prior question.

As an alternative to this conception of "answers" as rather docile conversational objects, it seems clear that respondents may on occasion invoke an array of devices aimed at, for example, postponing answers, dispersing accusations, or undoing the question's "sense" and "force." North's testimony in the fragment above provides a case in point. The "project" of Nields's first question is to get the Fifth Amendment plea on the record, and hence, out of the way. After naming its recipient ("Col. North"), it then moves immediately into a syntactic formulation that establishes the ensuing utterance as a direct question ("were you . . ."), and it packages "what that question refers to" in the form of *specific* activities done for *specific* purposes ("the use of proceeds of sales of weapons to Iran for the purpose of assisting the n- Contras in Nicaragua"). In this sense, it provides an interrogatory space for the placement of the Fifth amendment plea (which North then gives).

Nields's second question [at lines 045–048] begins the same way ("Col. North"), but—in contrast to the first—it gets formulated as an assertion ("you were involved") which is then repackaged as a question through a tagging operation ("is that correct?").

Where the force of the first question is primarily interrogative, the latter can more readily be heard as the first move in an accusatorial line of questioning. Given that accusatorial questions strongly prefer confirmatory responses, this second question—hearable in a game-positional sense as a mere reformulation of Nields's first question—has the effect of a rhetorical upgrade aimed at tightening the noose around the available response options of the witness. It prefigures confirmation, but to simply confirm would be to accede to the ambiguous terms of the accusation.

Nields's second question is tied to his initial question both by virtue of its sequential location (as a restatement of a game-initial question that has not yet been answered) and as an accusation that presupposes that the initial question has been heard and understood. That is to say, unless "two operations of great significance to the American people" is referentially connected to "the use of proceeds of sales of weapons to Iran for the purpose of assisting the Contras in Nicaragua," the second question could reasonably be heard as vague, or as a characterization that asks the witness to guess what the questioner has in mind.

In this case, North exploits the former possibility. "Two operations of great significance to the American people" is *not* taken up in its sequential and referential affiliations to "the use of proceeds of sales of weapons to Iran for the purpose of assisting the Contras in Nicaragua." Rather, it is treated as an *equivocal* specification of the "significance" of North's activities and, *ironically*, as a numerical minimization of that significance.

The rhetorical success of North's response [line 050], "At least two, yes sir.," consists in its analysis and use of Nields's second question as temporally and discursively *detachable* from the referential order of the first, and as an occasion for ironic commentary concerning the failures of Nields's game-initial question. It then extends that irony through a disciplined compliance with the strong illocutionary demands of accusations.

To summarize: while the sequential movement from preliminaries, through the final preliminaries, to the game-initial question, was, in some sense, scripted-in-advance—that is, it appears as a *mere* formality—*just how* the game-initial moves would be linked to their immediate backdrop in the final preliminaries *was not*. Nields's game-initial question presumes an order of "questioning" that traverses the line between "final preliminaries" and the actual, recognizable onset of interrogation. North's response refuses that movement, opting instead for a hearing of Nields's second question as a game-initial question *in its own right*.

As an "explicative transaction" this initial exchange sets the stage for the kinds of modulations, reversals, accusatorial dispersions, and categorical challenges we find strewn throughout the subsequent testimony. And it is at least in part through his adept use, *early on*, of margins of free-play available in the question/answer protocol, that North is able to enlist members of both the immediate and the televisual audience as partisans on his behalf.

With respect to Schegloff's analysis of the initial exchange between Bush and Rather, this example suggests that it is the principal task of such game-initial exchanges to provide for the transition from "preliminaries" to "game-specific activities," so that—far from being devoted to the absence of "preliminaries"—such exchanges will, as is possible and necessary, provide for a sense of "preliminaries" as *present in* and *relevant* to the initiation of "game-specific activities."

A second point of critical contact between the North testimony and Schegloff's analysis of the Bush/Rather "encounter" is raised by Nields's question at lines 068–071 and North's subsequent response in lines 073–075. Over the course of these two turns, the cameras are on North. This exchange, transcribed with an attention to North's bodily movements, runs as follows:

> Nields: =And one of them (.) in*volv*ed the support of the con-
>   tras (.) during the time
> →   the Boland Amendment was in effect, ((North shifts
>   forward, nods slightly and averts his eyes)) (0.4) and
>   another one involved the sale of arms to Iran.
>   (2.0)
> → North: [((shakes head))
>   Nields: [is 'at correct?
>   0.8)
> → North: ((nodding and moving forward)) Yes, (ih) it also involved
>   support for:: the democratic outcome in Nicaragua both
>   before an:d *af*ter the Boland Amendment was in effect.

Just at the end of the first complete turn-component of Nields's utterance, North shifts forward, nods his head slightly, and momentarily averts his eyes [first arrow]. In this case, North does not take the opportunity to speak, even though—in terms of a kind of interrogatory organization we find dispersed throughout the hearings—he clearly "could have."

Later in the hearings, we get the following exchange:

> Nields: I'd like yeh to take a look at the middle of the pa::ge (1.4) it
>   says:: (1.8) "S:e::cord teh ca:::ll, (1.4) a city in a foreign
>   country,"
>   (0.4)
> North: Ye(ih)s::,
>   (1.5)
> Nields: Then: underneath that it says (0.2) "Ben-Youssif:: start buy
>   orders at fourteen million dollars or *less:*,"

	(0.8)
North:	Ri:ght.
Nields:	While we're o:n that, that's thee uh, (0.8) Ben-Youssif is the person at thee: Israeli (.) purchasing office I take it?
	(0.8)
North:	He is.
	(0.6)
Nields:	And thee suggestion teh *buy:::* at fourteen million or *le:ss* has to do with thee re*por*ting requirements under the Arms and Export Control Act,
	(0.5)
North:	Thats: correct.
	(0.2)
Nields:	Th' idea being if it's under fourteen *mil*lion (.) you don't haf teh report teh Congress,
North:	Someone hed told me that, thet's ri:ght.

This exchange is fairly typical of these proceedings: a document is prof-fered and its sense is explicated over a series of assertions and confirmations concerning, for example, the wording of the document, its authorship and intended audience, its salience for the present inquiry, and so on. While questioner's utterances *may* deploy syntactic or intonational features of "questions," they need not always do so. Likewise, for answerer to await the "question" in questioner's utterances would tend to confound this particular interactional organization.

To say that in the previous example North clearly "could have" spoken at the point where instead he shifted forward, nodded slightly, and averted his eyes, is merely to note that Nields's utterance provides a place where confirmation would be an appropriate response, though with quite different consequences for the subsequent talk. There is an organizational basis, then, for claiming that North's bodily movements mark a "withholding" of an available turn-option. In this case, however, the availability of that option is not derived from the overall organization of "conversation," but is instead a demonstrably "live" possibility within the hearing's situated inquiries in so far as the assertion/confirmation pair figures as a methodic feature of interrogation.

Indeed, as we move through this exchange, there is some momentary awkwardness surrounding the two-second pause following the point at which Nields's utterance has come to a second possible completion. Throughout the duration of this pause, North maintains a steady gaze, focused on the questioner. He neither begins a response, nor indicates a failure of under-standing, but instead maintains the same posture and expression he had had at the beginning of the second component. That is, he treats Nields's utterance as, at this point, sequentially *non*implicative.

This brief hiatus is then ramified in the simultaneous occurrence of Nields's candidate repair ("is 'at correct?") and North's head shake [second arrow]. By formulating questioning's failure as the absence of an explicit questioning form, Nields's repair locates the trouble within the strong assertoric coloring of his utterance-thus-far. And, in fact, North's failure to treat the initial component of Nields's utterance as an assertion awaiting confirmation lends a basis to this reading. North's head shake, on the other hand, comes too early to be responsive to Nields' candidate repair. Instead, it responds to the utterance-thus-far as variously incomplete or unintelligible, and so initiates a sequence at cross purposes with the trajectory of trouble indicated by Nields's tagging operation.

The issue gets resolved in North's subsequent response. Here the strong confirmatory preference of Nields's prior question is, in the first instance, rather strongly affirmed by North's moving forward and nodding "Yes." But this momentary confirmation is then immediately elaborated as a "qualified confirmation," or better, a "confirmation with additions." North's response— "(ih) it also involved support for:: the democratic outcome in Nicaragua both before an:d *after* the Boland Amendment was in effect."—identifies the "incompleteness" of Nields's question in terms of a misformulation of the time frame during which North was engaged in organizing support for the Contras. In a sense, North's response treats the question-as-asked as a legitimate, but incomplete "assertion of fact." That is, it is treated as legitimate in as much as it is taken-up as a "question" requiring a direct response (and not, say, as an assertion that violates the Q-A-Q-A order of "questioning"), but it is treated as incomplete in so far as its factual account fails to mention that these activities were also being conducted *before* the Boland Amendment was in effect.[50] In another sense, however, the question-as-asked is here being treated as specifically "irreparable," and this circumstance goes to the heart of North's evident bafflement. Owing to the use Nields's question makes of the Boland Amendment—as both a significant marker of time and a measure of the significance of North's activities—a simple addendum to the two part list Nields has laid out is not sufficient for North's response. On the contrary, the answer he gives works to reformulate the entire sense of these activities at the precise juncture where Nields's "question" initially went awry: namely, at the end of the first component where—having failed to properly characterize the temporal occurrence and sense of North's activities—the possibility that North might simply confirm Nields's assertions had already been foreclosed. Hence, North's bodily movements at this particular "structural joint" in Nields' talk, while in part doing a kind of "withholding" of an available turn-option, do so with a specific attention to points of nonconfirmation, misformulation, disagreement, or incompleteness. As such, these movements are less concerned with the questioning or assertoric force of the "question" than with marking those points where some clarification, recasting, rebuttal, or correction is called for.

In and as an attention to some present stretch of talk, the reception of that talk, its organization, and sense, where it might lead, and so forth, are registered by the body. Its movements, noises, and gestures articulate a notational system that both records and remarks on the activities-at-hand. It is at least in this sense that "the body" is methodically produced as an intelligible, investigable, documentary phenomenon.

Returning to Schegloff's account of Bush's hands, lips, and jawbone: though it is not incumbent to Schegloff's argument that every such marked attention to the "structural joints" of speech be a case of a "withholding" of the turn-taking options of "ordinary conversation," it is essential that this be evidently the case with Bush. Now consider the extended transcript of the initial exchange between Rather and Bush:

(2) *Bush/Rather, 00:00*

	Rather:	. . . Today, Donald Gregg still works inside the White
		House as Vice President Bush's trusted advisor.
		((End of feature; start of live broadcast.))
000		(1.0)
001	Rather:	°hh Mister Vice President, tha:nk you for being
002		with us toni:ght, °hh Donald Gregg sti:ll serves
003		as y'r tru:sted advi#sor, =he w'z dee:ply involved
004		in running arms t'the Contras an' he didn' in*f*orm
005		you.=
006		{ (0.5)}
007	Rather:	{=°hhhh} + Now when President Rea:gan's, (0.2)
008		trusted advisor: Admiral Poindexter: (0.6) failed
009		to inform *hi*:m, (0.8) the President- (0.2)
010		*f*ired'im.hh
011		(0.5)
012	Rather:	Why is Mister Gregg still: (°) inside the White
013		Hou@se'n still a trusted advisor.=
014	Bush:	=Becuz I have confidence in im, (0.3) en becuz
015		this matter, Dan, . . .
11		. . . as you *well* *kn*ow:, 'n your *ed*itors
12		know:, has been *look*ed at by .hh the *ten million*

13	*do*llar *stud*y by thee: (.) Senat 'n thuh *Hou:*se, .hh
14	it's been *look*ed at by thuh *Tow*er Commission, .hh thuh
15	Rodr*i*guez testimony thet you put on here, I jus' think
16	it's out*rage*ous, because he was *totally* vindicated,
17	.hh *s*wore under *oath* thet 'e never talked to me about
18	.hh thuh Contras, 'n yet *this*: (.) report *you*'re
19	making which *you told me*:: er your *pe*ople did, you
20	have a Mister *C*ohen thet works for you, .hh was gonna
21	be a po*li*tical *pro*file. .hh now if *th*is is a po*li*tical
22	*pro*file fer an election, .hh uh: I have a very
23	different o*pi*nion ez to what one should *be:.* (d-)
24	Don Gregg w- *w*orked for *me:*, .hh because *I* don't
25	think he's *d*one anything *w*ro:ng. .h an' I think if
26	'e *ha:*d, this EXHAUSTIVE examination, .hh that went
27	into: thet'd gone into *by* thuh *S*enate, ( ) 'n *by* thuh
28	*H*ouse, ( ) would've *sh*owed it. ( ) And you've impugned
29	the: .hh eh *my* integrity by sug*gest*ing with one o'
30	your little *b*oards here, .hh that *I* didn't *tell* thuh
31	*t*ruth w- bout what-what uh Felix Rodr*i*guez. .h ya
32	didn't ac*cuse* me of it, ( ) but you *m*ade that
33	sug*gest*ion. and OTHER people in thuh *media*, =including
34	Mister *n*ick Brady, ( ) and HE 'as said thet-(.) *my*
35	(.) *v*ersion is corre:ct, .hh and so I *f*ind this tuh
36	be ay *re*hash .hh and a *li:*ttle bit (.) if you'll ex*c*use
37	me ay *mi*srepresented- *t*ation on thuh part of
38	CBS who said yer *d*oin political profiles .hh
39	on *all* thuh candidates, .h and then *y*ou- (0.2) come
40	up with something thet 'as been ex*haust*ively looked
41	into.
#	Bush brings hands together and mouth opens
+	Bush separates hands
@	Bush's lips part[51]

Schegloff's argument that over the course of Rather's initial utterance Bush and Rather can be seen to be "doing interview," and to be doing it by way of an articulated contrast with "ordinary conversation," hinges on the claim that Bush's bodily movements register a suspension of an "ordinary conversational" principle (the "principle of immediacy") in favor of the sequential requirements of the institutional setting-at-hand.

An alternative is to read Bush's bodily movements as marking segments of Rather's utterance as ambiguous, misformulated, misrepresentative, or in any of a number of ways, *contestable matters*, and hence, as items in need of elaboration. As with North, they are part of a notational system for marking discursive points at which some question has been proffered, but for which a simple confirmation will not do.

Read this way, the movements of Bush's hands, lips, and jawbone fail to support the foundationalist reading. On the contrary, the tension being played with is *not* between the sequential properties of "news interviews" and those of "ordinary conversation," but centers instead on the difference between "accusatorial" and "investigative" lines of questioning. Were Bush to offer some token confirmation at either of the first two "joints" marked in Schegloff's transcript, he would not only be providing for the assertion/confirmation order of interrogation, he would also be placing himself at a distinct disadvantage with respect to the emergent accusation borne by Rather's "question," since he would have confirmed, step-by-step, the chain of inferences on which that accusation was built. Given that a questioner might reasonably challenge objections registered in the course of asking a question on the grounds that the question itself has not yet been asked, prudence suggests that such an objection be simply registered for now, and then repackaged in respondent's turn as matters relevant to supplying that question's answer. It is in this sense that the "directness of an answer" can be made to turn on the *directness of the question*, and without necessarily "violating" any of the provisions of the Q-A-Q-A machinery, though these are matters that may require a great deal of local care and delicacy.[52]

CONCLUSION

In this chapter I have dealt with a specific intellectual enterprise both in general and in terms of a specific analysis that exemplifies certain foundational commitments of that enterprise. In part, this is what makes these commitments "foundational" in the most practical sense of that word: that they have provided the basis for an organized science of conversation. This means, of course, that the very attempt to raise these commitments for inspection and to describe the work they do within a set of arguments or analyses, will arouse suspicions. And, indeed, it would be rare for methodological questions of this sort to arise in an unmotivated way, and so to begin to ask is already to have entered into the possibility of critical evaluation.

I have argued that the conversation analytic specification of sequential organization offers one of the most promising cases available for the development of rigorous formal models of natural language use and social interaction. For this reason, wherever it can be shown that the operative assumptions of that discipline are, in important ways, developed independent of the local production of sense, order, intelligibility, and the like, then some headway will have been made down the antiformalist road.

In this chapter I have also begun to show how a vocabulary of rules for the conduct of social activities interlaces with the kinds of structural claims that are typical of foundationalist forms of inquiry. In the final chapter, I will again be considering Habermas's position concerning the prospects of developing a general theory of communicative action, but now with a renewed focus on the place occupied by the concepts of "rules" and "rule following" within his arguments.

5

Order Without Rules

Each of the three preceding chapters has dealt with a specific foundationalist conception of language and social practice. Chapters 2 and 3 challenged the central role of "the doctrine of literal expression" in the writings of Habermas and Searle. These critical arguments are heavily indebted to the work of Harvey Sacks and his colleagues in the field of conversation analysis. In Chapter 4, I examined methods of argument and demonstration in conversation analysis itself in order to bring to light certain foundationalist assumptions of that discipline, and to show how these assumptions get built into the phenomena under investigation.

At stake in these arguments is the question of how social order is produced and maintained, and centrally, what the rational properties of persons' actual conduct consist in. The "order without rules" thesis opposes accounts of social action in which the observable order(s) of language and cultural practice are envisaged as mere behavioral realizations of abstract rules (cognitive, linguistic, or social) which, it is argued, lie behind actual events and determine persons' conduct in situ. In contrast to approaches to social order in which the vocabulary of "rules" is invoked as a uniform explanatory construct, I have argued that the "rational properties of practical activities" cannot be secured from without, via methods of formal analysis, but are instead a feature of the endogenous logic(s) by which intelligible, coherent, orderly courses of social interaction are produced and recognized.

The suggestion that the "rational properties of practical activities" are locally determined typically occasions two objections. First, that lacking any reference to that which lies behind or precedes the moment-to-moment constitution of a setting's sense, this approach cannot account for the culturally acquired competencies, knowledges, experiences, and so forth, that parties to that setting already "have in place," as it were, prior to doing setting's work. Second, that lacking any reference to general rules or principles that make

121

possible training in a new practice, or translation between practices, this approach fails to account for how practices are reproduced and how they endure over time. Taken together, these two objections amount to the charge that while local determination might resolve the details of a setting's surface, it cannot get you the depth grammar of stable, reproducible practices.

Habermas's criticisms of Wittgenstein's notion of "language games" and of the central methodological policies of ethnomethodology are based on precisely these sorts of objections.[1] In both cases Habermas argues that the possibility of understanding *generally* requires a quasi-transcendental moment in which otherwise distantiated minds are brought into accord. In both cases he invokes Gadamerian hermeneutics as an analogy for the "everyday hermeneutics" of ordinary speech. In this chapter I will argue that this analogy trades on a conception of rules, and of the relationship of rules to the reproducibility of practices, that Wittgenstein has shown to be incoherent. The oddity here is that Habermas relies extensively on Wittgenstein's remarks on the subject in making a case for his (essentially Cartesian) conception of rules.

I begin with a brief characterization of features of the conception of rules generic both to classical philosophies of the subject and to their structuralist successors. I then attempt to demonstrate that Habermas's reading of Wittgenstein retains all the elements of the classical picture, *even though Wittgenstein's later writings signal a decisive break with this picture on just these points*. I conclude with a discussion of Wittgenstein's remarks on the use of the words *rule* and *same*, and how these concepts are, in his words, "interwoven."

THE CLASSICAL CONCEPTION OF RULES, OR "LANGUAGE'S TWO BODIES"

The question of how orderly, organized human activities get reproduced has long been regarded as the province of epistemology, or more recently, of cognitive science. This idea owes a heavy debt to the following four assumptions concerning the determinate structure of social activities:

1.   that social activities generically decompose into two parts— roughly speaking, the interior or cognitive part, and the exterior or behavioral part—and are in this sense analyzable as "paired phenomena";

2.   that these two parts, though *theoretically* distinct, are internally related on the analogy of a machinery and its products;

3.   that social activities involve a production process that can therefore be plotted temporally;[2] and

4. that since any specific machinery must predate its products, the "pair relation" between the cognitive and behavioral parts of social activity is therefore overwhelmingly unidirectional, with rules, thoughts, intentions, and the like, antecedent to their specific "behavioral realizations."[3]

By conceiving social activities, on the analogy of a production machinery, and hence, as generically "paired phenomena," questions of how linguistic and cultural practices are acquired, used, transmitted, and distributed can be conceived in keeping with the iterative capacities of machines. For this reason the idea of "rules of thought" is a primitive concept in the cybernetic vocabulary of human action.[4]

It makes little difference whether the relation between "rules" and their "behavioral realizations" is conceived on the model of causation (production rules), constraint (regulative rules), or enablement (constitutive rules) because the differences involve disputes over the *nature* of rules, and not over whether or not abstract rules, the basic idea of the representational picture of mind, are relevant to the reproduction of orderly, organized social activities.[5] These otherwise divergent approaches have in common the assumption that "rules of conduct" must play a foundational role in any robust account of human activity. In all of these cases, rules are methodically abstracted from practices and then reconfigured as substantial, generic, unproblematically reproducible features of orderly, organized social activities. Generality is achieved by enlisting specific, observable activities as representatives of the rulelike procedures and idealized plans of action that, it is said, collectively constitute the "corpus of knowledge" available within some particular language community or culture.[6]

In the name of formal methods, practices are stripped of all location, singularity, sensuality, memorability, and inflection. The result is a sanitized and stable, spectral presence that exists in the shadow of the body that moves, speaks, laughs, and smells.[7] The ideal body stands for the possibility of a "perfect unity" of all corporeal bodies. It is what they have in common; how they are the same. The spectral presence of the ideal body also serves as a constant reminder of the imperfect, finite, notoriously contingent operations of the corporeal body in and as its merely particular practices.[8] (It is in this sense that any "rules account" of language in general is implicit theology).[9]

Clearly, the classical conception of rules gains much in the way of formal clarity and procedural cleanliness. It also generates its own conceptual puzzles. Paramount among these is a series of puzzles that collects around what I will term the problem of the "sameness of meaning."

THE PROBLEM OF THE "SAMENESS OF MEANING"

"Sameness of meaning" becomes an issue wherever language is conceived as a generic medium for bringing otherwise distinct minds into momentary congruence around some stable set of linguistic expressions. Consider, for instance, Saussure's famous image of the "speaking circuit":[10]

In this picture of language, "speech" consists in the particular, local activities that make speakers' messages acoustically available to listeners. Language, by contrast, comprises a corpus of lexical items and syntactic procedures for the translation of *speakers'* meanings into meaningful linguistic expressions. It is available in *general* as a system of patterned regularities that is *invariant* with respect to any particular instance of use.[11]

This relation between "speech" and "language" recapitulates the terms of classic epistemology outlined in the previous section. "Speech" is conceived as the particular, contingent, relatively irregular product of "language." As "language's" poorer cousin, "speech" inevitably appears as a partial or imperfect embodiment of the ideal; a go-between or messenger whose communications are, by definition, mere translations of the original and not the original itself. The task for message receivers, then, is to use the sensorial information of living speech to figure out what the speaker, in and through the acts of speech, was all the time *trying* to say. Every "saying," then, is a kind of "trying to say"; a paraphrase or expression of the (speaker's) original meaning; and every "hearing" is, in turn, a listening for the original thoughts, feelings, and intentions standing, as it were, at the back of the (mere) "saying" of speech.

This means that listeners must attend to the "facts of speech" precisely for the ways in which they instantiate the order, or "code" of language. Here we find a kind of practical warrant for the idea that particular instances of "speech" are of theoretical interest only insofar as they exemplify the phenomena of "language."

This picture, however, introduces a moment of *radical uncertainty* into the very heart of the general conditions of communication. To the extent that listeners must rely on the elliptical facts of speech in reasoning about the meaning of speaker's utterances, it is unclear how they can be sure that their interpretations of those utterances are congruent with the speaker's original intentions. Any theory that begins by conceiving speech paraphrastically—that is, as cognition's intermediary—therefore must ask how a particular utterance comes to have a meaning that is "the same" for both a speaker and a listener.

It is typical of most modern linguistic inquiry, whether structuralist, truth-conditional, or hermeneutical in inspiration, that some version of the "sameness of meaning" problem lies at its core. In this respect, Habermas's theory of communicative action is no exception. What is novel to Habermas's approach is that his theory explicitly thematizes the "sameness of meaning" problem (qua problem), and then attempts to erect a general theory on the historically contingent possibility of its ultimate resolution. In this way, Habermas absorbs the classical conception of rules, along with the intractable puzzles it generates, into the general framework of the theory of communicative action.

It should be possible, then, to see how the classical conception of rules ramifies throughout the Habermasian system by retracing the steps by which he arrives at the "sameness of meaning" problem, and by looking to his arguments for its proposed resolution.

"SAMENESS OF MEANING" AS A PRECONDITION OF UNDERSTANDING

> The use of the same symbols with a constant meaning has to be not only given *as such*; it has to be knowable for the symbol users themselves. And this sameness of meaning can be secured only by the intersubjective validity of a rule that "conventionally" fixes the meaning of a symbol.
> —Habermas, *The Theory of Communicative Action*

Habermas begins the second volume of *The Theory of Communicative Action* with a discussion of Mead's theory of the emergence of symbolically mediated communication from the language of gestures. Habermas needs to situate the validity basis of speech—the claims to truth, rightness, sincerity, and intelligibility—within a theory of communication that is *general enough* to explain linguistic phenomena *phylogenetically*, without simultaneously discarding the idea, so heavily worked over in the first volume, that linguistic phenomena can be described adequately only in the "performative attitude" of one who is (at least potentially) a master of the particular practice(s) in question.

According to Habermas, Mead provides a viable account of the phylogenesis of speech, but his conception of symbolic exchange fails to grasp the internal relation between understanding and the normativity of expression. As Habermas sees it, the task is to revise Mead's theory so that the *achievement of intersubjective understanding* is placed at the center of the phylogenetic account of the emergence of language.

Habermas begins his reconstruction of Mead by arguing that Mead's notion of "taking the attitude of the other" fails to grasp certain basic relational preconditions of intersubjective understanding. To the extent that this argument is successful, it allows the intersubjective validation of claims to truth, rightness and sincerity—that is, the rational basis of speech—to emerge as an essential moment in the development of what, in Mead's terms, are the higher symbolic functions of language.

According to Habermas, Mead's theory of the emergence of language operates with a conception of meaning borrowed from research into animal behavior. The descriptions of animal researchers, Habermas argues, employ a system of "natural meanings" that ascribe meaning to patterns of behavior without assuming that the organism is itself aware of those meanings.[12] Meaning, then, becomes a matter of the functional role of patterned behavior within a system of innate drives and responses. For Mead, the transition from the language of gestures to symbolically mediated communication is thus analyzable primarily as what Habermas terms "the semanticization of natural meanings."[13] The problem with such ethologically prejudiced accounts of meaning, according to Habermas, is that they can never explain how meaning is grasped, so to speak, "from the inside":

> Insofar as nothing more is meant by ["taking the attitude of the other"] than that one native takes in advance the attitude with which the other will respond to its vocal gesture, it is not at all clear how languagelike symbols, vocal gestures with the *same* meanings, are supposed to arise from this . . . If the same gesture arouses in both a disposition to *like* (sufficiently similar) behavior, an observer can notice a concurrence in the way they interpret the stimulus, but this does not yet imply the formation of a meaning that is the same for the natives themselves . . . That both concur in the interpretation of the same stimulus is a state of affairs that exists in itself but *not for them*.[14]

Habermas then argues that Mead's reliance on a vocabulary of "natural meanings" leads to an attenuation or "one-sidedness" in his conception of the process by which "objective meanings are internalized."

Looked at in another way, Mead portrays social actors as good behavioral scientists: "taking the attitude of the other" involves making *inferences* about shared meanings by observing the patterned responses of the other, and internalizing the relation between the gesture and the response. For Habermas, it is not enough that meanings merely *appear* to be shared, they must be *experienced as identical*. In other words, he wants to show that members of a language community not only must be good behavioral scientists; they must be good hermeneuticians as well.

To this end he argues that there are three transformations that need to take place in the movement from the language of gestures to symbolically mediated communication:

> First, gestures are transformed into symbols through replacing the meanings that exist for individual organisms with meanings that are the same for both natives. Second, the behavior of natives changes in such a way that an interpersonal relation between speaker and addressee replaces the causal relation between stimulus-response-stimulus—in interacting with one another, natives now have a communicative intent. Finally, there is a transformation of the structure of interaction, in that the natives learn to distinguish between acts of reaching understanding and actions oriented to success.[15]

Habermas conceives each step as a phase in a developmental process organized around the species necessity of learning about and reproducing the deep interconnections between language use and social relations.[16] In the first step natives "take the attitude of the other" inasmuch as they have internalized "a segment of the objective meaning structure" sufficient to respond to the same stimulus in the same way. In the second step, they enter a developmentally more advanced phase of "taking the attitude of the other," namely, that of "reciprocal relations between speaker and hearer." As a result, they can begin to differentiate, for example, between genuine communicative activities (i.e., activities addressed to others) and "consequence-oriented actions" (i.e., activities aimed at bringing something about in the world).

The ability to differentiate between communicative and consequence-oriented actions is, in turn, presupposed by what Habermas terms a "third way of taking the attitude of the other." This third way is "constitutive for natives ascribing to the same gesture an *identical* meaning rather than merely undertaking interpretations that are objectively in agreement." Habermas, then, believes that the possibility of a *presumptive identicality of meaning* wants explaining; although this possibility is intrinsic to the logical development of symbolically mediated communication, Mead's theory fails to specify its developmental preconditions "in any precise way."[17]

Habermas once again traces this shortcoming in Mead to his impoverished vocabulary of meaning. According to Habermas, with the first two ways of "taking the attitude of the other," a native can only *predict* how alter will respond to a verbal gesture (in the same way that a behavioral scientist might predict the patterned responses of organisms), but cannot yet know—that is, be practically certain—that the meanings the two of them assign to the gesture are the same. This is the case because their relation is not yet secured normatively. Therefore "meaning" has not yet obtained as an *ethical*, and hence socio-logically binding, force:

> There is an identical meaning when ego knows how alter *should* respond to a significant gesture; it is not sufficient to expect that alter *will* respond in a certain way.[18]

Throughout the discussion of Mead, the notion of "identical meaning" is doing some awfully heavy lifting in the service of Habermas's argument. First, the idea of "identicality," placed, as it is, at the end of the developmental process, makes that process retrospectively available as (and only as) the coming-to-be of meaning identical with itself. Hence, the biohistory of language becomes a moment within the history of understanding, where "understanding" is conceived *hermeneutically* as the experience of merging nonidentical worlds, and *dialectically* as a contingent outcome of the developmental history of the species to date.[19]

Second, the unity of mind implied by the philosophically loaded conception of "understanding" requires that *genuine* agreement, or Agreement, be distinguished from its more common forms: for instance, that we agree about this or that aspect of some contract and are, as is often said, "of one mind" *about that*, but not necessarily about all the other elements of the contract. In this case, "agreement" is being used to contrast those things about which we can say "they are (provisionally) settled," from those things about which further negotiation is required. The provisionality of agreement here has to do with the possibility that agreements, though ratified, ultimately may need revision, reevaluation, renegotiation, and so forth. So, too, "taking something to have been settled" may turn out to have been based on a misunderstanding, disagreement, or miscommunication—for instance, about what can constitute a settlement in this case or what that "something" that was settled might have been. In such cases, it might be said, "we only *thought* that we had agreed."

The idea of "identical meaning," then, is a reification of the occasional distinction between, for example, "agreeing" and "thinking that we agree." In this way, the question of whether or not agreement has been successfully accomplished and can be relied on is made a general precondition of all meaningful speech. Habermasian agreement is not *about* anything in particular; rather, it is a part of a venerable tradition of considering concepts apart from any conceivable context of their application: that is, of considering concepts per se. Habermasian agreement, then, is the idea of "identical meaning" conjoined with the idea of "agreement per se."

Finally, the idea of "identical meaning" prefigures a conception of linguistic and cultural "attunement"—or what Wittgenstein called "agreement in form of life"[20]—that recapitulates the terms of classical epistemology by abstracting "meaning" from any particular practice in which the issue of "what this or that utterance, word, or gesture means" conceivably might arise.

In sum, the idea of "identical meaning" is the pivotal move in Habermas's assimilation of Wittgenstein's remarks on rules and rule following to a Mead-inspired natural history of communicative action. On the one hand, it identifies what is lacking in Mead's account of the logical genesis of "symbolically mediated communication," and does so in relational terms, such that Habermas's subsequent account of "rules for the use of symbols" arguably develops an idea immanent in Mead's own thought. On the other hand, the idea of "identical meaning" prefigures a specific reading of Wittgenstein's rules argument: namely, that the possibility of the presumed identicality of meaning will be found to congeal, as it were, in the rational expectations associated with "rules for the use of symbols."[21]

In the following two sections I argue that this reading so severely tailors Wittgenstein's remarks on rules and rule following to its own purposes that the design and weave of the original garment are lost in the process. In the first section I attempt to clarify the link that Habermas sees between a critique of Wittgenstein's notion of language-games and the proposal that the theory of communicative action be modeled after the limit case of translation. In the second section I consider Wittgenstein's remarks on the concepts of "rule" and "same," arguing that there is a systematic "lack of fit" between Habermas's theory of communicative action and Wittgenstein's remarks on rules and rule following that can in turn be traced to their quite different conceptions of the relation between rules and the reproducibility of practices.

"SPHERES OF LANGUAGE" AND THE
LIMIT CASE OF TRANSLATION

In the second volume of *The Theory of Communicative Action*, Habermas takes up Wittgenstein's remarks on rules and rule following, in his words, "to elucidate the connection between identical meanings and intersubjective validity."[22]

Recalling the discussion from chapter 1, Habermas had criticized Wittgenstein for failing to provide a theory of language that could account for the reproduction of linguistic and cultural knowledge. In *On the Logic of the Social Sciences* he argued that Wittgenstein conceived language games as "invariant linkages of symbols and activities" that were "monadically sealed" from one another. On this reading, the effect of Wittgenstein's critique of the various doctrines of logical positivism is the displacement of one seamless logic by another. The idea of the existence of a multiplicity of language games, each having its own discrete logical structure, is no less ahistorical than the idea of a logical calculus that Wittgenstein believed had "bewitched" his philosophical predecessors. According to Habermas, the "one-sidedness" in Wittgenstein is the result of his failure to account for the movements, or *translations*, that are possible between the different "spheres of language."

What disturbs Habermas most about the "spheres of language" picture, which he (incorrectly) attributes to Wittgenstein, is that it seems inevitably to lead to a cultural conservatism with respect to the transmission and reception of linguistic and cultural knowledge. His argument is as follows: if translation between the different spheres of language is necessary not only for learning new practices or mastering a diversity of language games, but also for the continued reproduction of particular practices across time—that is, for the intergenerational transmission and reception of linguistic and cultural traditions—then the possibility of translation must be implicated a priori in the mastery of any practice whatsoever; that is, it must be a possibility that all the discrete language games have in common.[23]

The significance of this idea, for Habermas, is that it introduces a reflective, rational element into the reproduction of linguistic and cultural practices. Translation becomes a limit case for any practice wherein the rules of that practice are not only acquired or inculcated, but also reflected on and questioned. On this account, by failing to incorporate the possibility of translating between the different language games as an a priori feature of linguistic practice, Wittgenstein fails to provide for the possibility of critical reflection, and hence, ends up with a picture of language where competency in a practice comes to be identified with obeying rules "blindly."

This reading is supported in several otherwise competitive or even hostile quarters of social theory. Lyotard, for instance—in an argument designed to undermine Habermas's "consensualist theory of meaning"—adopts the "spheres of language" conception of language games in order to advance a theory of language in line with Foucault's image of the heterogeneity of "discursive formations."[24] By construing Wittgenstein's notion of "language games" as a prototheoretical formulation of heterogeneous systems of rules, Lyotard preserves the core of the "impulse to systematic theorizing"—the possibility of giving a rules account of language—precisely when he believes he has transcended it.[25]

On the significance of obeying rules "blindly," Bloor has argued that the idea of blind obedience cannot be reconciled with the idea of critical reflection.[26] Bloor differs from Habermas in that he uses this as a starting point for a behaviorist reading of Wittgenstein in which the culturally bounded, incommensurable language games are treated as discrete Durkheimian social systems. Neither Bloor nor Habermas consider that the analysis of "obeying a rule blindly" may be as much about the logical grammar of "obedience" as that of "rule," where to "*obey*" a rule (order, command, etc.) means, among other things, that what is specifically forgone is the critical posture of one concerned over the reasonability of the rule, its likely consequences, and so on. The confusion here is the result of treating the discussion of "blind" rule following as having laid the basis for a general theory of action, rather than as conceptual point about specific cases for which it can rightly be said "one obeys without thinking."

I mention these other sources for two reasons. First, I wish to show that Habermas's reading of Wittgenstein, though strained, is not his alone. Second, I wish to record what we have already accepted once we adopt the reading common to Habermas, Lyotard, and Bloor: (1) that Wittgenstein's "rules argument" contains an implicit theory of language,[27] and (2) that because there is a theory there, but only an implicit one, Wittgenstein's philosophy stands all the more urgently in need of systematic reconstruction.

This assumption is the starting point for Habermas's revisionist reading of Wittgenstein in *The Theory of Communicative Action*. Throughout the first volume of that text, Wittgenstein is celebrated as the theorist who first proposed the "deep interconnection" between meaning and the conditional validity of speech activities.[28] In the second volume Habermas uses Wittgenstein to forge a link between the problem of the "sameness of meaning" and our common ability to follow rules.

Recall that Habermas ends his discussion of Mead with the following problem. Mead takes us a long way toward understanding the socio-evolutionary basis of intersubjective understanding (and hence, of "communicative action"). On his account of "taking the attitude of the other," however, natives can only warrant the *expectation* that they share a common meaning, but they cannot *know* that this is so. In Habermas's terms, there is a "third way" of taking the attitude of the other that Mead had overlooked: the institutionalization of "rules for the use of symbols" such that natives "can now consider in advance whether in a given situation they are using a significant gesture in such a way as to give the other no grounds for a critical response."[29]

Once it has been granted that at the higher stages of linguistic and cultural development natives encounter their own language as objective structures of discrete practices, then the matter of acquiring a language can be conceived easily on the analogy of mastering the rules of a game, with the following qualification: in the case of language, one must master a whole host of games; some of these games are closely connected, whereas others bear little relation to each other.

According to Habermas, the ability to follow a rule implies a certain mastery of the game in which that rule has a meaning (or "force"). This means that the conditions under which a rule can be said to have been mis-applied or misunderstood, must be *internalized* such that any game activity is susceptible, as it were, to critique in advance of its performance. In this sense, for Habermas, *every competent performance at least potentially is open to critique*. It is the *immanence of critique* within the general structure of rule following that leverages Habermas's proposal that the intelligibility of action requires the development of processes of criticism; processes that rest ultimately on the possibility of an achieved consensus.

The part that Wittgenstein is meant to play in this argument is perhaps clearest in the following passage:

> Wittgenstein's famous argument against the possibility of subjects following rules for themselves alone, so to speak, has its place here: "And to *think* one is obeying a rule is not to obey a rule. Hence it is not possible to obey a rule 'privately': otherwise thinking one was obeying a rule would be the same thing as obeying it." The point of this consideration is that S cannot be sure whether he is following a rule at all if there is no situation in which his behavior is exposed to critique by *T*—a critique that is in principle open to consensus. Wittgenstein wants to show that the identity and the validity of rules are systematically interconnected. To follow a rule means to follow the *same* rule in *every* single case. The identity of the rule in the multiplicity of its realizations does not rest on observable invariants but on the intersubjectivity of its validity.[30]

Habermas is by no means the first to take Wittgenstein's argument against the possibility of obeying a rule "privately" as laying the basis for a consen-sualist theory of meaning.[31] What this passage makes particularly clear, however, is how the consensualist reading interlaces with the classical conception of rules outlined at the beginning of this chapter.

From this perspective, Wittgenstein's argument, culminating in the famous "paradox" of ¶201—"no course of action could be determined by a rule, because every course of action can be made out to accord with the rule"[32]—can only be read as an argument about the *indeterminacy of rules*.[33] This is exactly how Habermas reads it.

Before ¶201, however, Wittgenstein had been operating with a philo-sophically loaded conception of rules, namely the Tractarian conception of language as a calculus of meaning-rules. The paradox of ¶201 appears "paradoxical" only on this conception of rules, which requires that a determinate relation exist between any rule and the course(s) of action it determines, regulates, or (as has been argued here) *constitutes*. Hence, it is only on the classical conception of rules that concerns arise over the generic indeterminacy of rules.

These are exactly the kinds of concerns Habermas attributes to Wittgenstein when he writes: "Wittgenstein wants to show that the identity and the validity of rules are systematically interconnected." Anyone looking to Wittgenstein's later work will search in vain for his writings on the "identity of rules." Rather, those remarks that appear to be concerned even remotely with matters relevant to Habermas's discussion of the "identity of rules" are aimed at showing that such formulations are miscast. So, for instance, in the course of his argument concerning the public criteria of being in pain, Wittgenstein notes:

> The substitution of "identical" for "the same" (for instance) is another typical expedient in philosophy. As if we were talking about shades of meaning and all that were in question were to find words to hit on the correct nuance.[34]

The point is that philosophical puzzles arise when we overlook vast and significant differences in conceptual usage in order to exploit a surface similarity—in this case, the occasional relation between "identical" and "same." The questions raised by such conceptual slippages, Wittgenstein goes on to argue, are not the business of philosophy, but rather, are "its raw material . . . something for philosophical *treatment*."

Habermas's claim that, "to follow a rule means to follow the *same* rule in *every* single case" only makes sense if we presume, first of all, that the "identity of rules" represents a cogent formulation of some philosophical puzzle; and second, that it formulates an issue that is always and everywhere relevant to the stable and concerted conduct of social activities. His claim that "the identity of the rule in the multiplicity of its realizations does not rest on observable invariants but on the intersubjectivity of its validity" *deepens* the place occupied by the classical conception of rules within his theory of action by proposing a *sociological* solution to the "paradox" of ¶201. On Habermas's reading, then, far from offering a radical challenge to the possibility of providing rule-based accounts of language, Wittgenstein showed instead that such accounts must be conjoined with and supplemented by a general theory of social action. This reading would place Wittgenstein squarely within the classical tradition that treats rules as foundational to the possibility of organized, orderly social activities.

So far I have attempted to show how Habermas's reading of Wittgenstein's "rules argument" retains the central elements of the classical conception of rules. In what follows I will argue that the principal effect of

Wittgenstein's remarks on rules and rule following is the *subversion* of the privilege that the concepts of "rule" and "rule-governance" have traditionally enjoyed in our thinking about language, logic, and the sciences of human action.

WITTGENSTEIN ON AGREEMENT, RULES, AND THE "SAME"

> The word "agreement" and the word "rule" are *related* to one another, they are cousins. If I teach anyone the use of the one word, he learns the use of the other.

> The use of the word "rule" and the use of the word "same" are interwoven. (As are the use of "proposition" and the use of "true.")
> —Wittgenstein, *Philosophical Investigations*

For someone interested in giving a rule-based account of the reproduction of meaning,[35] these remarks might be taken to mean that the relation between "rules" and "identical meanings" is powerful, determinate, and decisive for the question "How do we mean?" This is only possible, however, if these remarks are read *classically* (as *explanatory accounts*, or statements reporting the results of philosophical analysis), rather than as fragmentary offerings designed to initiate courses of *nonclassical* inquiry.

Wittgenstein's work contains a reflexive element that the classical reading is forced to overlook. Wittgenstein's writing is colored continually by a detailed awareness and recognition of its own textuality; that is, by its embeddedness without repair in specific social technologies for reading and writing, and especially, for reading and writing *philosophy*.[36] This writing is done in painstaking anticipation of the possibilities, contingencies, and determinations of its possible readings. Therefore, one must see not only what some passage says, but also how it says it, and how that "saying" always instructs a reading as well:

> Sometimes a sentence can be understood only if it is read at the *right tempo*. My sentences are all supposed to be read *slowly*.[37]

It is worth considering, then, how and to what extent what is radical to Wittgenstein's thought is indifferent to the classical trade in explanatory theorizing, historical reconstructions, and the like, just because it is engaged instead in the far more ambitious project of cultivating a *nonclassical pedagogy of reading*.

As Hunter, for one, has pointed out, the difficulties of reading Wittgenstein are due not only to his well-known fondness for economy of expression, but also to his habit of ending paragraphs with questions, or with suggestions for thought-experiments (the reader being left to carry them out with scarcely a hint as to where they might lead).[38]

I have already discussed how ¶¶224 and 225 can be read as supporting the proposal that the "identicality of meaning" is secured through conventional agreements concerning rules for the use of symbolic expressions. This reading, however, merely submits to the *aphoristic force* of these passages without clarifying what it means, for instance, to speak of words as "cousins" or of the uses of words as "interwoven." Both paragraphs make powerful, if extraordinarily cryptic, claims about the facts of language. Both fail to clarify what the significance of these facts might be. Both passages, as it were, have holes which can be filled only by laboring through to the end of some line of inquiry. So, for instance, with ¶225:

> The use of the word 'rule' and the use of the word 'same' are interwoven. (As are the use of 'proposition' and the use of 'true.')

The point of this passage is not to establish a singular relation between the word "rule" and the word "same," much less to allow the substitution of "identical meaning" for "same" and then to investigate the relation between "rules" and "identical meanings," as if there were such a relation existing apart from the logical grammar of the concepts in question.

On the face of it, the passage consists of a claim about two words: that the use of rule and the use of *same* are "interwoven." The question is "What is meant by saying they are 'interwoven' and what is the significance of this relation?" The analogy to which Wittgenstein alludes parenthetically at the end of this passage may perhaps provide a clue.

Elsewhere he writes on the relation between the words *proposition* and *true*:

> At bottom, giving "This is how things are" as the general form of propositions is the same as giving the definition: a proposition is whatever can be true or false. For instead of "This is how things are" I could have said "This is true." (Or again "This is false.") But we have
>
> > 'p' is true = p
> > 'p' is false = not-p
>
> And to say that a proposition is whatever can be true or false amounts to saying: we call something a proposition when *in our language* we apply the calculus of truth functions to it.

Now it looks as if the definition—a proposition is whatever can be true or false—determined what a proposition was, by saying: what fits the concept 'true,' or what the concept 'true' fits, is a proposition. What *engages* with the concept of truth (as with a cogwheel), is a proposition.

But this is a bad picture. It is as if one were to say "The king in chess is *the* piece that one can check." But this can mean no more than that in our game of chess we only check the king. Just as the proposition that only a *proposition* can be true or false can say not more than that we only predicate "true" and "false" of what we call a proposition. And what a proposition is is in one sense determined by the rules of sentence formation (in English, for example), and in another sense by the use of the sign in the language-game. And the use of the words "true" and "false" may be among the constituent parts of this game; and if so it *belongs* to our concept 'proposition' but does not 'fit' it. As we might also say, check *belongs* to our concept of the king in chess (as so to speak a constituent part of it). To say that check did not *fit* our concept of the pawns, would mean that a game in which pawns were checked, in which, say, the players who lost their pawns lost, would be uninteresting or stupid or too complicated or something of the kind.[39]

Consider, for instance, how the pieces of a jigsaw puzzle fit together. There are the edge pieces and the interior pieces, the spaces for specific pieces arising out of the adjacent positioning of other pieces, the clues offered by the picture to be constructed, and so on. Now imagine that a piece is found and placed into a space. We go on to the next piece, and only then find another piece that also would have fit into the space where we have just laid the previous piece. Now we must revise our notion of how this puzzle is put together, of what it means for a piece to "fit"—that is, of the complications involved in playing this game. (For instance, although two pieces might fit the same space, it may turn out that one of them makes any subsequent move impossible—and here we must say "It only seemed to fit.") Thus, "discovering a fit," at least in the old way, is no longer sufficient in itself for making a correct move. And if we cannot find other criteria for distinguishing between the two pieces, then we might find it difficult to proceed (for instance, if the puzzle had no predetermined shape, or if all the pieces were the same size and color). Here we are seeking to learn what the game conditions of a jigsaw puzzle are or can be; how what is "puzzling" about a jigsaw puzzle interlaces with a vocabulary of color and shape; how this interlacing designates a field for the various permutations of "jigsaw"; and where it no longer makes sense or is interesting to work with something as a puzzle (where, you might say, you were only working with it "as if" it were a puzzle).

As a first cut at the question, "How is the use of the word *rule* interwoven with the use of the word *same*?," we might say that "same" belongs to our concept of *rule* wherever the iterability of a rule might reasonably be brought into question:

> Suppose someone gets a series of numbers 1,3,5,7, . . . by working out the series $2x + 1^1$. And now he asks himself: "But am I always doing the same thing, or something different every time?" If from one day to the next you promise: "To-morrow I will come and see you"—are you saying the same thing every day or every day something different?[40]

If the questions posed by this passage appear absurd, this is because it is unclear what might serve as an occasion for having the kind of doubts they presuppose.[41]

If I generate a series of numbers using the formula $2x + 11$, then it makes no sense to ask whether or not I am doing the same thing each time I generate a new number, since the fact that I am using *the* formula means that I am not, for instance, using *many* formulae, or using *none*. Even if I go back to check my work, I can only do so by applying the rule once again. If I find that I have made a mistake, it is not because I have failed to use the formula, but because I have used it *incorrectly*.

Similarly, if you make a promise, day in day out, using the same words, under what conditions does it make sense even to ask whether you are doing the same thing each time? That you have "promised" each time already formulates the iterative character of your activities. (Alternatively, if every day for 30 days you promise that "tomorrow I will come and see you," but you never come, how could you respond when, on the thirty-first day, the promisee said "but you always say the same thing"?)[42]

The common property of these two descriptions is that both describe practices whose *iterability is part of the descriptions*. That is to say, "using a formula to generate a number series" and "promising day in and day out that I will come and see you tomorrow" describe practices that are reproducible *by definition*. It is part of the definition of "$2x + 1^1$," that the formula can be applied to different numbers, yielding different results, or to the same number, yielding the same result. These are among the adequate grounds, or *criteria*, for the successful reproduction of the practice. It is *not* consequential for that practice what clothes are worn, what language is spoken, what day it is, whether the number series is written out or spoken, or—within certain limits—how quickly or slowly some calculation is accomplished. Not that these features are somehow excluded, or "bracketed," by the apt conduct of "generating a series" (as if "$2x + 1^1$," in addition to doing its work as a mathematical expression, were also responsible for suspending these other "imaginable" relevancies). Rather, they simply are not a part of it.[43]

A second point of ¶226 is that the relation Wittgenstein is explicating between the uses of the words *rule* and *same* is *asymmetrical* in the following sense: whereas "doing the same thing" is part of what it means to "follow a rule," in the way that "discoverable fit" is part of what it means to be able to work with a jigsaw puzzle piece, the concept of "rule" is *not* part of the definition of "doing the same thing." We can see this by contrasting certain features of the first and second parts of ¶226.

On the surface, both remarks appear to describe a practice that involves following a formula or rule: you generate a series of numbers 1,3,5,7, . . . by working out the series $2x + 1^1$; you promise someone something by saying "Tomorrow I will come and see you." But generating a series of numbers 1,3,5,7, . . . is *what it means* to work out the series $2x + 1^1$, whereas "Tomorrow I will come and see you" is neither a *result* of "promising" nor a *formula* by which "promising" is done. "Tomorrow I will come and see you" is not *how* promising is done, nor *what it means* to promise; rather, it is an example of "promising" *simpliciter*—no more and no less than what is being promised.

CONCLUSION

Wittgenstein's ¶226 makes perspicuous that the logical grammar of "doing the same thing" can be explicated independent of the idea of following a rule or formula, or of producing correct results. In this sense, orders of situated practice will routinely outstrip any conceivable "rules account" of their conduct. This "drop of grammar" has profound consequences not only for the cognitivist program of representing "intelligence" as systems of rules, but also for any argument—including Habermas's—which presumes that the vocabulary of "rules" and "rule following" is generically relevant to the reproducible conduct of orderly social activities.

In this chapter I have attempted to show how Habermas's reading of Wittgenstein retains all the important elements of the classical conception of rules. In this respect, Habermas is by no means alone. And it is significant that several commentators, despite their apparent differences, have come to agree that Wittgenstein's later work demonstrates the indeterminacy of rules and the dependency of reason upon systems of consensual ratification.

This is a reading Wittgenstein seems clearly to have anticipated in the statement cited earlier regarding the nature of linguistic agreement:

> "So you are saying that human agreement decides what is true and what is false?"—It is what human beings *say* that is true and false; and they agree in the *language* they use. That is not agreement in opinions but in form of life.[44]

These remarks are connected to Wittgenstein's claim that grammar is *arbitrary*. By this he does not mean that grammar is chaotic, or that its order makes no difference; rather, grammar is not answerable to the terms and conditions by which we justify claims or validate opinions. It is not subject to the agreements of the community because it provides the *conditions of intelligibility* that make discursive achievements such as "agreement over facts" or "the validation of opinions" possible in the first place. Grammar is, in this sense, *beyond justification*.[45]

I began this study by citing Wittgenstein's famous remarks concerning the "abolition" of logic. Recall that in this passage Wittgenstein asserts that linguistic communication requires "agreement not only in definitions, but also . . . in judgments." He then continues:

> This seems to abolish logic, but does not do so.—It is one thing to describe the methods of measurement, and another to obtain and state results of measurement. But what we call "measuring" is partly determined by a certain constancy in results of measuring.[46]

Here Wittgenstein first distinguishes between descriptions of methods and the practice they concern. He then argues that the very sense and stability of "measuring" is dependent on obtaining "a certain constancy in results"; that is, on seeing how this occasion of measuring is the same as measuring on other occasions, by seeing how the results, while not *identical*, are obtained in the same way. (The teacher says "it goes like this," and then does something. The student has to learn to see what has been done; to see it as an element in the practice; and to see what it is about what is done that is the same and what is different, from occasion to occasion, for that practice.) Discerning the methodical organization of measuring is therefore only contingently related to being able to produce 'methods descriptions' of how one is to proceed.

Much of this discussion hinges on the issue of whether in learning the *rules* of a practice one also and inevitably learns the practice itself. Perhaps it could be said, after all, that if I say I know the rules of chess, but when asked to play I am unable to do so, then I have lied or was confused, and that this is so because knowing the rules of chess and being able to play the game are related as a claim to its criteria of assessment. Then again, I might know the rules of chess—how the pieces may be moved, who goes first, that play alternates, and so on—but I might be said to play the game rather badly. And playing the game badly may have nothing to do with needing to learn some further rules, but instead may be explained by a lack of experience, practice, or aptitude.

When we seek to know how practices are instructably reproducible, however, we are looking not for the set of conditions necessary and sufficient for playing the game *poorly*, but for those features of the practice that are related criterially to its *mastery*. For this reason, the classical conception of "rules" is ill-suited to the demands of explicating the endogenous logic(s) of practical social life.

Conclusion

> Our mistake is to look for an explanation where we ought
> to look at what happens as a 'proto-phenomenon.' That is,
> where we ought to have said: *this language-game is played.*
> —Wittgenstein, *Philosophical Investigations*

In this study I have attempted to supply a critique of the conception of rules currently in ascendancy within theories of language use and social action. These arguments have focused on a critique of the notion that the stability and reproducibility of social activities can be described adequately in terms of systems or sets of rules that comprise those activities' formal and context-free properties. As an alternative to this picture, I have argued that we should not be concerned, in the first instance, with describing activities' "rules of conduct," but that we ought instead to seek to identify criteria that are routinely invoked for determining that some specific activity is a recognizable instance of doing some organized practice, and more important, for displaying an evident *mastery* of that practice. Hence, the proposal being advanced in this study is that we abandon orders of inquiry organized around the endless search for general rules of thought and action in favor of investigations aimed at making clear how the heterogeneous and differently related practices of social life are acquired and mastered.

As was mentioned earlier, there are two common objections to the proposal that the search for general rules or standards of thought and action ought to be abandoned in favor of inquiries into "rational action" as a situated and contingent feature of practical social life. The first is that this strategy is limited by its focus on local context. It therefore cannot account for the culturally acquired competencies, knowledge, prejudices, and the like, that parties to an occasion have in their possession, as it were, prior to their engagement with the persons, circumstances, and material environment that constitute the local occasion-at-hand. The second is that, owing to its lack of reference to culturally acquired, internalized rules of conduct that hold *in general* from setting to setting, this approach cannot account for how practices are reproduced, endure, and remain relatively stable over time.

Both of these objections suffer from the same logical difficulty: in order to construct the trans-situational stability of practices as a problem, it is necessary to stipulate the existence of a general medium, or "supercontext," within which the various, heterogeneously organized contexts of interaction are located. Thus, elucidations of grammatical relations are held answerable to idealized images of grammar, and are seen as incomplete in the absence of a general theory of language. The problem of trans-situational stability is thus introduced by way of a tautology: it is a result of the requirement that the isolated, empirical facts of language be stabilized theoretically, and yet, it is only when we are speaking theoretically—that is, in terms of the super-context of "language-in-general"—that the issue of formal linkage between the different, separable, local contexts of action arises.

Within social theory, there are, broadly speaking, two ways in which Wittgenstein's remarks on "rules" and "rule-following" have been under-stood. The choice between these two positions—what, following Lynch,[1] I will call the "skepticist" and the "antiskepticist" readings—seems to depend, among other things, on varying levels of commitment to the classical project of explanatory theorizing. The skepticist reading interprets Wittgenstein's arguments in the *Philosophical Investigations* as demonstrating that human behavior is *underdetermined* by rules of logic. This is the position taken by Kripke in his famous critique of Wittgenstein's number series argument that was outlined in the previous chapter. According to Kripke, the "paradox" of ¶201 not only challenges the Platonic conception of truth, logic, and ration-ality, it also leads to a form of radical skepticism in which the relationship between rules and human behavior is generally called into question.

In a recent exchange with David Bloor, Lynch outlines the somewhat salutary consequences of the skepticist position for the project of social scientific explanation:

> Given that mathematics (in this case, elementary arithmetic) is among our most rigorously rule-governed activities, then it appears that Wittgenstein is making a powerful argument for turning to sociology and other empirical sciences to explain order in mathe-matics. What holds for rules can also be said to hold for theories in the natural sciences: they are underdetermined by facts, since no theory can be supported unequivocally by a finite collection of experimental results.[2]

Via the skepticist reading, the transcendental categories of truth, logic, and reason are replaced by the sociological categories of norm, structure, and convention. Formally speaking, however, the structure of logical compulsion remains the same: actions are determined by formal structures that are external to their specific contexts of production, and are thus susceptible to classical forms of causal explanation.

As an alternative, Lynch advances an antiskepticist reading on behalf of an ethnomethodological approach to social studies of scientific knowledge. According to Lynch, the skepticist's crucial error is to confuse Wittgenstein's critique of the *Platonic* conception of rules, in which mathematical formulae are conceived as independent of forms of human conduct, with the assertion that rules are therefore *generally insufficient* with respect to the determinate organization of language and social practice. Against this interpretation, Lynch argues that the demonstration of the practical nature of mathematical reasoning does not, in Wittgenstein's words, "abolish logic," but that it forces us instead to reconsider how we conceptualize "rules," and what we mean by "logical compulsion." The fact that practices can be shown to be *causally underdetermined* by rule formulations does not mean that rules have no special relation to actual courses of human conduct. The error is to conceive "rules" and "rule-following" too narrowly, and to insist that rules must either have a uniform, causal relation to human conduct, or they must be radically indeterminate, and are therefore related to practices only as post hoc formulations and/or rationalizations of conduct. On the antiskepticist reading, rules are neither abstract structures that lie behind and determine human conduct, nor are they logically weak formulations that stand in need of social structural supplement. Rather, rules (and their cognates: principles, maxims, orders, etc.) have "force" as matters of deployable structure within definite orders of social practice. When we "teach," when we "inform," when we "describe," "direct," "criticize," and so forth, we make recourse— at specific points and for a variety of specific purposes—to a vocabulary of rules. Rules gain their sense from within these praxiologically "thick" textures of human conduct, and are, in turn, understood in relation to those activities which they, in no small part, work to organize and describe. From this perspective, the theoretical puzzles associated with "radical indeterminacy" arise less out of concrete relations between rules and practical action than from the historically specific demands of producing general theories of human behavior grounded in a vocabulary of rules.

As soon as we begin to approach rules not as "superconcepts," but as ordinary conceptual objects having appropriate occasions of use, we immediately run up against certain basic assumptions of the social sciences, since the abandonment of the search for rules as standards of explanation of social order signals the abandonment of sociology's foundational project. The arguments that have been made concerning the link between the fetishization of the concept of "rules" as an explanatory construct and the foundationalist aspirations of the social sciences are meant to have consequences on two main fronts.

The first and perhaps broader target is that of contemporary critical theory. Here Habermas's attempt at linking a theory of democratic will-formation to a pragmatic theory of meaning provided a kind of "test case" for examining the more general question of whether empirical investigations of natural language use can provide a basis for a communicative ethics that is, in some sense, derivative of the performative logic of language.

Initially I criticized Habermas not for trying to forge such a connection, but for pinning his hopes on a rather weak and indefensible version of formal pragmatics. In chapters 2 and 3, I argued that Sacks's observations on the sequential organization of indexical expressions seriously undermined the core logical assumptions of the pragmatic theory of meaning based in the theory of speech acts. While this is certainly not the first place that "the doctrine of literal expression" has come under attack, it is consequential for my later argument that these criticisms issue from within the body of lectures that served as precursors for what would later become the science of conversation analysis.

By the end of chapter 3, the possibility of forging a link between a theory of the normative preconditions for open, rational discourse, and an empirical science aimed at recovering the procedural rationality of everyday conversation, comes into full view. And indeed, it is part of the argument of chapter 4 that this possibility is in the process of being realized from both sides: not only does Habermas need to identify an empirical-analytic complement for his formal pragmatic theory of meaning, the discipline of conversation analysis, for its part, has shown increasing interest in identifying sequential structures that are basic to the overall organization of talk and social interaction. In short, there is an "elective affinity" between these two enterprises around the possibility of producing a foundational account of the procedural rationality of everyday conversation.

If the guiding thread of this study has been the critique of the appropriation of the vocabulary of rules as a privileged theoretical construct for explaining social order, then the guiding irony is that the discipline of conversation analysis, which, in its formative stages was closely linked to the ethnomethodological critique of social scientific foundationalism, should end up on course for a rendevous with classical social theory.

Throughout these discussions I have tried to clarify the terms of an emergent complicity between Habermas's theory of communicative action and the empirical and scientistic aspirations of what I have termed "the organization of talk." I have sought to provide the rudiments of a genealogy of the forms of scientific inquiry, analysis, and demonstration that are, in many ways, unique to the discipline of conversation analysis, in order to trace the procedures by which instances of everyday practice get assimilated to talk's foundational structure.[3] The next step is to recast this critique of the foundationalist tendencies of contemporary conversation analysis in terms of a program of analysis that retains Sacks's fundamental interest in questions of logic and social order while avoiding the drift into the waters of normal social science.[4]

Notes

INTRODUCTION

1. Jürgen Habermas, *The Theory of Communicative Action, Vol. I: Reason and Rationalization of Society*, Thomas McCarthy (trans.) (Boston: Beacon Press, 1984); Jürgen Habermas, *The Theory of Communicative Action, Vol. II: Lifeworld and System*, Thomas McCarthy (trans.) (Boston: Beacon Press, 1987).

2. Seyla Benhabib and Fred Dallmayr (eds.), *The Communicative Ethics Controversy*, (Cambridge, Massachusetts: MIT Press, 1990).

3. For a superb discussion of this polarization in late-twentieth-century social theory see Lawrence Hazelrigg, "Is There a Choice Between 'Constructionism' and 'Positivism'?," *Social Problems*, 33 (1986):1–13.

4. Jürgen Habermas, *The Philosophical Discourse of Modernity*, Frederick G. Lawrence (trans.) (Cambridge, Massachusetts: MIT Press, 1987).

5. Ludwig Wittgenstein, *Philosophical Investigations*, Third Edition, G.E.M. Anscombe (trans.) (New York, New York: Macmillan Publishing Co., Inc., 1958), ¶200.

6. Harold Garfinkel, *Studies in Ethnomethodology* (Englewood Cliffs, New Jersey: Prentice-Hall, 1967), p. 33.

7. Jeff Coulter, *Mind in Action* (Oxford, England: Polity Press, 1989); Michael Lynch, *Scientific Practice and Ordinary Action: Ethnomethodology and Social Studies of Science* (Cambridge, England: Cambridge University Press, 1993); Graham Button, Jeff Coulter, John R. E. Lee, and Wes Sharrock, *Computers, Minds, and Conduct* (Oxford, England: Polity Press, 1995).

8. See Jürgen Habermas, *On the Logic of the Social Sciences*, S. Nicholsen and J. Stark (trans.) (Cambridge, Massachusetts: MIT Press, 1988), pp. 117–144; Habermas, *The Theory of Communicative Action, Vol. I*, op. cit., pp. 115–116; and Habermas, *The Theory of Communicative Action, Vol. II: Lifeworld and System*, op. cit., pp. 15–22.

9. See Habermas, *On the Logic of the Social Sciences*, op. cit., pp. 98–100.

10. This "openness" of the theory of communicative action to the practical-historical contingencies of reason is apparent, for instance, in Habermas's rejection of the search for "ultimate justifications" that characterizes the work of his close colleague Karl-Otto Apel. On this issue, see Jürgen Habermas, "Discourse Ethics: Notes on a Program of Philosophical Justification," pp. 43–115 in Jürgen Habermas, *Moral Consciousness and Communicative Action*, Christian Lenhardt and Shierry Weber Nicholsen (trans.) (Cambridge, Massachusetts: MIT Press, 1990), esp. pp. 82 ff. For a discussion of the neo–Kantian elements latent in Habermas's concept of "discursive justification" see Thomas McCarthy, "Practical Discourse: On The Relation of Morality to Politics," pp. 51–72 in *Habermas and the Public Sphere*, Craig Calhoun (ed.) (Cambridge, Massachusetts: MIT Press, 1992).

11. Habermas, *The Theory of Communicative Action, Vol. I*, op. cit., pp. 102–141; and Habermas, *On the Logic of the Social Sciences*, op. cit., pp. 89–189.

12. Garfinkel, *Studies in Ethnomethodology*, op. cit.; Harold Garfinkel and Harvey Sacks, "On Formal Structures of Practical Action," pp. 338–366 in J. C. McKinney and E. A. Tiryakian (eds.), *Theoretical Sociology: Perspectives and Developments* (New York, New York: Appleton-Century-Crofts, 1970).

13. See Hannah Fenichel Pitkin, *Wittgenstein and Justice* (Berkeley, California: University of California Press, 1972); James C. Edwards, *Ethics Without Philosophy: Wittgenstein and the Moral Life* (Tampa: University Presses of Florida, 1982); Paul Johnston, *Wittgenstein and Moral Philosophy* (London, England: Routledge, 1989).

14. Most seminally, in the notion of the "Lebenswelt pair" described by Livingston, and Livingston and Garfinkel, in their studies of the work of mathematical proofs. See Eric Livingston, *The Ethnomethodological Foundations of Mathematics* (London: Routledge and Kegan Paul, 1986) and Eric Livingston and Harold Garfinkel, "Notation and the Work of Mathematical Discovery," unpublished paper, Department of Sociology, UCLA, 1983.

15. Peter Winch, *The Idea of a Social Science and Its Relation to Philosophy*, 2nd ed. (Atlantic Highlands, New Jersey: Humanities Press International, 1990).

16. Max Weber, *Economy and Society: An Outline of Interpretive Sociology, Vol. 1*, Guenther Roth and Claus Wittich (eds.) (Berkeley, California: University of California Press, 1978), p. 4.

17. Ibid., pp. 24–25.

18. Winch, *The Idea of a Social Science and its Relation to Philosophy*, op. cit., p. 44.

19. Wittgenstein, *Philosophical Investigations*, op. cit., ¶241.

20. Winch, *The Idea of a Social Science and Iits Relation to Philosophy*, p. 52.

21. Hunter extends this argument on behalf of what he terms the "self-sufficiency of language" to purposes-at-hand; that is, that it is important to notice that most of the time our words, and, by implication, our actions, are simply done and understood for what they are, without recourse to any supplemental "interpretation" or "translation." See J. F. M. Hunter, "'Forms of Life' in Wittgenstein's *Philosophical Investigations*," *American Philosophical Quarterly*, 5 (1968):233–243.

22. Winch, *The Idea of a Social Science and Its Relation to Philosophy*, op. cit., p. xiii.

23. Ibid., pp. xiii–xiv.

24. We also distinguish between "following the rules," in the sense of using certain rules as a consultative basis for acting, and "following the rules," in the sense that one is not being overtly disobedient. So, for instance, we might say of a small child, that he "followed the rules all day," but we do not thereby mean "whenever he acted, he did so through the application of the relevant rule."

25. Gordon Baker, "Following Wittgenstein: Some Signposts for *Philosophical Investigations*," ¶¶143–242, pp. 31–71 in Steven Holtzman and Christopher Leach (eds.), *Wittgenstein: To Follow a Rule* (London, England: Routledge & Kegan Paul, 1981), p. 47.

26. John R. Searle, *Speech Acts: An Essay in the Philosophy of Language* (Cambridge, England: Cambridge University Press, 1969); Kent Bach and Robert M. Harnish, *Linguistic Communication and Speech Acts* (Cambridge, Massachusetts: MIT Press, 1982).

27. Winch, *The Idea of a Social Science and Its Relation to Philosophy*, op. cit., p. xv.

28. Habermas, *On the Logic of the Social Sciences*, op. cit., pp. 148–149.

29. Ibid., p. 149.

30. Ibid., p. 146.

31. Winch, *The Idea of a Social Science and Its Relation to Philosophy*, op. cit., p. 100. See also, Peter Winch, "Understanding a primitive society," *American Philosophical Quarterly*, 1 (1964):307–324.

32. Baker, "Following Wittgenstein," op. cit., p. 43.

33. Winch, *The Idea of a Social Science*, op. cit., p. xvi.

34. Ibid., p. 100.

35. Ibid., p. xvi.

36. In "Understanding a Primitive Society," Winch, op. cit., asserts that to say of a society that it has a language means also that it has a concept of rationality, only that the concept it has may be vastly different from our own.

37. Habermas, *The Theory of Communicative Action, Vol.* I, op. cit., p. 331.

38. Ibid., pp. 124–125.

39. Richard Rorty, "Habermas and Lyotard on postmodernity," pp. 161–175 in R.J. Bernstein (ed.), *Habermas and Modernity* (Cambridge, Massachusetts: MIT Press, 1985).

1. THE "BINDING FORCE" OF EVERYDAY SPEECH

1. Jürgen Habermas, *The Theory of Communicative Action, Vol. I: Reason and Rationalization of Society*, trans. Thomas McCarthy (Boston: Beacon Press, 1984), p. 10.

2. Jürgen Habermas, "Does Philosophy Still Have a Purpose?," pp. 1–19 in *Philosophical-Political Profiles*, Frederick G. Lawrence (trans.) (Cambridge, Massachusetts: MIT Press, 1983), p. 16.

3. "Does Philosophy Still Have a Purpose?," op. cit., p. 14. See also Jürgen Habermas, "Dogmatism, Reason, and Decision: On Theory and Praxis in Our Scientific Civilization," pp. 253–282 in *Theory and Practice*, John Viertel (trans.) (Boston: Beacon Press, 1973).

4. Habermas, *The Theory of Communicative Action, Vol..* I, op. cit., pp. 377–378.

5. "Does Philosophy Still Have a Purpose?," op. cit., p. 14.

6. Habermas, "Law and Morality," in *The Tanner Lectures on Human Values, VIII*, Kenneth Baynes (trans.) (Salt Lake City: University of Utah Press, 1988). These lectures provide a more detailed discussion of themes first elaborated in *The Theory of Communicative Action, Vol. I*, op. cit., chapter II, section 4, pp. 243–271, "The rationalization of law: Weber's diagnosis of the times."

7. *Tanner Lectures*, p. 219.

8. This is an extremely abbreviated account of the argument of pp. 223–230. A more extended treatment of these issues can be found in Habermas, *The Theory of Communicative Action, Vol..* I, op. cit., pp. 243–271.

9. *Tanner Lectures*, p. 227.

10. *Tanner Lectures*, p. 227.

11. *Tanner Lectures*, p. 229.

12. *Tanner Lectures*, p. 230.

13. See Habermas, *The Theory of Communicative Action, Vol. II*, pp. 301 ff.

14. Richard Gunn, "Rethinking Organization," in Richard Gunn and Gordon Brewer, *The Politics of Organization* (Edinburgh, Scotland: First of May Publications, 1980), p. 19.

15. See Harold Garfinkel, *Perception of the Other*, Unpublished Ph.D. Thesis. (Cambridge, Massachusetts: Harvard University, 1952) and "The Rational Properties of Scientific and Commonsense Activities," pp. 262–283 in *Studies in Ethnomethodology* (Englewood Cliffs, New Jersey: Prentice-Hall, 1967). See also Harold Garfinkel, "Respecification: Evidence for Locally Produced, Naturally Accountable Phenomena of Order, Logic, Reason, Meaning, Method, Etc. in and as of the Essential Haecceity of Immortal Ordinary Society (I)—An Announcement of Studies," pp. 10–19 in G. Button (ed.), *Ethnomethodology and the Human Sciences* (Cambridge, UK: Cambridge University Press).

16. A number of these studies are collected in three Volumes that appeared in the early 1970s: Jack Douglas (ed.), *Understanding Everyday Life: Toward the Reconstruction of Sociological Knowledge* (Chicago: Aldine, 1970); David Sudnow (ed.), Studies in Social Interaction (New York: Free Press, 1972); and Roy Turner (ed.), *Ethnomethodology* (Harmondsworth: Penguin, 1974). A more recent collection of "ethnomethodological classics" edited by Jeff Coulter includes papers by Garfinkel, Sacks, and others that originally appeared in journals or in other, nonethnomethodological collections, as well as reprints from these three volumes. See Jeff Coulter (ed.), *Ethnomethodological Sociology* (Vermont: Edward Elgar Publishing, 1990).

17. This theme is explicit in Sacks's early essay on "sociological description." See Harvey Sacks, "Sociological Description," *Berkeley Journal of Sociology*, 8 (1963):1–16.

18. Wes Sharrock and Bob Anderson, "Epistemology: Professional Skepticism," pp. 51–76 in Graham Button (ed.), *Ethnomethodology and the Human Sciences* (Cambridge, UK: Cambridge University Press, 1991). These experiments closely parallel arguments later developed by Dreyfus concerning the conceptual limitations of cybernetic models of human cognition. See Hubert Dreyfus, *What Computers Can't Do: The Limits of Artificial Reason*, rev. ed. (New York: Harper and Row, 1979) [Reprinted as *What Computers Still Can't Do: A Critique of Artificial Reason* (Cambridge, Massachusetts: MIT Press, 1992)]. On the relationship between the ethnomethodological and the Dreyfusarian perspectives, see Lucy Suchman, *Plans and Situated Actions: The Problem of Human/Machine Communication* (Cambridge, England: Cambridge University Press, 1987).

19. Sharrock and Anderson, op. cit., p. 61.

20. In the interest of clarity, I have chosen to refer to these orders of inquiry as "empirically guided" rather than as simply "empirical." This rather cumbersome language is occasioned by the fact that these inquiries, while plainly based in rigorous observational studies of real-worldly events, so clearly fail to conform to the central tenets and textual conventions of

what has come to be treated as "empirical" within the mainstream of American social science. In the present context, "empirically guided studies" designates a way of working that stands in marked contrast to these prevailing traditions, while sacrificing *nothing* of what empirical studies are or ever could have been in terms of their analytic rigor or scientificity.

21. This, I take it, is what Rorty means when he characterizes Habermas's pursuit of normative grounding as "scratching where it does not itch." See Richard Rorty, "Habermas and Lyotard on postmodernity," pp. 161–175 in Richard J. Bernstein (ed.), *Habermas and Modernity* (Cambridge, Massachusetts: MIT Press, 1985), p. 164.

22. Garfinkel first opened up this line of investigation in his study of jurors' situated methods of reasoning reported in Harold Garfinkel, "Some Rules of Correct Decision Making That Jurors Respect," chapter 4 in *Studies in Ethnomethodology*, op. cit., pp. 104–115.

23. Michael Lynch and David Bogen, *The Spectacle of History: Speech, Text, and Memory at the Iran-Contra Hearings* (Durham, North Carolina: Duke University Press, 1996).

24. This overview draws on two closely related discussions, the first of which appeared as "On the Problem of Understanding Meaning in the Empirical-Analytic Sciences of Action," in Habermas, *On the Logic of the Social Sciences*, op. cit., pp. 89–170. These remarks adumbrate Habermas's later discussion in the *Theory of Communicative Action* (Habermas, "The Problem of Understanding Meaning in the Social Sciences," *The Theory of Communicative Action, Vol. I*, op. cit., pp. 102–141).

25. Habermas, *The Theory of Communicative Action, Vol. I*, op. cit., p. 106.

26. Habermas, *On the Logic of the Social Sciences*, op. cit., p. 95.

27. Hans-Georg Gadamer, *Truth and Method* (New York: Seabury Press, 1975).

28. See Karl-Otto Apel, *Toward a Transformation of Philosophy*, Glyn Adey and David Frisby (trans.) (London: Routledge and Kegan Paul, 1980), p. 2.

29. Habermas, *On the Logic of the Social Sciences*, op. cit., p. 144.

30. Habermas, *The Theory of Communicative Action, Vol. I*, op. cit., pp. 107–110.

31. Anthony Giddens, *New Rules of Sociological Method: A Positive Critique of Interpretive Sociologies* (London: Hutchinson, 1976).

32. Habermas, *The Theory of Communicative Action, Vol. I*, op. cit., p. 110.

33. Note, however, that this discussion is predicated on our willingness to accept a crisp distinction between the human and the natural sciences, a distinction that presumably is warranted by the fact that the materials on

which the social sciences are based—for example, situated actions and cultural artifacts—come preinterpreted and embedded within some local field of action, while the empirical substrate of the natural sciences does not. While this strategy may work to defend the human sciences against the naive empiricism of positivist sociology, the distinction between the natural and the hermeneutic sciences has been roundly attacked as a philosophical idealization and a relic by post-Kuhnian philosophers and sociologists of science. See, for instance, Ian Hacking, *Representing and Intervening* (Cambridge, England: Cambridge University Press, 1983) and Michael Lynch, *Scientific Practice and Ordinary Action: Ethnomethodology and Social Studies of Science* (Cambridge, England: Cambridge University Press, 1993). See also Mary Hesse, "Science and Objectivity," pp. 98–115 in J. B. Thompson and D. Held (eds.), *Habermas: Critical Debates* (Cambridge, Massachusetts: MIT Press, 1982) for a critique of the particular use to which Habermas puts this distinction.

34. Ibid., p. 112.

35, Ibid., p. 137.

36. See Peter Winch, *The Idea of a Social Science* (London: Routledge & Kegan Paul, 1958), and "Understanding a Primitive Society," *American Philosophical Quarterly*, 1(1964):307–324.

37. Ethnomethodologists are keen to point out that "ordinary" social actors take a presumptive interest in the ongoing workings of society, even though the view obtained may be radically different from what prevails in professional sociology. Ethnomethodology thus directs our attention toward methods of sociological inquiry wherever they are encountered, irrespective of the professional sociological credentials of their users. It is this agnosticism with respect to professional sociology's epistemological status that lies behind the policy of ethnomethodological indifference: ethnomethodological studies are carried out in pointed disregard for professional sociology's claimed monopoly on methods of sociological inquiry because these methods—*broadly* understood—constitute the topic(s) of investigation.

38. W. W. Sharrock and R. J. Anderson, "On the Demise of the Native: Some Observations on and a Proposal for Ethnography, *Human Studies*, 1982, 5:119–135. See also the related discussion in W. W. Sharrock and R. J. Anderson, "Criticizing Forms of Life," *Philosophy*, 1985, 60:394–400.

39. Ibid., p. 122.

40. The "incommensurability thesis" is generally associated with Winch's arguments in *The Idea of a Social Science*, op. cit., and "Understanding a Primitive Society," *American Philosophical Quarterly*, op. cit. Sharrock and Anderson argue, however, that the formulation that ties the issue of "incommensurability" to a reification of "culture" misconstrues Winch's original position, which is directed more against the use within social anthropology of

correspondence theories of truth as standards of cultural comparison. Whether this is so or not, Winch certainly has expended a good deal of effort trying to extricate himself from the implications of this thesis. See, for instance, the exchange between Winch and Jarvie in I. C. Jarvie, "Understanding and Explanation in Sociology and Social Anthropology," pp. 231–248 in Robert Borger and Frank Cioffi (eds.), *Explanation in the Behavioral Sciences* (Cambridge, England: Cambridge University Press, 1970), and Peter Winch, "Comment," pp. 249–259 in Robert Borger and Frank Cioffi (eds.), *Explanation in the Behavioral Sciences* (Cambridge, England: Cambridge University Press, 1970).

41. Sharrock and Anderson, "On the Demise of the Native," op. cit., p. 124.

42. Gilbert Ryle, "The World of Science and the Everyday World," pp. 68–81 in *Dilemmas* (Cambridge, England: Cambridge University Press, 1954).

43. Ibid., p. 75.

44. Ibid., p. 76.

45. Ibid., p. 77.

46. Sharrock and Anderson, "On the Demise of the Native," op. cit., p. 124.

47. Dusan Bjelic, "'Frenching' The 'Real' and Praxiological Therapy: An Ethnomethodological Clarification of the New French Theory of Media," pp. 231–257 in Paul Jalbert (ed.), *Media Studies: Ethnomethodological Approaches* (Washington, D.C.: University Press of America, 1999).

48. Ibid., p. 242.

49. Ibid., p. 242.

50. Ibid., p. 242.

51. Of particular importance in this regard are Pollner's studies of "mundane reasoning." See Melvin Pollner, *Mundane Reason: Reality in Everyday and Sociological Discourse* (Cambridge, England: Cambridge University Press, 1987) and Melvin Pollner, "Explicative transactions: Making and Managing Meaning in Traffic Court," pp. 227–255 in G. Psathas (ed.), *Everyday Language* (New York: Irvington Press, 1979).

52. For example, Habermas conceives indexical expressions as "sentences in which terms such as 'I' and 'you,' 'here' and 'now,' 'this' and 'that' appear . . ."; that is, as a narrow subset of logically incomplete lexical items (Habermas, *The Theory of Communicative Action, Vol. I*, op. cit., p. 124). Ethnomethodologists, by contrast, have sought to exploit the indexical properties of speech for what they tell us about how settings are composed, oriented to, and understood by social actors. By opting for a narrow conception of indexicality, in line with the prevailing canon of formal linguistics, Habermas is able to retain the idealization of decontextualized, literal

sentence meaning, but at the price of being unable to thematize the indexical properties of speech as a topic of socio-logical analysis. I shall return to this argument in much greater detail in chapter 3.

2. FORMAL PRAGMATICS AND THE LOGIC OF CONVERSATION

1. Jürgen Habermas, "Toward a Critique of the Theory of Meaning ," pp. 57–87 in Jürgen Habermas, *Postmetaphysical Thinking: Philosophical Essays*, William Mark Hohengarten (trans.) (Cambridge, Massachusetts: MIT Press, 1992), p. 79.

2. Garfinkel and Sacks, "On Formal Structures of Practical Action," op. cit.

3. Harvey Sacks, *Lectures on Conversation, Vols. I and II*, Gail Jefferson (ed.) (Oxford, England: Blackwell Publishers, 1992).

4. For an analysis that explores the sequential operation of Habermasian validity claims see Lynch and Bogen, *The Spectacle of History*, op. cit., chapter 4: "The Truth- Finding engine," pp. 122–153.

5. Habermas, *The Theory of Communicative Action, Vol. I*, op. cit., Chapter III: "Intermediate Reflections: Social Action, Purposive Activity, and Communication," pp. 273–337. See also Jürgen Habermas, "What Is Universal Pragmatics," pp. 1–68 in Jürgen Habermas, *Communication and the Evolution of Society*, Thomas McCarthy (trans.) (Boston, Massachusetts: Beacon Press, 1979).

6. Habermas, *The Theory of Communicative Action, Vol. I*, op. cit., pp. 328–331.

7. For a critique of this formalist approach to the analysis of speech acts see G. P. Baker and P. M. S. Hacker, *Language, Sense & Nonsense* (Oxford, England: Basil Blackwell, 1984), chapter 3: "Sense and Force: The Pathology of the Species," pp. 80–120.

8. Habermas, *The Theory of Communicative Action, Vol. I*, op. cit., pp. 331–332.

9. See Jürgen Habermas, "Moral Development and Ego Identity," pp. 69–94 in Habermas, *Communication and the Evolution of Society*, op. cit.

10. Habermas, *The Theory of Communicative Action, Vol. I*, op. cit., p. 10.

11. Ibid., p. 297.

12. Ibid.

13. Habermas, *Communication and the Evolution of Society*, op. cit. p. 41.

14. Habermas, *The Theory of Communicative Action, Vol. I*, op. cit., p. 329.

15. Ibid., pp. 335–336.
16. Garfinkel and Sacks, "On Formal Structures of Practical Action," op. cit.
17. Coulter, "Logic: Ethnomethodology and the Logic of Language," op. cit., pp. 34–35.
18. Ibid., p. 35.
19. Harvey Sacks, Emanuel Schegloff, and Gail Jefferson, "A Simplest Systematics for the Organization of Turn-Taking for Conversation," pp. 7–55 in Jim Schenkein (ed.), *Studies in the Organization of Conversational Interaction* (New York, New York: Academic Press, 1978), p. 45.
20. Ibid.
21. Jeff Coulter, "Logic: ethnomethodology and the logic of language," pp. 20–50 in Graham Button (ed.), *Ethnomethodology and the Human Sciences* (Cambridge, England: Cambridge University Press, 1991), p. 39.
22. Ibid., p. 35.
23. Habermas, *The Theory of Communicative Action, Vol. I*, op. cit., p. 331.
24. Ibid., p. 337.
25. Ibid., p. 297.
26. Ibid., pp. 325–327.
27. Ibid., p. 362.
28. Jeff Coulter, "Contingent and *A Priori* Structures in Sequential Analysis," *Human Studies*, 6 (1983):4:361–376.
29. Ibid., p. 367.
30. Coulter, "Contingent and *a Priori* Structures in Sequential Analysis," op. cit., p. 365.
31. Ibid., p. 366.
32. Habermas, *The Theory of Communicative Action, Vol. I*, op. cit., p. 331.
33. Ibid., pp. 322–323.
34. Emanuel Schegloff, "Between Macro and Micro: Contexts and Other Connections," pp. 207–234 in J. C. Alexander, B. Giesen, R. Münch and N. J. Smelser (eds.), *The Micro–Macro Link* (Berkeley: University of California Press, 1987), pp. 218–219.
35. Habermas, *The Theory of Communicative Action, Vol. I*, op. cit., p. 106.
36. I mean to distinguish this from the Schutzian notion of "background knowledge" in which cultural and linguistic expectations are conceived as matters of more-or-less stored cognition. The difference between this and a practice-based account of "relevant background" is made clear by Garfinkel in the following passage:

There is a feature of members' accounts that for them is of such singular and prevailing relevance that it controls other features in their specific character as recognizable, rational features of practical sociological inquiries. The feature is this. With respect to the problematic character of practical actions and to the practical adequacy of their inquiries, members take for granted that a member must at the outset "know" the settings in which he is to operate if his practices are to serve as measures to bring particular, located features of these settings to recognizable account. They treat as the most passing matter of fact that members' accounts, of every sort, in their logical modes, with all of their uses, and for every method for their assembly are constituent features of the settings they make observable. Members know, require, count on, and make use of this reflexivity to produce, accomplish, recognize, or demonstrate rational-adequacy-for-all-practical-purposes of their procedures and findings. (Garfinkel, *Studies in Ethnomethodology*, op. cit., p. 8).

37. Jürgen Habermas, "Interpretive Social Science vs. Hermeneuticism," pp. 251–269 in N. Hahn and R. N. Bellah (eds.), *Social Science as Moral Inquiry* (New York, New York: Columbia University Press, 1983), p. 258.

38. Habermas, *The Theory of Communicative Action, Vol. I*, op. cit., p. 10.

39. Seyla Benhabib, "Afterword: Communicative Ethics and Current Controversies in Practical Philosophy," pp. 330–369 in Seyla Benhabib and Fred Dallmayr (eds.), *The Communicative Ethics Controversy* (Cambridge, Massachusetts: MIT Press, 1990), p. 340.

40. Ludwig Wittgenstein, *Philosophical Investigations*, 3rd ed., G. E. M. Anscombe (trans.) (New York: Macmillan Publishing Co., 1958), ¶241.

41. Ibid., ¶124.

42. Benhabib, "Afterword: Communicative Ethics and Current Controversies in Practical Philosophy," op. cit., p. 337.

43. Habermas, *Communication and the Evolution of Society*, op. cit., pp. 31–32.

44. Habermas, *The Theory of Communicative Action, Vol. I*, op. cit., p. 337.

3. THE DOCTRINE OF LITERAL EXPRESSION AND THE THEORY OF SPEECH ACTS

1. Jürgen Habermas, *Communication and the Evolution of Society*, Thomas McCarthy (trans.) (Boston, Massachusetts: Beacon Press, 1979), p. 17.

2. John R. Searle, *Speech Acts: An Essay in the Philosophy of Language* (Cambridge, England: Cambridge University Press, 1969).

3. The relevant discussions can be found in Habermas, *Communication and the Evolution of Society*, op. cit., pp. 1–68 and Jürgen Habermas, *The Theory of Communicative Action, Vol. I: Reason and Rationalization of Society*, Thomas McCarthy (trans.) (Boston: Beacon Press, 1984), pp. 320–337.

4. Searle, *Speech Acts: An Essay in the Philosophy of Language*, op. cit., p. 4.

5. J. L. Austin, *How to Do Things with Words* (Cambridge, Massachusetts: Harvard University Press, 1962).

6. In an effort to refine Austin's formulations, Searle adopts the language of necessary and sufficient conditions and the criteria of the "distinctness" and "disjunctiveness" of analytical categories as a priori constraints on the theory of speech acts. For similar reasons, he rejects what he terms "the jargon of 'family resemblance'" (Searle, *Speech Acts: An Essay in the Philosophy of Language*, op. cit., p. 55). Elsewhere, he makes explicit his claim to be writing that theory of language which "Austin did not live long enough to develop himself" (John R. Searle, "Reiterating the differences," *Glyph*, 1(1977):198–208).

Habermas is likewise committed to the idea that the inability to provide for formally discrete categories of speech activity represents a major shortcoming in Austin (Habermas, *The Theory of Communicative Action, Vol. I*, op. cit., p. 319*ff.*). For both Searle and Habermas, the obvious way to improve on Austin is to bring his intuitive and "loose" categories of speech activity into line with a regimentarian conception of the logic of language.

7. Habermas correctly points to speech act theory as a pivotal move against the "long dominant view that sentences get *literal meaning* only by virtue of the rules for using the expressions contained in them" (Habermas, *The Theory of Communicative Action, Vol. I*, op. cit., p. 335). However, he immediately pulls back from the consequences of a radically contextualized account of speech:

> For each type of speech act there are *general* contextual conditions that must be met if the speaker is to be able to achieve illocutionary success. But these general contextual conditions could supposedly be derived in turn from the literal meaning of the linguistic expressions employed in the standard speech acts. (Ibid., pp. 335–336)

Instead of allowing that "contextual conditions" are themselves the contingent products of speech and social activity, Habermas allows only that the problematic idealization of "syntactic and semantic indicators" needs to be replaced by the (no less problematic) idealization of "*general* contextual conditions . . . derived . . . from the literal meaning of linguistic expressions employed in the standard speech acts." Though he is correct in noting that without this idealization formal pragmatics would lose its object domain, that prospect is not by itself sufficient warrant for presuming the existence of some "context-in-general."

8. In one of his more famous programmatic passages, Wittgenstein writes:

> We must do away with all *explanation*, and description alone must take its place. And this description gets its light, that is to say its purpose, from the philosophical problems. These are, of course, not empirical problems; they are solved, rather, by looking into the workings of our language, and that in such a way as to make us recognize those workings: *in despite* of an urge to misunderstand them. The problems are solved, not by giving new information, but by arranging what we have always known. Philosophy is a battle against the bewitchment of our intelligence by means of language. (Ludwig Wittgenstein, *Philosophical Investigations*, 3rd ed., G. E. M. Anscombe [trans.] [New York, New York: Macmillan Publishing Co., 1958], ¶109.)

For a detailed discussion of the confluence between Wittgenstein's "descriptivist" posture and the ethnomethodological policy of "indifference" see David Bogen and Michael Lynch, "Social Critique and the Logic of Description: A Response to McHoul," *The Journal of Pragmatics*, 14 (1990):131–147.

9. Searle, *Speech Acts: An Essay in the Philosophy of Language*, op. cit., p. 20.

10. Ibid., pp. 20–21.

11. G. P. Baker and P. M. S. Hacker, *Language, Sense & Nonsense* (Oxford, England: Basil Blackwell, 1984), Chapter 3: "Sense and Force: The Pathology of the Species," pp. 80–120.

12. In a footnote to his seventy–two page rant in reply to Searle ("Reiterating the Differences," op. cit.), Derrida makes passing reference to Austin's essay "Three Ways of Spilling Ink":

> In it Austin analyzes the differences between "intentionally," "deliberately," "on purpose (purposely)." I refer to it here in a kind of *oratio obliqua*. After a paragraph explaining why it "would be wholly untrue . . . to suggest that 'unintentionally' is the word that 'wears that trousers,'" Austin underlines the word *limited* in the passage that follows (where "my idea of what I'm doing" is compared to "a miner's lamp on our forehead"): "The only general rule is that the illumination is always *limited*, and that in several

ways. It will never extend indefinitely far ahead . . . Moreover, it does not illuminate *all* of my surroundings. Whatever I am doing is being done and to be done amidst a background of *circumstances* (including of course activities by other agents) . . . Furthermore, the doing of it will involve *incidentally* all kinds of minutiae of, at the least, bodily movements, and often many other things besides." (Jacques Derrida, "Limited inc abc," *Glyph*, 2 [1977]:162–254, p. 253.)

It is, of course, unclear how seriously we ought to treat Derrida's invocation of Austin's authority here, or better, how we ought to treat it seriously—that is, as anything more than a rhetorical snarl at Searle's ("Sarl's") "auto–authorization" as the "legitimate heir" to Austin (Ibid., p. 168*ff*.).

13. Habermas, by contrast, makes an explicit attempt to move beyond this monadic conception of speech activities by identifying the constitutive role that utterance uptake plays in the production and recognition of intelligible speech. The problem for Habermas, then, is to provide for *standardized forms of uptake*, such that the intelligibility of utterances does not hinge entirely on empirically contingent responses. In a footnote to his early study of the logic of speech acts, Habermas writes:

> A communication theory that is supposed to reconstruct conditions of action oriented to reaching understanding requires as its basic unit of analysis, not necessarily pairs of complementary speech actions—that is, reciprocally performed and accepted speech actions—but at least a speaker's utterance that can not only be understood but accepted by at least one additional speaking and acting subject. (Habermas, *Communication and the Evolution of Society*, op. cit., p. 216.)

By reducing "uptake" to the binary logic of yes/no responses to speakers' validity claims, Habermas can allow for the dialogical constitution of speech activities without destabilizing his object domain to such a degree that talk of utterances in "standard form" becomes incoherent. It should be noted, however, that this reduction is inconceivable apart from the stipulation that speech acts in "standard form" invariably operate like claims; that is, as activities that are *generically* constrained by the optionalities of "acceptance" or "rejection." It is somewhat strained, however, to say that when someone asks a "question," that an "answer" represents an "acceptance" of that question. Likewise with the other speech acts, for which there are a variety of discrete response options—"commands," for instance, are not "accepted" or "rejected," but rather, are "obeyed" or "disobeyed"—each of these doing some rather fine work distinguishing the immense variety of activity-types as well as the particular social relations they imply. On this view, the entire language of "validity claims" represents a monumental attempt at repairing the doctrine of literal expression in the face of the consequences of radical indexicality.

14. For a discussion of the implications of the multiplex structure of utterances for linguistically informed theories of speech activity see Emanuel Schegloff, "On Some Questions and Ambiguities in Conversation," pp. 28–52 in J. M. Atkinson and J. Heritage (eds.), *Structures of Social Action* (Cambridge: Cambridge University Press, 1984).

15. Searle, *Speech Acts: An Essay in the Philosophy of Language*, op. cit., p. 20.

16. I do not mean by this that there are *no* distinctions to be had between "saying something" and "meaning it," but rather, that such distinctions, where they occur, are neither idle nor generic. We say things, and *mean* them (or not), relative to issues of clarification, emphasis, justification, explanation, and the like, and this means simply that the difference between "saying" and "meaning" does not admit of generic distinctions—much less a *single* generic distinction—as if it were a logical precondition of each and every speech situation. By supposing, for instance, that in order to (sincerely, nondefectively) say something a speaker must always and already *mean* it, Searle commits himself to a conception of utterance meaning as a matter of subjective intent. On the confusions engendered by this picture, see Stanley Cavell, *Must We Mean What We Say?* (New York: Charles Scribner's Sons, 1969) and Frank B. Ebersole, *Meaning and Saying: Essays in the Philosophy of Language* (Lanham, Maryland: University Press of America, 1979).

17. The language of "remedy" is taken from Garfinkel's and Sacks' formulation of the "infinite task" of practical sociological reasoning:

> Wherever and by whomever practical sociological reasoning is done, it seeks to remedy the indexical properties of practical discourse; it does so in the interests of demonstrating the rational accountability of everyday activities; and it does so in order that its assessments be warranted by methodic observation and report of situated, socially organized particulars of everyday activities, which of course include particulars of natural language.
>
> The remedial practices of practical sociological reasoning are aimed at accomplishing a thoroughgoing distinction between objective and indexical expressions with which to make possible the substitution of objective for indexical expressions. At present that distinction and substitutability provides professional sociology

its infinite task. (Harold Garfinkel and Harvey Sacks, "On Formal Structures of Practical Action," pp. 338–366 in J. C. McKinney and E. A. Tiryakian [eds.], *Theoretical Sociology: Perspectives and Developments* (New York: Appleton-Century-Crofts, 1970), p. 339).

In this light, Searle's insistence on the translatability of indexical expressions into standard and "exact" sentence-types represents a singular move within a species of situated sociological reasoning. This method is no less *practical* simply because it thrives within the self-evidently "technical" discourse of "the philosophy of language."

18. Searle, *Speech Acts: An Essay in the Philosophy of Language*, op. cit., p. 16.

19. Ibid., p. 19.

20. On some distinctions between "saying literally" and "saying in so many words" see Mats Furberg, *Saying and Meaning* (Oxford: Basil Blackwell, 1971).

21. Searle, *Speech Acts: An Essay in the Philosophy of Language*, op. cit., p. 25.

22. Wittgenstein, *Philosophical Investigations*, op. cit., ¶88. At one point in his argument Searle cites this same passage in order to argue, against Goodman, that synonymy is a conceptual relation that appeals to practical (and not philosophical) criteria for its use and ratification (see Searle, *Speech Acts: An Essay in the Philosophy of Language*, op. cit., pp. 9–10). Given this, it is all the more curious that he would claim, some nine pages later, that even where speakers use indexical expressions, they could always, at least in principle, say *exactly* what they mean (Ibid., pp. 19–20).

23. Harvey Sacks, "Fall 1967, Lecture 14: Paraphrasing; Alternative Temporal References; Approximate and Precise Numbers; Laughter; 'Uh huh,'" pp. 739–747 in Harvey Sacks, *Lectures on Conversation, Vol. I*, Gail Jefferson (ed.) (Oxford, England: Blackwell Publishers, 1992).

24. Ibid., p. 740.

25. Ibid., p. 742.

26. Harvey Sacks, "Fall 1967, Lecture 7: Intentional Mis-address; Floor seekers," pp. 675–684 in Harvey Sacks, *Lectures on Conversation, Vol.. I*, op. cit.

27. Ibid., p. 675.

28. Ibid.

29. The classic statement of the rules for speaker selection appears in Harvey Sacks, Emanuel Schegloff, and Gail Jefferson, "A simplest system-

atics for the organization of turn-taking for conversation," *Language*, 50 (1975):696–735.

30. Watson argues that an examination of the interactional uses of pronouns suggests that the very idea that pronouns form a "set" may be formally incoherent:

> We have, for instance, the issue of the third person singular pronouns 'he' and 'she,' which do not just partition by person and number but also by membership categories from the collection . . . 'sex.' There is a strong sense in which these pronouns explicitly map onto a set of descriptions in a way which is not the case for others of the set. Indeed, 'he' and 'she' share these properties with *other* sets, not their 'own.'
>
> . . . Instances of 'interactional' issues in the selection and use of pronouns or other proterms can readily be found, and these issues indicate that pronouns are not all of a piece. As we have just observed, the personal pronoun 'you' may . . . be used interactionally as an address term in, for instance, the process of selecting a next speaker in a conversation, as when the present speaker turns to some other party to the conversation and says 'You agree, don't you?.' However, the personal pronoun 'he' or 'she' is not *routinely* usable in this way; rather, 'she'/'he' are what we call 'designators.' (Rod Watson, "Interdisciplinary considerations in the analysis of pro-terms," pp. 261–289 in G. Button and J. R. E. Lee [eds.], *Talk and Social Organization* [Clevedon, England: Multilingual Matters], pp. 266–267.)

31. Sacks, "Fall 1967, Lecture 7: Intentional Mis-address; Floor Seekers," op. cit., p. 676.

32. Sacks's studies of "membership categorization" provide the most well-known and striking set of counterexamples. See Harvey Sacks, "An initial investigation of the usability of conversational data for doing sociology," pp. 31–74 in David Sudnow (ed.), *Studies in Social Interaction* (New York: Free Press, 1972); Harvey Sacks, "On the Analyzability of Stories by Children," pp. 329–345 in J. J. Gumperz and D. Hymes (eds.), *Directions in Sociolinguistics: The Ethnography of Communication* (New York: Holt, Reinhart and Winston, 1972); Harvey Sacks, "Hotrodder: A Revolutionary Category," pp. 7–14 in G. Psathas (ed.), *Everyday Language* (New York: Irvington Press, 1979); Harvey Sacks and Emanuel Schegloff, "Two Preferences in the Organization of Reference to Persons in Conversation and Their Interaction," pp. 15–21 in G. Psathas (ed.), *Everyday Language* (New York: Irvington Press, 1979).

Sacks's work on the organization of stories told in conversation is equally rich in this regard. Consider, for instance, the following rather unremarkable monologue:

> "Well I got out to my car at five thirty I drove around and at first I had to go by the front of the store, . . . And there was two police cars across the street, and a colored lady wanted to go in the main entrance there where the silver is and all the (gifts and things), and they wouldn't let her go in, and he hadda *gun*. He was holding a *gun* in his hand a great long gun. . . . And then over on the other side, I mean to the *right*, of there, where the employees come out, there was a whole, oh, must have been eight or ten employees standing there, because there must of been a- It seemed like they had every entrance *ba*rred. I don't know what was going on. Some kind of a *ki*ller was in there." (Harvey Sacks, "Winter 1970, Lecture 2: Conveying Information; Story-Connective Techniques; Recognition-Type Descriptors; 'First Verbs'; Understanding; Differential Organization of Perception," pp. 675–684 in Harvey Sacks, *Lectures on Conversation, Vol. II*, Gail Jefferson [ed.] [Oxford, England: Blackwell Publishers, 1992], pp. 178–179.)

Sacks's subsequent analysis of this story focuses upon the ways in which "place-indexical terms" ("the front of the store," "across the street," "the main entrance," and so on) are used to organize the story into a connected series of events. As he continues:

> Consider such a connection as "And over on the other side, I mean to the right of there, where the employees come out . . . there must of been eight or ten employees standing there . . . ," as a kind of a way to connect up the employees with what is going on in a just-that's-the-way-they-are fashion. That is, the way to bring these other people and these other events into the story connectedly is to put them as being "on the other side," as compared to, perhaps, not putting them in the story at all. So the place-indexical terms bind the story together such that whatever takes place in the course of the narrative is taking place in-this-story. Such techniques may not be required, nor may it be required that the technique is used as massively as this one is; but it is nonetheless a non–incidental sort of technique to use. (Ibid., p. 179)

One consequence of this analysis is that references to persons are not only indexically tied to, for example, the narrational cogency of some story-now-underway, but further, that the local intelligibility of references to persons will, at times, hinge on their relevance to some other indexical order; in this case, to an order of place-indexical terms. In Sacks's view, there is neither a *single* method for doing adequate reference, nor a set of generic formulae for determining when adequate reference has been accomplished. Rather, "referring" is itself a radically situated achievement, involving, *inter alia*, sequential techniques for the interarticulation of indexically tied expressions.

33. Sacks, "Fall 1967, Lecture 7: Intentional Mis-address; Floor Seekers," op. cit., p. 677.

34. Ibid.

35. Ibid., p. 678.

36. Ibid.

37. Searle, *Speech Acts: An Essay in the Philosophy of Language*, op. cit., p. 16.

38. Sacks, "Fall 1967, Lecture 14: Paraphrasing; Alternative temporal references; Approximate and Precise Numbers; Laughter; 'Uh Huh,'" op. cit., pp. 739–740.

39. Searle, *Speech Acts: An Essay in the Philosophy of Language*, op. cit., p. 182. The collapse of this distinction and its reconstruction along the lines of a validity based theory of meaning is essential to Habermas's attempt to develop a formal pragmatics with political implications. Hence, the success or failure of Searle's "proof" that descriptive statements entail specific normative commitments is, for Habermas, no idle matter.

40. Ibid., p. 177.

41. Ibid.

42. Ibid., p. 185.

43. Harold Garfinkel, "A Conception of, and Experiments with, "Trust" as a condition of stable concerted actions," pp. 187–238 in O.J. Harvey (ed.), Motivation and Social Interaction (New York: Ronald Press, 1963), p. 195.

44. Ibid.

45. The following account by Oliver Sacks of a conversation with one of his patients, "Dr. P.," makes clear how descriptions within the "empiricist mode" are specifically at odds with the requirements of commonsense understanding:

> "What is this?' I asked, holding up a glove.
>
> "May I examine it?" he asked, and, taking it from me, he proceeded to examine it as he had examined the geometrical shapes.
>
> "A continuous surface," he announced at last, "infolded on itself. It appears to have"—he hesitated—"five outpouchings, if this is the word."
>
> "Yes," I said cautiously. "You have given me a description. Now tell me what it is."

"A container of some sort?"

"Yes," I said, "and what would it contain?"

"It would contain its contents!" said Dr. P., with a laugh. "There are many possibilities. It could be a change purse, for example, for coins of five sizes. It could . . ."

I interrupted the barmy flow. "Does it look familiar? Do you think it might contain, might fit, a part of your body?"

No light of recognition dawned on his face.

(Oliver Sacks, *The Man Who Mistook His Wife for a Hat* [New York: Harper & Row, 1987], p. 14.)

46. The idea of "brute linguistic facts" interlaces with Searle's physicalist conception of linguistic phenomena, which is evidenced in the second sentence of his essay on speech acts: "How is it possible that when a speaker stands before a hearer and emits an acoustic blast . . . the speaker means something; the sounds he emits mean something; the hearer understands what is meant; the speaker makes a statement, asks a question, or gives an order?" (Searle, *Speech Acts: An Essay in the Philosophy of Language*, op. cit., p. 3). By posing the question in this way, Searle implies that there is an essential connection to be made between the "brute (acoustic) facts" of language (the emission of sounds or wave forms) and the realization of intelligible social activities (questions, answers, and the like), and that establishing this connection is the principle task of the philosophy of language. The problem here is that in order to create the gap between "brute (acoustic) facts" and "intelligible social activities"—which provides the necessary theoretical space for the theory of speech acts—Searle must suppress the differences between, for example, "saying something" and "making sounds." We say of babies, for instance, that they are only "making sounds" precisely when they have not yet learned to speak, and though it seems clear that "making sounds" is thus a kind of proto-speech, this does not mean that when we are "speaking" we are all the time also "making sounds" any more than it would be correct to say that when we are walking we are all the time crawling as well. A "sound" might "mean something" if it is the sound of an oncoming train and I am on the tracks, but it is only under rather special circumstances (explaining poetry, for example) that one might say that the "sounds" of language bear meaning. When we ask, 'who (or what) did the caller *sound* like?,' we are asking a question about the *voice* and not the *actions* of the speaker, and most likely after attempts at determining the identity of the caller through other means have failed. These and like conceptual confusions arising out of the physicalists' conflation of vocabularies of behavior with vocabularies of meaning are discussed in Frank Ebersole, *Meaning and Saying: Essays in the Philosophy of Language* (Lanham,

Maryland: University Press of America, 1979), pp. 113–156 and Jeff Coulter, *Rethinking Cognitive Theory* (New York: St. Martin's Press, 1983), pp. 5–42.

47. See Baker and Hacker, *Language, Sense & Nonsense*, op. cit., pp. 106–107 for similar criticisms of the rhetoric of "indirect speech." Clearly any detailed treatment of the relation between 1 and 2—either as a textual artifact or as a legitimate abstract of possible events-in-the-world—would show that it is a far more complicated and variable relation than the characterization "evidence" might suggest.

48. Although Searle spends a good deal of time addressing the various relativist and skepticist objections to his position, he is unable to do so without supposing the "brute facticity" of reports (see Searle, *Speech Acts: An Essay in the Philosophy of Language*, op. cit., pp. 188–198). In contrast to Searle, I mean to contest both the idea that there are such things as decontextualized descriptions of "brute linguistic facts" and the idea that if descriptions are not, at essence, statements of "brute fact" then they must be something like "brute fictions."

49. Anita Pomerantz, "Presenting 'raw data' as a conversational practice," paper presented to the American Sociological Association's annual meetings, 1981.

50. Ibid., pp. 5–6.

51. Notice that this point also connects with the earlier discussion concerning the interactional uses of paraphrase in the following respect: that for C to assert that she was told that Leamington is the second stop it is not necessary that someone actually said, for example, "Leamington is the second stop."

52. Gail Jefferson, "At first I thought . . . ," paper presented to the Conference on Conversation and Discourse Analysis, Temple University, Philadelphia, Pennsylvania, 1985.

53. On the use of meaning-adequate descriptions in the construction of accountably "ordinary" experiences see Harvey Sacks, "On Doing 'Being Ordinary'," pp. 225–246 in J. M. Atkinson and J. C. Heritage (eds.), *Structures of Social Action* (Cambridge, England: Cambridge University Press, 1984).

4. THE ORGANIZATION OF TALK

1. R. J. Anderson and W. W. Sharrock, "Analytic Work: Aspects of the Organisation of Conversational Data," *Journal for the Theory of Social Behavior*, 14 (1984):103–124.

2. Harold Garfinkel, Michael Lynch, and Eric Livingston, "The Work of a Discovering Science Construed with Materials from the Optically

Discovered Pulsar," *Philosophy of the Social Sciences*, 11 (1981):131–158; Michael Lynch, Eric Livingston, and Harold Garfinkel, "Temporal Order in Laboratory Work," in Karin Knorr-Cetina and Michael Mulkay (eds.), *Science Observed: Perspectives on the Social Study of Science* (London and Beverly Hills: Sage, 1985); Michael Lynch, *Art and Artifact in Laboratory Science* (London: Routledge and Kegan Paul); Eric Livingston, *The Ethnomethodological Foundations of Mathematics* (London, England: Routledge & Kegan Paul, 1986); Dusan Bjelic and Michael Lynch, "The Work of a Scientific Demonstration: Respecifying Goethe's and Newton's Theories of Prismatic Color," pp. 52–78 in G. Watson and R. Seiler (eds.), *Text in Context: Contributions to Ethnomethodology* (London and Beverly Hills: Sage, 1992); Dusan Bjelic, "The Praxiological Validity of Natural Scientific Practices as the Criterion for Identifying Their Unique Social-Object Character: The Case of the Authentication of Goethe's Morphological Theorem," *Qualitative Sociology*, 15 (1992):221–245; Michael Lynch, *Scientific Practice and Ordinary Action: Ethnomethodology and Social Studies of Science* (Cambridge, England: Cambridge University Press, 1993).

3. The crucial distinction here is the focus, in the case of the present argument, on the conditions under which such demonstrations are produced as available outcomes of *reading*.

4. Harvey Sacks, "On Doing 'Being Ordinary,'" pp. 413–429 in J. Maxwell Atkinson and John Heritage (eds.), Structures of Social Action (Cambridge, England: Cambridge University Press, 1984), p. 413.

5. Emanuel Schegloff, "From Interview to Confrontation: Observations of the Bush/Rather Encounter," *Research on Language and Social Interaction*, 22 (1989/90):215–240.

6. Stanley Fish, "Anti-foundationalism, Theory Hope, and the Teaching of Composition," in Stanley Fish, *Doing What Comes Naturally* (Durham: Duke University Press, 1989).

7. The classic statement of this discovery appears in Sacks, et al.'s overview of the systematics of turn-taking, where they write, "[i]t appears likely that conversation should be considered the basic form of speech-exchange system, with other systems on the array representing a variety of transformations of conversation's turn–taking system, to achieve other types of turn-taking systems" (Harvey Sacks, Emanuel Schegloff, and Gail Jefferson, "A Simplest Systematics for the Organization of Turn-Taking for Conversation," *Language*, 50 (1974):696–735, p. 730.) Note that it matters little for this argument whether this analytic substrate continues to be called "conversation," or comes to be known by some more technical name (e.g., mundane "talk-in-interaction"). Its functional role as analytic substrate remains the same in either case.

8. Schegloff, "From Interview to Confrontation: Observations of the Bush/Rather Encounter," op. cit., pp. 217–18.

9. In their study of astronomers' work, Garfinkel et al. use the anecdote of "Shils's complaint" as a way of describing what they see as the contemporary situation of inquiry in the social sciences:

> In 1954 Fred Strodtbeck was hired by the University of Chicago Law School to analyze tape recordings of jury deliberations obtained from a bugged jury room. Edward Shils was on the committee that hired him. When Strodtbeck proposed to a law school faculty to administer Bales Interactional Process Analysis categories, Shils complained: "By using Bales Interaction Process Analysis I'm sure we'll learn what about a jury's deliberations makes them a small group. But we want to know what about their deliberations makes them a jury." (Garfinkel, et al., "The work of a discovering science construed with materials from the optically discovered pulsar," op. cit., p. 133.)

They add that sociology has remained unresponsive to Shils's complaint; in their words, that "[t]echnical methods for turning Shils's complaint into an agenda of researchable phenomena are not available in the social sciences" (Ibid., p. 133).

10. Schegloff, "From Interview to Confrontation: Observations of the Bush/Rather Encounter," op. cit., p. 221.

11. Ibid., pp. 219–220.

12. Lave argues that the idea of "just plain folks" is an artifact of those forms of intellectual "colonialism" typical of the human sciences. Her frequent use of the term, she writes, is done in the spirit of a double irony: "on the colonialist's distance and condescension . . . and on the belief of ["just plain folks"] that the rubric is appropriate" (Jean Lave, *Cognition in Practice* (Cambridge, England: Cambridge University Press, 1988), p. 191). Whatever the merits of Lave's initial insight into the use of that concept, it is difficult to see how her usage gets around the apparent puzzles of writing about persons-in-general since, in order to formulate the second irony, she is forced to use "just plain folks" in the ordinary (nonironic) sense that the first irony rejects out of hand. In this regard, Sacks's strategy of respecifying person-categorical terms as members' categories seems to be a far more promising line of analysis.

13. Roland Barthes, "L'Effet de réel," *Communications*, 11 (1980): 84–89. Note that by conceiving the transcript as a genre of realism I am proposing an alternative to skeptically inclined arguments such as Atkinson's (Paul Atkinson, "Ethnomethodology: A Critical Review," *Annual Review of*

Sociology, 14 (1988):441–65), which point out that the transcript is not the event, but is a representation of the event, without being able to clarify how it is that transcript's "documentary method" does its work.

14. Gérard Genette, Narrative Discourse: An Essay in Method, Jane E. Lewin (trans.) (Ithaca, New York: Cornell University Press, 1980), p. 164.

15. Ibid.

16. Ibid., p. 165.

17. Ibid.

18. This point becomes especially clear when using more advanced recording technologies. Such technologies routinely give back so much of what was "there to be seen or heard" that ordinary hearings of an event get lost within an overflow of ambient acoustic detail. This fact provides an endless source of material nuisance for recording engineers whose job it is to recover the essentially unrecoverable detail of "live" events.

19. The notion of "emplotment" is borrowed from the historian, Hayden White. Following Lévi-Strauss, White claims that there is no such thing as a bare historical record or unmotivated collection of facts, but that, on the contrary, the mere assembly of a specific grouping of dates into a working chronology already prefigures the story that will be made of them—in his terms, the "plot structure" of the narrative to be told. The notion of "emplotment" is intended as a contrast to the idea that the collection and assembly of historical data involves a mere "plotting" of dates and events. Instead, each event is *there* just because it is already a part of an emergent narrative that makes its inclusion relevant and necessary. See Hayden White, *Metahistory: The Historical Imagination in Nineteenth Century Europe* (Baltimore: Johns Hopkins University Press, 1973).

20. This point recapitulates Benjamin's famous discussion of the disjuncture between representational art and methods of photography: that photography, and later filmmaking, collapses the "natural distance" between painting and reality, and so dissolves its connection to the traditional demands of representation, placing in their stead a set of techniques for apprehending reality under a "new law" of decomposition, inscription and assembly. (Walter Benjamin, "The Work of Art in the Age of Mechanical Reproduction," pp. 217–251 in Walter Benjamin, *Illuminations*, Hannah Arendt (ed.), H. Zohn (trans.) (New York: Schocken Books, 1969), pp., 232–234.) Likewise, audio- and video-taped recordings do not *describe* lived events, they *record* them. For this reason, the techniques for producing electromagnetic records are responsive to criteria of adequacy that are orthogonal to traditional criteria of descriptive adequacy.

21. Schegloff, "From Interview to Confrontation: Observations of the Bush/Rather Encounter," op. cit., p. 220.

22. Elsewhere Schegloff argues that the ability to deliver on this claim is what distinguishes conversation analysis from "positivistic" social science. See Emanuel Schegloff, "Between Macro and Micro: Contexts and Other Connections," pp. 207–234 in Jeffrey C. Alexander, Bernhard Giesen, Richard Münch and Neil J. Smelser (eds.), *The Micro-Macro Link* (Berkeley, California: University of California Press, 1987), pp. 218–219.

23. Schegloff, "From Interview to Confrontation: Observations of the Bush/Rather Encounter," op. cit., p. 220.

24. Schegloff notes, for instance:

If there is a single, most fundamental component of what is considered an "interview," both in vernacular or common-sense conceptions of that term and in more technical accounts, it is that one party asks questions and the other party gives answers. (Ibid, p. 218).

See also similar statements in Steven E. Clayman, "Displaying Neutrality in Television News Interviews," *Social Problems*, 35 (1988):474–492; Steven E. Clayman and Jack Whalen, "When the Medium Becomes the Message: The Case of the Rather-Bush Encounter," *Research on Language and Social Interaction*, 22 (1989/90):241–272; David Greatbatch, "A Turn-Taking System for British News Interviews," *Language in Society*, 17 (1988): 401–430; John Heritage and David Greatbatch, "On the Institutional Character of Institutional Talk: The Case of News Interviews," pp. 93–137 in Deirdre Boden and Don Zimmerman (eds.), *Talk and Social Structure* (Cambridge, England: Polity Press, 1991).

25. Schegloff, "From Interview to Confrontation: Observations of the Bush/Rather Encounter," op. cit., p. 220.

26. Ibid., p. 221.

27. Ibid., p. 220.

28. Ibid., p. 220–221.

29. Ibid., p. 221–222.

30. Ibid., p. 223.

31. Ibid., p. 222.

32. Ibid., p. 238n.5.

33. This phrase is taken from the title of Glucksmann's review of *Reading Capital*. Glucksmann argues that Althusser "makes Marx speak" by playing two structuralist discourses off each other, even though both voices are those of Louis Althusser. See André Glucksmann, "A Ventriloquist Structuralism," pp. 282–314 in *Western Marxism: A Critical Reader* (London, England: Verso, 1978).

34. Schegloff, "From Interview to Confrontation: Observations of the Bush/Rather Encounter," op. cit., p. 224.

35. Emanuel A. Schegloff, "On Some Questions and Ambiguities in Conversation," pp. 28–52 in J. Maxwell Atkinson and John Heritage (eds.), Structures of Social Action (Cambridge, England: Cambridge University Press, 1984), pp. 29–30.

36. J. F. M. Hunter, "'Forms of Life' in Wittgenstein's *Philosophical Investigations*," *American Philosophical Quarterly*, 5 (1968):233–243, p. 237.

37. This claim is derivative of the argument, outlined in chapter 3, that the data of conversation analysis consists in "parties' understandings of prior turns' talk" (Sacks *et al.*, "A Simplest Systematics for the Organization of Turn-Taking for Conversation," op. cit., p. 729). As Coulter has pointed out, however, there is often an asymmetry between technical and vernacular characterizations of speech activities such that "what for speaker amounts to a 'long-winded digression' may be, for the analyst, a 'delicately organized side-sequence.'" This asymmetry makes the claim to be working with "parties' understandings" untenable. For this reason, Coulter proposes that the subject matter of conversation analysis "consists in conversational objects and their logical relations, rather than in the study of members' understandings.'" Jeff Coulter, "Contingent and *A Priori* Structures in Sequential Analysis," *Human Studies*, 6 (1983):361–376, p. 371.

38. Schegloff, "On Some Questions and Ambiguities in Conversation," op cit., pp. 34–35.

39. Emanuel A. Schegloff and Harvey Sacks, "Opening Up Closings," *Semiotica*, 7 (1973):289–327, pp. 295–296.

40. Schegloff, "From Interview to Confrontation: Observations of the Bush/Rather Encounter," op. cit., p. 223.

41. Ibid., p. 222.

42. Michael Lynch and David Bogen, *The Spectacle of History: Speech, Text, and Memory at the Iran-Contra Hearings* (Durham, North Carolina: Duke University Press, 1996).

43. *Taking the Stand: The Testimony of Lieutenant Colonel Oliver L. North* (New York, New York: Pocket Books, 1987), p. 4.

44. Ibid., pp. 2–3.

45. Ibid., p. 3.

46. This argument also dispenses with the idea that the "directness" of an answer can be given a decontextualized accounting. In their analysis of the Bush/Rather "encounter," Clayman and Whalen claim, for instance, that where, in his first turn, Bush begins addressing the video–clip, he "does not confine himself to simply answering the question," and therefore "has departed from the strict provisions of the interview turn–taking system" (Clayman and Whalen, "When the medium becomes the message: The case of the Rather–Bush encounter," op. cit., p. 250). An alternative would be to see Bush's extended reply as a formulation of Rather's utterance as more

than just a "question," and as a response that targets the rather blatant linkage between Rather's initial utterance and the video-clip that immediately preceded it. Given this agenda, Bush's reply is *extremely* direct, responding first to the very last query in Rather's question, and then moving immediately into the thick of issues raised by the video-clip for just how they bear on the immediate matter-at-hand of what the auspices are (or are to be) of *this* interview.

47. See Lawrence D. Wieder, *Language and Social Reality: The Case of Telling the Convict Code* (The Hague: Mouton, 1974).

48. Melvin Pollner, "Explicative Transactions: Making and Managing Meaning in Traffic Court," pp. 227–255 in George Psathas (ed.), *Everyday Language* (New York, New York: Irvington Press, 1979).

49. Bjelic's analysis of the dialogue between Socrates' and Thrasymachus demonstrates the ancients' recognition and use of turn-taking as just such a "live" rhetorical force. See Dusan Bjelic, *On the Social Origin of Logic*, Unpublished Ph.D. Dissertation, Department of Sociology, Boston University, 1989.

50. Lynch details a family of devices for assenting to the illocutionary force of some prior utterance while at the same time recasting its sense and implications (what—trading off of Wittgenstein's famous discussion of the "duck-rabbit"—he calls the "dawning of an aspect"). Michael Lynch, "Closure and Disclosure in Pre-Trial Argument," *Human Studies*, 5 (1982): 15–33.

51. This is a composite of transcripts taken from Schegloff, "From Interview to Confrontation: Observations of the Bush/Rather Encounter," op. cit., p. 221–222 and Clayman and Whalen, "When the Medium Becomes the Message: The Case of the Rather-Bush Encounter," op. cit., p. 249.

52. This reading is bolstered by Bush's subsequent utterance. There Bush begins by addressing himself to the final clause of Rather's previous utterance. His response treats Rather's utterance as a "question," but as a "question" in need of some monumental unpacking given an objection to its buried presuppositions and its explicit connections to a chain of accusations available from the video–clip that had been run just prior to the onset of questioning. Clayman and Whalen argue that Bush's initial utterance is a sort of "turn-type departure," with rather mild force in terms of the degree to which it stretches, or gives up on the "strict provisions of the interview turn-taking system":

Although Bush engages in a nonanswering type of action, he does this *in conjunction with* answering. This stands as an alternative to doing something *instead of* answering; that is, to reject matters raised by the question in favor of embarking on a wholly indepen-

dent line of talk. . . . By choosing the former course of action, Bush
departs from the question-answer framework only to a degree and
continues to honor its constraints while introducing additional
unsolicited information. (Clayman and Whalen, "When the medium
becomes the message: The case of the Rather-Bush encounter," op.
cit., pp. 250–51)

In characterizing Bush's utterance as a "non-answering type of action"
and as a response that, while honoring the "constraints" of the "question-
answer framework," nevertheless introduces "unsolicited information," the
authors presume that "questions" and "answers" can be given a canonical
specification in line with, for instance, the "solicitation function" of a question and the "direct response function" of an answer. Whether or not Bush's
response provided "unsolicited information" depends on what you figure
Rather's "question" was up to, what kind of response it called for, and
hence, what in fact that question "solicited." Although these are contentious
and delicate matters, they are by no means outside of the limits of producing
appropriate, continuous, and orderly sequences that retrospectively can be
said to have filled out an organization of "questions" and "answers."

5. ORDER WITHOUT RULES

1. Habermas's criticisms of Wittgenstein's notion of "language games"
are discussed at length in the Introduction and chapter 1. His most comprehensive statement on ethnomethodology can be found in Jürgen Habermas,
*The Theory of Communicative Action, Vol. I: Reason and Rationalization of
Society*, Thomas McCarthy (trans.) (Boston: Beacon Press, 1984), pp.
124–141.

2. See Lucy A. Suchman, *Plans and Situated Actions: The Problem of
Human-Machine Communication* (Cambridge, England: Cambridge University Press, 1987). Suchman's study demonstrates ethnographically how the
model of linear production forces a reduction of the temporal relations
involved in the real–worldly execution of plans.

3 Suchman argues that the development of the cognitive scientific
conception of "intelligence" follows a similar course:

A leading idea in cognitive science is that mind is best viewed as
neither substance nor insubstantial, but as an abstractable structure
implementable in any number of possible physical substrates.
Intelligence, on this view, is only incidentally embodied in the
neurophysiology of the human brain. What is essential about
intelligence can be abstracted from that particular, albeit highly
successful substrate and embodied in an unknown range of alter-

native forms. The commitment to an abstract, disembodied account of cognition, on the one hand, and to an account of cognition that can be physically embodied in a computer, on the other, has led to a view of intelligence that takes it to be first and foremost mental operations and only secondarily, and as an epiphenomenon, the "execution" of situated actions. (Lucy A. Suchman, "Representing practice in cognitive science," pp. 301–321 in Michael Lynch and Steve Woolgar [eds.], *Representation in Scientific Practice* [Cambridge, Massachusetts: MIT Press, 1990], p. 304)

Notice that in this account "abstractable structure" is conceived as neither substantial nor insubstantial, but as that which is the same about, or essential to, "intelligence" across the array of its instantiations. Hence, "the body" of cognitive science is contingently related to "intelligence" as a physical site that is adequate for, though inessential to, its situated realization(s).

4. See, for instance, Fodor's argument for the theoretical necessity of equipping minds with a generic, representational system of this kind in Jerry Fodor, *The Language of Thought* (Cambridge, Massachusetts: Harvard University Press, 1975), pp. 27–53.

5. On this argument, Habermas's critique of the instrumentalist fallacy implicit in both Marxian and Weberian theories of action, and his attempt to move beyond the traditional aporias of critical theory by recovering and elaborating forms of noninstrumental, communicative action implicit in the rules of speech, nonetheless remains committed to the classical approach to social action—that is, of identifying the essential nature of human activity with the elaboration of systems of abstract rules—and simply *extends* that approach to the field of communicative practice.

6. Zimmerman's and Boden's statement of the "context–sensitive" yet "context-free" nature of sequential organization is exemplary in this regard:

Whenever, wherever, and by whomever, turns have to be taken, encounters have to be opened and closed, questions asked and answered, requests made and granted or denied, assessments offered and seconded, and so forth, the organization of talk provides the formal resources to accomplish these interactional tasks, and deploys those resources in a manner that is sensitive to just what circumstances and participants happen to be at hand—which is to say *locally*. The shape of talk found in a specific site thus reflects the context-sensitive (and thus particularized) application of a more general, context-free (and thus anonymous) interactional mechanism. (Don H. Zimmerman and Deirdre Boden,

"Structure-in-action: An introduction," pp. 3–21 in Don H. Zimmerman and Deirdre Boden [eds.], *Talk & Social Structure: Studies In Ethnomethodology and Conversation Analysis* [Berkeley, California: University of California Press, 1991], p. 8)

In this passage, agency is transferred to the mechinery that organizes and supplies the medium of interaction. It is no longer persons, but "the organization of talk" that accomplishes the transfer of turn and the shaping of utterances. As was discussed in the previous chapter, this transfer of agency and entitlements from actors in contingent contexts to the operations of a context-free structure of rules is a canonical move in the development of a foundationalist science of linguistics.

In a related argument, Callon shows how, in the context of their practical-scientific work, researchers mobilize specific observations and specimens as representative of classes of phenomena under investigation. Callon's use of the concept of "representation" is linked to the notion of an ideal polity: that the specimens used by scientists—in this case a sampling of sea scallops—are representative of "scallops" in the same way as elected officials are representative of their respective constituencies. See Michel Callon, "Some Elements of a Sociology of Translation: Domestication of the Scallops and the Fishermen of St. Brieuc Bay," pp. 196–233 in John Law (ed.), *Power, Action and Belief* (London, England: Routledge and Kegan Paul, 1986).

7. Habermas takes this one step further by conceiving reason as that which transcends not only the particularities of *speech* but also particular *languages*. "Reason," he continues, "which is always bound up with language, is also always beyond its languages. Only by destroying the particularities of *languages*, which are the only way in which it is embodied, does reason live in *language*" (Jürgen Habermas, *On the Logic of the Social Sciences*, Shierry Weber Nicholsen and Jerry A. Stark [trans.] [Cambridge, Massachusetts: MIT Press, 1991], p. 144).

8. Sacks, among others, has remarked on this feature of writing generalized descriptions of social behavior (what might best be called their "ethical charge"):

> The nasty consequence of writing generalized descriptions is that one makes of particular objects 'versions' of the general object. One then deals with any object in the world as 'imperfect' (as a version of an ideal object in an ideal world). For example, when behavior does not conform to the behavior described as rational, the object is talked of as partly 'irrational.' (Harvey Sacks, "Sociological description," *Berkeley Journal of Sociology* 8 [1963]:1–16, pp. 13–14)

9. This means, however, that the corporeal body, in its locality, singularity, and sensual being, retains its subversive position *vis-à-vis* the idea of "the unity of mind." Wherever, whenever, and in just those ways that the witnessable activities of the corporeal body fail to correspond to some rulelike formulation for determining, for example, their motive and sense, the unity of mind is threatened. For this reason, epistemological examinations of how linguistic and cultural knowledge gets reproduced do not, as has often been supposed, founder on the problem of "other minds." Rather, they come to grief on the far more intractable problem (for both classical epistemology and Christian theology) of "the flesh" and of the desire of other *bodies*.

10. Ferdinand de Saussure, *Course in General Linguistics*, C. Bally, A. Sechehaye and A. Riedlinger (eds.), W. Baskin (trans.) (New York, New York: McGraw–Hill, 1959), p. 11.

11. Saussure (Ibid., p. 13) speaks of a kind of "average" form of expression: "all will reproduce, not exactly of course, but approximately, the same signs united with the same concepts."

12. This view is challenged fundamentally by Crist's recent study of animal researchers which indicates tremendous variation in researcher's attributions of understanding to animals. See Eileen Crist, *The Significance of Language in Portraying Animals: Anthropomorphism and Mechanomorphism in Behavioral Studies* (Philadelphia, Pennsylvania: Temple University Press, in press).

13. Habermas, *The Theory of Communicative Action, Vol. II: Lifeworld and System*, op. cit., p. 8.

14. Ibid., p. 12.

15. Ibid., p. 9.

16. Notice that these three stages of development also recapitulate the transition, at the level of *method*, from an objectivist behavioral science, through an intermediate stage of interaction analysis, to the familiar telos of methods of "rational interpretation."

17. Ibid., p. 14.

18. Ibid.

19. Elsewhere, Habermas argues that "the concept of translation is itself dialectical." (Habermas, *On the Logic of the Social Sciences*, op. cit. p. 144). His meaning is summarized in his account of what Gadamer calls the "hermeneutic experience": that in and through the process of translation we come to recognize both the *limits* of particular languages and the means by which languages can transcend their own internal limitations. "Hermeneutic experience," according to Gadamer, "is the corrective through which thinking reason escapes the spell of language; and it is itself linguistically constituted." (Ibid.).

20. Ludwig Wittgenstein, *Philosophical Investigations*, 3rd ed., G. E. M. Anscombe (trans.) (New York: Macmillan Publishing Co., 1958), ¶241.

21. Habermas, *The Theory of Communicative Action, Vol. II: Lifeworld and System*, op. cit., p. 15.

22. Ibid., p. 16.

23. This conception of "language games" not only reduces what would seem, on Wittgenstein's account, to be a richly textured, heterogeneous field of linguistic and social practices—some of which are contiguous, overlapping or mutually elaborative, others of which may be only distantly related or disjunct—to the bland cartography of a two-dimensional plain occupied by monadically sealed-off "spheres of language," it also enacts a reduction of the practice(s) of *translation* by conceiving "translating from one language–game into another" as the name for a general, singular method of bringing discrete practices into relation (as if the relation between addition and subtraction was in principle the same as that between German and French).

24. Jean-François Lyotard, *The Postmodern Condition: A Report on Knowledge*, G. Bennington and B. Massumi (trans.) (Minneapolis, Minnesota: University of Minnesota Press, 1984).

25. This point is made forcefully by Samuel Weber, in his Introduction to Lyotard's and Thébaud's *Just Gaming*:

> One of the convictions that dominates [Lyotard's] argument . . . is that there is an irreducible singularity and multiplicity of the different language games. Each game is thought to have its own delimited and delimitable rules, which constitute its determinate singularity. This argumentation is undoubtedly directed against the totalitarian pretensions of totalizing thought. But does not the concept of absolute, intact singularity remain tributary to the same logic of identity that sustains any and all ideas of totality? As soon as we affirm that each game is *absolutely different* from all the others, in theory if not in fact, we are in danger of being caught in the trap we wished to remove from the game. For wanting to determine singularity as the other of the other can only end in the same, in the identical, in the "pure" and the "specific [*propre*], as Hegel demonstrated very well in relation to the notion of "pure" difference. (Samuel Weber, "Literature: Literature—Just Making It," afterword to J.-F. Lyotard and J.-L. Thébaud, *Just Gaming*, W. Godzich [trans.] [Minneapolis: University of Minnesota Press], p. 103).

26. David Bloor, "Left and Right Wittgensteinians," pp. 266–282 in Andrew Pickering (ed.), *Science as Practice and Culture* (Chicago, Illinois: University of Chicago Press, 1992).

27. Compare Anscombe's analysis of the differences between the "belief in and practice of a 'formal' science of grammar" and Wittgenstein's grammatical investigations in Anscombe, G. E. M. 1981. "A Theory of Language?," pp. 148–58 in I. Block (ed.), *Perspectives on the Philosophy of Wittgenstein* (Cambridge, Massachusetts: MIT Press, 1981).

28. So, for instance, Habermas writes:

[An interpreter] can understand the meaning of communicative acts only because they are embedded in contexts of *action* oriented to reaching understanding—this is Wittgenstein's central insight and the starting point for his use theory of meaning. (Habermas, *The Theory of Communicative Action, Vol. I: Reason and Rationalization of Society*, op. cit., p. 115).

29. Habermas, *The Theory of Communicative Action, Vol. II: Lifeworld and System*, op. cit., p. 15.

30. Ibid., p. 18.

31. See, for instance, Christopher Peacocke, "Rule-following: The Nature of Wittgenstein's Arguments," pp. 72–95 in S. H. Holtzman and C. M. Leich (eds.), *Wittgenstein: To Follow a Rule* (London, England: Routledge & Kegan Paul, 1981). See also Wright's argument in the same volume concerning the logical weight of appeals to a "solicitable community of assent." Crispin Wright, "Rule-following, objectivity and the theory of meaning," pp. 99–117 in *Wittgenstein: To Follow a Rule*, op. cit., pp. 100–106.

32. Wittgenstein, *Philosophical Investigations*, op. cit., ¶201.

33. The most notorious example of this is Kripke's treatment of ¶201 as having laid the basis for "a new form of philosophical skepticism" (Saul Kripke, *Wittgenstein on Rules and Private Language* (Cambridge, Massachusetts: Harvard University Press, 1982)). Kripke's skepticist position has been roundly criticized in a number of quarters. See especially G. P. Baker and P. M. S. Hacker, *Scepticism, Rules and Language* (Oxford, England: Basil Blackwell, 1984).

34. Wittgenstein, *Philosophical Investigations*, op. cit., ¶254.

35. So, for instance: "understanding a symbolic action is linked with the competence to follow a rule" (Habermas, *The Theory of Communicative Action, Vol. II: Lifeworld and System*, op. cit., p. 17).

36. I am using "social technologies" in the sense given by Havelock's analysis of Plato's *Republic* as an attempt to displace an entire poetic form of

intellectual life. See Eric A. Havelock, *Preface to Plato* (Cambridge, Massachusetts: Harvard University Press, 1963).

37. Ludwig Wittgenstein, *Culture and Value*, G. H. Von Wright (ed.), Peter Winch (trans.) (Chicago, Illinois: The University of Chicago Press, 1980), p. 57e.

38. J. F. M. Hunter, *Essays After Wittgenstein* (Toronto, Canada: University of Toronto Press, 1973).

39. Wittgenstein, *Philosophical Investigations*, op. cit., ¶136.

40. Ibid., ¶226.

41. As Wittgenstein notes, doubts of this kind arise when we attempt to evaluate expressions in one language-game by the criteria of another:

> If he now said, for example: "Oh, I know what 'pain' means; what I don't know is whether *this*, that I have now, is pain"—we should merely shake our heads and be forced to regard his words as a queer reaction which we have no idea what to do with. (It would be rather as if we heard somebody say seriously: "I distinctly remember that some time before I was born I believed . . .)
>
> That expression of doubt has no place in the language–game; but if we cut out human behavior, which is the expression of sensation, it looks as if we might *legitimately* begin to doubt afresh. My temptation to say that one might take a sensation for something other than what it is arises from this: if I assume the abrogation of the normal language-game with the expression of a sensation, I need a criterion of identity for the sensation; and then the possibility of error also exists. (Ibid., ¶288)

42. See also Norman Malcolm, "Wittgenstein's *Philosophical Investigations*" pp. 65–103 in G. Pitcher (ed.), *Wittgenstein: The Philosophical Investigations* (Garden City, New York: Anchor Books, 1966), pp. 70–75.

43. This is the "bracketing" fallacy evident, for instance, in Pollner's use of the concept of "world," and in his discussions of the *ceteris paribus* clause (as if engaging in some practice involves holding all other practices—or "worlds"—at bay). Melvin Pollner, *Mundane Reason: Reality in Everyday and Sociological Discourse* (Cambridge, England: Cambridge University Press, 1987). For a critical discussion of this line of argument see David Bogen, "Beyond the 'limits' of *Mundane Reason*," *Human Studies*, 13 (1990):405–416.

44. Wittgenstein, *Philosophical Investigations*, op. cit., ¶241.

45. See G. P. Baker and P. M. S. Hacker, *Wittgenstein: Rules, Grammar and Necessity: Vol. 2 of an Analytical Commentary on the Philosophical Investigations* (Oxford, England: Basil Blackwell, 1985), p. 329–338.

46, Wittgenstein, *Philosophical Investigations*, op. cit., ¶242.

CONCLUSION

1. Michael Lynch, "Extending Wittgenstein: The Pivotal Move from Epistemology to the Sociology of Science," pp. 215–265 in Andrew Pickering (ed.), *Science as Practice and Culture* (Chicago, Illinois: University of Chicago Press).

2. Ibid., p. 223.

3. See also, Michael Lynch and David Bogen, "Harvey Sacks' Primitive Natural Science," *Theory, Culture & Society*, 11 (1994):65–104; Michael Lynch, "Molecular Sociology," pp. 203–264 in Michael Lynch, *Scientific Practice and Ordinary Action: Ethnomethodology and Social Studies of Science* (Cambridge, England: Cambridge University Press, 1993).

4. See Michael Lynch and David Bogen, "Methodological Appendix: Postanalytic Ethnomethodology," pp. 262–287 in Michael Lynch and David Bogen, *The Spectacle of History: Speech, Text, and Memory at the Iran-Contra Hearings*, Duke University Press, 1996.

Author Index

Subject Index